Placing the Suspect Behind the Keyboard

Placing the Suspect Behind the Keyboard

Using Digital Forensics and Investigative Techniques to Identify Cybercrime Suspects

Brett Shavers

Harlan Carvey, Technical Editor

AMSTERDAM • BOSTON • HEIDELBERG • LONDON
NEW YORK • OXFORD • PARIS • SAN DIEGO
SAN FRANCISCO • SINGAPORE • SYDNEY • TOKYO

SYNGRESS.

ELSEVIER

Syngress is an Imprint of Elsevier

Acquiring Editor: *Chris Katsaropoulos*
Development Editor: *Heather Scherer*
Project Manager: *Malathi Samayan*
Designer: *Matthew Limbert*

Syngress is an imprint of Elsevier
225 Wyman Street, Waltham, MA 02451, USA

Library of Congress Cataloging-in-Publication Data
Application submitted.

British Library Cataloguing-in-Publication Data
A catalogue record for this book is available from the British Library.

For information on all Syngress publications
visit our website at http://store.elsevier.com

ISBN: 978-1-59749-985-9

Transferred to Digital Printing in 2013

Contents

Acknowledgments

The forensic community has grown in size in the past years, so to give thanks to the many that have kept me focused, encouraged me, and shared their knowledge is a longer list than I could share in a few pages. There are some that cannot go without public acknowledgement, for without their support as friends and confidants, this book would not have been but a fleeting thought.

I cannot thank Harlan Carvey enough for agreeing to be the Tech Editor for this book. Harlan is the rare person that not only has legendary expertise in the field, but also has a great heart as a person and family man. Troy Larson, another digital forensics legend, for his foreword to my book. Dave Stenhouse, one of the best persons I know to bounce ideas on the tough cases. Going back a few years, I thank the finest partner a detective could have, Mark Klinke. Mark is one of those investigators that will dig and not stop until the case is finished, all the while doing an absolute great job. I tend to think his tenacity in purpose rubbed off a bit on me. I'd also like to thank a dear friend, Brad Tofthagen, who constantly reminds me through his actions, that personal integrity and honor is something to keep strong, no matter the cost or effort. My constant calls, emails, and bothersome requests over the years, and in particular for this book, are appreciated.

As for my number one supporter, I thank my wife Chikae, as she has endured my endless discussions of computer jargon and excitement of finding forensic artifacts in my cases. Her limitless support was instrumental and probably the main reason I started and finished this book. I attribute my success and the success of our children to her tireless efforts and patience to encourage all of us to drive on.

About the Author

Brett Shavers is a former law enforcement officer of a municipal police department. He has been an investigator assigned to state and federal task forces. Besides working many specialty positions, Brett was the first digital forensics examiner at his police department, attended over 2000 hours of forensic training courses across the country, collected more than a few certifications along the way, and set up the department's first digital forensics lab in a small, cluttered storage closet.

Brett has been an adjunct instructor at the University of Washington's Digital Forensics Program, an expert witness and digital forensics consultant, a prolific speaker at conferences, a blogger on digital forensics, and is an honorary member of the Computer Technology Investigators Network. Brett has worked cases ranging from child pornography investigations as a law enforcement investigator to a wide range of civil litigation cases as a digital forensics expert consultant. And even though it's been more than two decades since wearing the uniform, he's still a Marine.

About the Technical Editor

Harlan Carvey (CISSP) is Vice President of Advanced Security Projects with Terremark Worldwide, Inc. Terremark is a leading global provider of IT infrastructure and "cloud computing" services, based in Miami, FL. Harlan is a key contributor to the Engagement Services practice, providing disk forensics analysis, consulting, and training services to both internal and external customers. Harlan has provided forensic analysis services for the hospitality industry, financial institutions, as well as federal government and law enforcement agencies. Harlan's primary areas of interest include research and development of novel analysis solutions, with a focus on Windows platforms.

Harlan holds a bachelor's degree in electrical engineering from the Virginia Military Institute and a master's degree in the same discipline from the Naval Postgraduate School. Harlan resides in Northern Virginia with his family.

Foreword

I first met Brett Shavers several years ago at a training event that he had organized. At the time, Brett was a police officer—one of a handful among the local jurisdictions with the training and skill to take on digital forensic investigations. I had no idea then how often our paths would cross or how valuable his support could be. Brett has since become a leader in the digital forensic community of the Pacific North West, presiding over our local professional organization (www.ctin.org), running his own consulting company, writing papers and training materials, and maintaining websites devoted to Windows FE and RegRipper. In fact, that the world knows anything of my little internal project, Windows FE, has more to do with Brett's work and enthusiasm than my own efforts. I am, therefore, quite honored that Brett asked me to write a foreword to this book.

To best describe the value of *Placing the Suspect Behind the Keyboard*, I need to put the book in context. When I started my career many years ago, there was only one book available on the subject of what we now call digital forensics. That book was primarily focused on how to investigate certain types of computer crime under the laws that existed two decades ago. Its emphasis was law, with very little presented regarding technical detail, investigative techniques, or, strictly speaking, digital forensics.

In the late 1990s, a few technical books about "computer forensics" began trickling out, and then, slowly, more have trickled out every year since. The early books presented the digital forensics more as a collection of generally applicable tips and tricks than technical deep dives into the varieties of electronic evidence. Over time, however, articles and books on forensics adopted a more solid and scientific approach, and began taking on a broader range of forensics topics with greater detail and systematic focus on particular subject matters. Thus, we have moved from those early books on "computer forensics" to books about the forensics particularities of specific platforms, e.g., "windows forensics," to books that focus on specific parts of specific platforms, e.g., "registry forensics." This has been a good thing.

Particularly valuable over the past few years has been the evolving trend of books and articles to focus on distinct "artifacts," that is, the trace evidence that computer or user activities create in memory, leave on disk, or send over the network. Armed with a good knowledge of artifacts, a competent forensics investigator can develop a surprisingly accurate and detailed account of what has happened on a computer system or digital device. Internet history, file usage, data deletion, program execution, IP addresses, even geolocation of devices, are all facts available to the digital investigator to decipher a blow-by-blow account what has been done with a computer or device. Despite all this, there is a limit to the conclusions that can be supported by digital evidence alone.

Putting a specific person at the keyboard at a specific time, often one of the most critical issues to be proved, just happens to be one of those things that digital evidence rarely can accomplish on its own. This is not as obvious as it should be, since it is deceptively easy to confuse the computer owner or an account name for a real person behind the keyboard when a deed was done. But account names are not people, and computer owners are not the only people who use their computers. Thus, confusion can have catastrophic consequences when it leads to people being prosecuted or punished in error. It can also lead to investigators being sued for defamation. New forensics investigators are therefore frequently admonished to confine their conclusions to what is supported by the digital evidence they know well, and avoid making unsupported assumptions about the person behind the keyboard, about whom they often know very little to nothing.

Placing the Suspect Behind the Keyboard shows how to bridge the gap between digital and physical evidence to "make the connection between the act and the actor" and establish the person responsible for what was found on the computer. As the book illustrates, sometimes this connect can be made by interviewing witness who can place a person at a place and a specific time. Sometimes the connection must be reconstructed from physical evidence, such as other records gathered from the suspect or third parties. Sometimes, establishing the connection may even require surveillance. Non-law enforcement investigators might consider many of these suggestions as out-of-scope, but this would ignore that all these investigative techniques are important tools to understand, as they all have a place in particular investigations. An investigator who limits the world of evidence to the confines of a hard drive is going to miss evidence. To miss evidence, particular important evidence, is to fail at investigation.

About mid-way through the book, *Placing the Suspect Behind the Keyboard* expands beyond the topic of the title to the all-important program of building a good case. Although there is a research-like aspect to digital forensics, forensics is ultimately about proving or disproving things, not simply dissecting artifacts or building timeline. To succeed at digital forensics, one must be able to do more than pick apart the details. A good investigator must be able to marshal the facts to an end, which involves a bit of organization, an eye for relevancy, and the ability to present technical data to a non-technical audience. All of these topics are addressed, and Mr. Shavers suggestions are practical and useful.

Don't let the word "suspect" in the title make you think this is a book primarily for law enforcement. Although the burdens of proof and rules of evidence collection may differ between criminal and civil investigations (which includes internal corporate investigation), the burden of finding and making sense of the facts does not, particularly when it comes to placing a person behind the keyboard. *Placing the Suspect Behind the Keyboard* is full of useful guidance for digital forensics investigators of all types.

Troy Larson
Microsoft Network Security

Preface

This book was inspired over a decade ago when I was a new detective. The biggest obstacle I faced was that of attribution. In every case to which I was assigned, attributing a crime to a suspect was the main focus. Some cases were easy. Other cases, seemingly impossible. Even just the identification of a suspect was next to impossible in some cases. But in every case, I did my best to identify the suspect and attribute criminal behavior appropriately.

I'm probably no different than most investigators; in that experiencing a horrific crime scene has some effect on the effort I put forth in investigations. After recovering evidence in the first child pornography case assigned to me, I was determined and driven to follow the evidence, identify the suspect, and collect enough evidence to close the case with charges. Seeing the personal damage caused to victims by the sliver of darkness in human nature is more than enough motivation to make sure a case is done right, the first time.

In this age of technology, where the Internet has increased the ease of crime through enabling transfer of contraband, harassment, bullying, intrusions, and facilitating terrorism through electronic communication, investigators need to accomplish the very important goal of *Placing the Suspect Behind the Keyboard*. The identification of a crime and victim does not further our justice system if we do not also identify the suspects.

The intention of this book is to be a guide to that end of placing the suspect behind the keyboard through a combination of digital forensics techniques and more traditional, non-technical investigative methods. Throughout the book, consider that the investigator and the forensic examiner may be the same person or more than two separate people, depending upon the size of their organization. However, their goal is the same and their cooperation with each other should not have half an inch of light between them or their common goal of a successful case conclusion.

Each chapter in this book is independent of the others, but all are interconnected through the same theme and purpose. The principles and concepts cover the best case scenarios and the worst case scenarios. Sometimes, the best evidence is out front in plain sight and the investigator has all the legal authority to seize it. Other times, the evidence may not exist, or be accessible, or able to be interpreted. Rather than giving in, take a step back and reflect on your investigation. There is a clue waiting for you to find it, and follow it. *This is a book of clues.*

Although the theme of this book primarily supports criminal investigations, many of the same methods and processes can be used in civil litigation and internal corporate matters. The primary differences being the legal authority in certain methods of investigations may be different between civil and criminal cases.

I also intentionally focused on the mindset of conducting an investigation, as it is your ideas and intuition that solve cases. Using software and hardware just helps you exploit your ideas eventually into physical evidence. Considering that my first forensic lab was literally a small storage closet converted into a cramped digital forensic lab, remember that it is the person, not the gear, which solves cases. Think of your ability as becoming the Pablo Picasso of forensics. Picasso's art and skill in painting didn't rely upon the kind of paint brush or the number of colors he used. He relied upon his mind. You as the examiner or investigator can do the same.

The principals outlined in the book are meant to be principals, not an absolute checklist, but a guide. The principals can be applied today just as much as they can be applied tomorrow. It is my sincerest intention that by reading this book, you have found one thing that will make your work easier and one thing that makes a case. If you learned one thing that saves you many hours of time, that will have been worth the time reading the book.

But if you learned just one small thing, just that one small *Eureka!* moment which blasts your case wide open, then your time reading this book was more than worthwhile to you. It was worthwhile to the victims in that one case, whether it be a child, a parent, or a business. *And it definitely will impact the suspect, that same suspect you placed behind the keyboard.*

Introduction

CONTENTS

The goal of this book is to describe investigative methods in *Placing the Suspect Behind the Keyboard*. Perhaps one of the most important aspects presented as a continuing theme is the constant building of a case worthy of court presentation through the means of visual displays, concise and easy to understand descriptors, and validated collection of evidence. A best case example is having an evidence collection consisting of both direct and indirect (circumstantial) evidence. Electronic evidence, usually consisting of an analysis of activity on a computer system attributed to any number of computer users, could be either circumstantial or direct evidence, or a combination of both.

Obtaining inferences of user activity from a forensic analysis of a computer system is typically circumstantial as it requires the finder of fact, such as a jury, to make the connection between the act and the actor. The testimony of a witness that observed a suspect at the computer during the alleged act would be direct evidence. The combination of both types of evidence helps make a case. After all, a great case is worthless if the perpetrator is not brought to justice.

Today's investigators are acutely aware of the value of electronic evidence. It is commonplace to expect finding a number of electronic devices involved in most crimes. Along with the expectation that digital devices not only store information about a crime, but are also used to facilitate crimes, non-digital forensic investigators are aware that collecting and analyzing digital evidence is an instrumental piece of the collective investigative process.

As you read through this chapter, keep in mind that depending upon the type of digital evidence, the type of investigation, and whether the suspect has been already identified, the manner of collection of the data will differ. The investigator needs to know what electronic information is most important to the case in order to appropriately collect it. This chapter gives options and suggestions on gathering electronic evidence that can be used to support findings in an investigation, most of which will be discussed in more detail in further chapters.

You will also be exposed to various approaches to computer systems based upon the needs of the investigation and the current state of the machines approached. Depending upon the totality of the situation, each approach requires different methods of data acquisition. Whether the case is criminal or civil and the system status being on ("live box") or off ("dead box"), each circumstance defines the examiner's actions.

In addition to obtaining electronic evidence to determine which crimes and activity occurred, the mindset to have when faced having to collect electronic evidence should also be, *"What digital information do I need to place the suspect behind the keyboard?"* That's what this chapter is about, getting a grip on where to look, what to look for, and how to collect it.

DIGITAL EVIDENCE COLLECTION

Investigations involving digital evidence follow the same rules of evidence as any other investigation. Digital evidence, much like non-digital physical evidence, should be seized according to evidentiary procedures of the investigator's agency and legal rules of evidence. As a general rule, any type of evidence collection should be done with the least detriment to its condition. Exceptions aside, the collection of digital evidence most always involves creating a working copy of the data contained on electronic storage media from which an analysis is conducted. It is always preferable to work on a copy, or forensic image, than touch the original storage media to prevent changing the original evidence.

The forensic image is a file format that contains every bit of data on the original storage media, such as a hard drive or flash drive. The format of a forensic image is chosen by the examiner creating the image which can be in any number of file formats, such as the Unix "Data Description format" (dd) or "Advanced File Format," in which the forensic image file contains a bit stream copy of all data from the storage media.

The acquisition of digital evidence has different implications and objectives as compared to the method of seizure and preservation of non-physical evidence. Not so many years ago, the most common method to seize electronic data was only to "pull the plug" on the suspect computer and create a forensic image or exact clone of the storage media. Given subsequent research in the field of digital forensics, this is not the only method, or even the preferred method, as evidence will be lost if a "live" computer system is shut down without first capturing volatile memory. With a running computer system, the investigator must make a choice of an acquisition method. Any method chosen will allow for the collection of some information but will also not allow for the collection of other data.

The following methods of data collection are simply options to consider in the different situations the investigator will face. Depending upon the goals of the investigation, specific measures in data acquisition must be taken. Case examples will be discussed in which *the manner of digital evidence acquisition may have an impact on whether or not a suspect can be placed behind the keyboard.* As the intention of this book is showing how to place the suspect behind the keyboard, investigators should be aware of options of evidence seizure. Electronic evidence is different than any other type of evidence. If a computer system is running, you can compare it to a living being, because the data is changing as you stand and look at it. Knowing reasonable methods of acquiring the evidence for a given situation is important and beneficial to the investigation. Before bagging and tagging electronic evidence, take time to think of the consequences of your choices.

As to the best method to seize electronic evidence, it is up to the investigator to decide which method is most reasonable when approaching the computer systems at each scene. Each case is different. Each computer system configuration is different. And each investigator is different. The totality of the circumstances at the time will determine which method will be a reasonable choice.

Those tasked with collecting electronic evidence need to be acutely aware that computer systems that are running are constantly changing data naturally. These changes may be minimal variations occurring through normal operating system tasks, or the changes can be dramatic depending upon specific programs that may be employed. A word processing application will have minimal impact on a live system, however, an application such as a data wiping program or a malicious software program will have a destructive impact on a system.

Any human interaction with a live system by an examiner compounds the changes already being made on the system. No matter how small the interaction may be with a live system, there will be an impact on the system through the examiner's actions. These impacts potentially include both the destruction and the creation of electronic data, and individually in volatile memory and hard drive storage. Either way, if the system is on, the data is changing and anything you do or don't do will still result in changes to the data. So what are your options?

SIMPLE FILE COPYING

In some cases, copying files by dragging them from the evidence computer to an external hard drive may be appropriate. Such an instance usually occurs in a civil case where the only importance may be the content of the copied files and the computer user is not in debate. Simple file copying will alter the metadata of the files and if the evidence computer is live, then the data on that system will also be altered. In those situations where simply file copying is warranted, the use of specialized software to at least maintain the original metadata is advised. Yet, in the many civil cases and certainly in every criminal case, this is not an acceptable method for collecting electronic evidence.

Frequently, parties to litigation have agreed to custodians of specific computers and disputes as to the users have been concluded. However, there remains the possibility that a custodian of a computer may deny specific actions that occurred on his or her computer. In that instance, the examiner must now work to place a person behind the keyboard for the questioned instances of activity.

Using simple file copying of only user created files leaves little electronic evidence from which to work, besides the copied files. Unless the examiner copies data that bolsters user activity, such as event logs and registry hives, basic user created files, such as word processing documents, leave little for an examiner to investigate if the need arises after the fact.

Where a file copying utility will be used on a suspect's computer, the choice of the tool should be one that has the most minimal impact on the files, such as a DOS application like "Upcopy" from Maresware (see Figure 1.1, Upcopy available freely from http://www.dmares.com). Among many of its features, Upcopy maintains the file's metadata as well as verifies copied files through hashing and creating a log file.

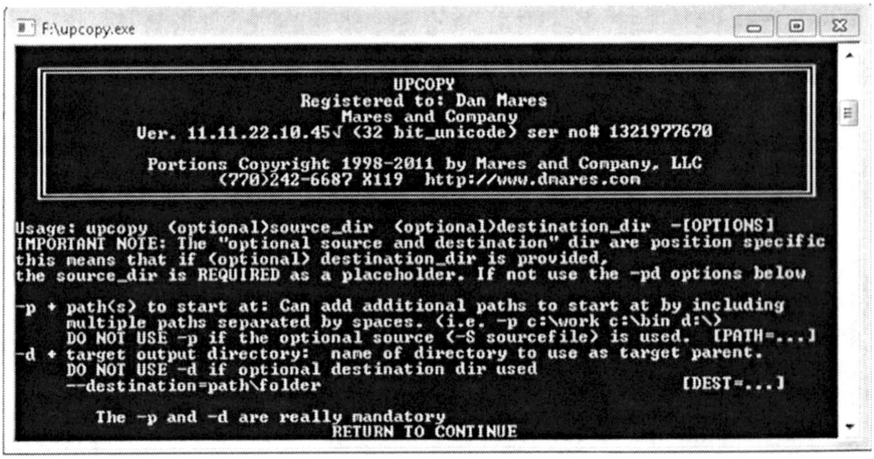

FIGURE 1.1 Upcopy from Maresware, http://www.dmares.com.

For best practices of data collection, even in those civil electronic discovery instances where simple file copying is approved rather than a complete forensic collection of a hard drive, steps can be taken that will constitute a more complete collection. As an example, hard drives containing files for electronic discovery collection can be removed, connected to a forensic workstation, and copied using forensic applications.

Another option could be to boot the custodian computer to a forensic operating system using external boot media like a compact disk modified not to alter any evidence devices. Having access without risk of changing the files can allow collecting the files using a forensically sound process.

Collecting data haphazardly without a process may eventually cause problems should the veracity of the data collected be called into question. Copying files through any method such as drag and dropping files or using file copying software is the least comprehensive method of collecting data. Before you decide to copy files on a live computer, remember that you only have one chance to collect the evidence reasonably. Every other attempt on a live machine results in the original evidence being higher at risk of modification.

"DEAD BOX" APPROACHES

Sometimes the easiest decision to make is the one you don't have to make. Investigators that approach computer systems that are not running ("dead") upon arrival have their decision on the method of acquisition decided already. In most criminal cases, *these computers are not to be turned on by the responding investigator*, but instead they are imaged using write protection to the evidence hard drive. Sometimes, it may be a necessary and acceptable practice to boot the system and create a forensic image from the live system. These cases usually happen in corporate and civil litigation matters or where the system is encrypted.

The steps to creating a dead box image could involve removing the hard drive and connecting it to a hardware write blocker or booting into a forensic operating system. Write protecting the evidence hard drive is accomplished using hardware write protection devices, an example seen in Figure 1.2. Evidence hard drives are connected to forensic computer systems using hardware write protection devices; much like an adaptor may connect a hard drive through a USB cable to a computer. However, unlike a basic adaptor, a hardware write protection device prevents modifications to the evidence hard drive as the device only allows data to be read from the evidence source.

Along with the hardware write blockers, software developed to create forensic images is used to read or copy the evidence data. Although there are countless

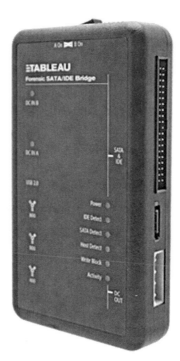

FIGURE 1.2 Tableau SATA/IDE Bridge Hardware write blocking device (photo courtesy of Forensic Computers, Inc., http://www.forensiccomputers.com).

applications developed for data duplication, data acquisition, and backing up data, nearly all forensic analysts will use applications specifically developed for creating forensic images. Most commercial vendors of forensic suites, in addition to open source software developers, also provide applications to create forensic images applications. Table 1.1 lists several examples of commonly used software applications developed with the ability to create forensically sound images of electronic data.

Table 1.1 Examples of Software Developed to Create Forensic Images of Media

FTK Imager	http://www.accessdata.com
Encase Forensics	http://www.guidancesoftware.com
X-Ways Forensics	http://www.x-ways.net
ProDiscover	http://www.techpathways.net
Guymager	http://guymager.sourceforge.net/
SMART Linux	http://www.asrdata.com
Macquisition	http://www.blackbagtech.com

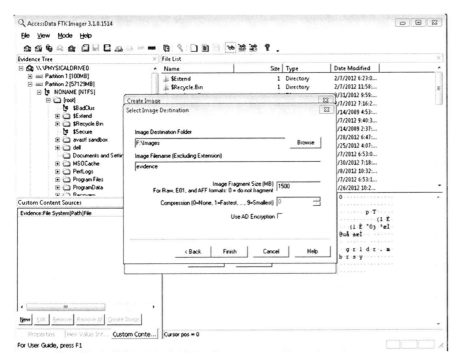

FIGURE 1.3 FTK Imager from Accessdata, dialog box for creating an image of physical media (http://www.accessdata.com).

Forensic imaging applications are naturally used in conjunction with a write protection device ("dead" box acquisitions). Most of these same forensic imaging applications can also be used on a live machine when necessary. Figure 1.3 shows an example of FTK Imager from Accessdata, which can create forensic images with hardware write blockers in the 'dead box' approach as well as be able to capture volatile memory and hard drive imaging from a live machine.

Another approach option for imaging is booting the suspect computer with specially modified boot media such as *a forensic boot disk*. A forensic boot disk is a CD/DVD/USB/floppy that contains an operating system from which a computer will run to avoid using and accessing the computer's internal hard drive. Even though the "floppy" hasn't been supplied with current computer systems, nor even as an option, there is still a possibility of encountering a system that may require a forensic floppy boot to exist.

The operating system on the boot media can be one of many forensically modified versions of Linux, Windows, or DOS. The primary modification required in a forensic boot media is that configuration which prevents mounting the evidence drive or otherwise allowing modification of data on the evidence hard drive. Many of these forensic boot media are freely available online or can be built and customized by individual examiners (see Table 1.2).

Once a computer has been booted to the forensic operating system, an image of the computer hard drive can be created and saved onto an attached external hard drive. Forensic boot media provides write protection of the evidence hard drive(s) through software configurations.

In order to use a forensic boot media, the BIOS of the suspect computer system is first modified by the examiner to boot the forensic media rather than boot the hard drive in the computer. This method of booting an evidence computer carries a risk of inadvertently booting the suspect system causing modification of files on the evidence drive if precautions are not taken to control the booting process. Failing to control the booting process runs the risk of booting your evidence to its operating system, changing thousands of files on the hard drive.

During a search warrant or civil evidence collection, you may feel either a self-induced pressure or actual external pressures to hurry up. Being rushed causes mistakes to be made, items overlooked, and regret after you leave the scene for doing a less than reasonable job. Booting a computer to a forensic disk is one of those times where being rushed will cause problems. To avoid inadvertently booting the evidence computer's operating system, test it first.

First, disconnect the evidence hard drive in the computer by unplugging the cable to all hard drives in the computer. Next, boot the computer to the BIOS. Change the boot order with the hard drive being last. The first boot media will be your forensic operating system on a CD or USB drive. The second boot media should be any other drive other than the hard drive. If there is a floppy drive, choose the floppy as the second media. Save your changes, exit, and shut down the computer.

Your forensic boot disk is placed in the CD drive, or if you are using a USB drive, plug it in. Any remaining drives can be filled with empty media, such as

Table 1.2 Examples of Pre-Configured Forensic Boot Media

Raptor	http://www.raptorforensics.com
DEFT	http://www.deftlinux.com
CAINE	http://www.caine-live.net
Windows FE	http://winfe.wordpress.com
Backtrack	http://www.backtrack-linux.com
Paladin	http://www.sumuri.com
SMART Linux	http://www.asrdata.com
Farmer's Boot CD	http://www.forensicbootcd.com

a blank floppy disk. Boot the computer and make sure your forensic operating system boots. If it does, shut down the system, reconnect the hard drive, and boot the system to your forensic disk.

A reason for filling any other drives with blank media, like the floppy drive, is to give an added layer of protection if the boot process somehow bypasses your forensic CD. Maybe the blank media will be caught in the booting process and prevent booting the evidence drive and if that happens, you will know that although your boot media was skipped, your blank media prevented evidence from being changed. Then go through this process again, maybe with another bootable media.

Figure 1.4 shows the Raptor Forensics Boot Operating System, one of many variations of a modified Linux operating system capable of running from a CD/DVD/USB.

Dead box imaging also applies to digital media that is not connected to a computer system, such as external hard drives, USB flash drives, compact disks, and other small media. The concepts of write protection are the same since the small media would not be in operation (not powered on).

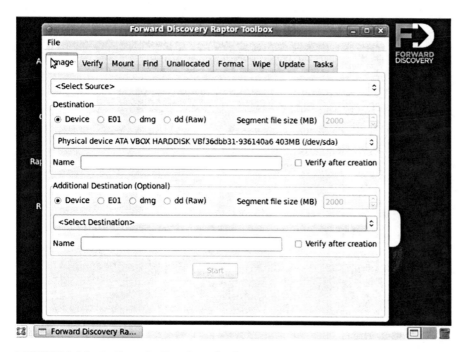

FIGURE 1.4 Raptor Forensics Boot Operating System, by Forward Discovery, http://www. raptorforensics.com.

Through write protection, these small media are connected to a forensic workstation and imaged much like a computer hard drive.

On the face of simply imaging a hard drive, it would seem to be an easy task. But I would rather compare it to steering a ship through the Suez Canal. Maybe steering the ship is only a few inches of turning the wheel left and right to keep the boat straight, but there is no such thing as a small mistake with those few inches of wheel sway.

Although this is an oversimplified analogy, the point is that imaging seems easy until it isn't. Software that worked on one drive may not work on another. Hardware that worked on one drive may not work on another drive of the same type. Computer systems with RAID configurations add complexity that may have to be solved with multiple imaging attempts in order to capture useable data depending upon the type of RAID, and whether it is a software or hardware RAID.

Failing hard drives during imaging is only one small part of imaging problems. In most instances, capturing a RAID through the live system is the surest method of capturing the RAID data, as there are occasions where individually acquired RAID hard drives are problematic to reconstruct outside of their original setup.

The hard drive itself may be a collection issue solely based on the size of the drive and the amount of data stored. A single desktop computer system can have terabytes of data storage across multiple hard drives. Creating forensic bit for bit images of each drive may not be practical or allowable with time constraints. In network systems in which even larger storage systems exist, it may be physically impossible to image every bit of data. Sparse or targeted collections may be the most reasonable method in these situations.

The bottom line is that the easy forensic imaging situations are becoming less and less common. You should not be surprised that if everything seems easy, you might be overlooking something.

"LIVE BOX" APPROACHES

Approaching a computer system that is running ("Live box") creates a time sensitive situation in which a decision must be made as to the method of data collection. As an investigator ponders this decision, changes to the data on the evidence drive are occurring. Therefore, to not make a decision or to slowly make a decision *allows* that data to continue to be modified by the operating system or any open applications.

Depending on future needs of the investigation that requires digital evidence to place the suspect behind the keyboard, the data in physical memory may

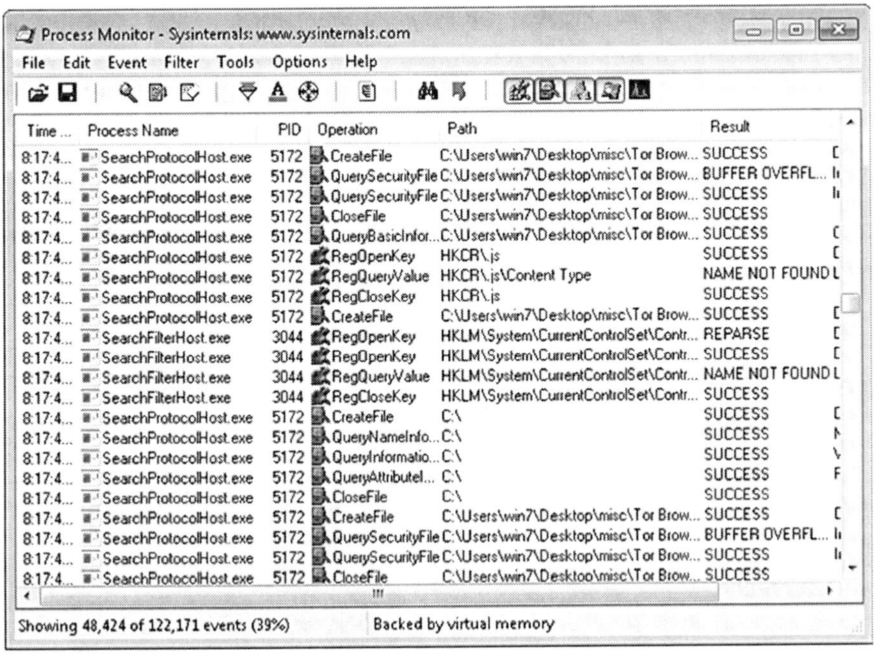

FIGURE 1.5 Process Monitor, Windows Sysinternals, http://www.technet.microsoft.com.

be crucial to obtain. To show an example of processes naturally occurring on a running system, Figure 1.5 is a screen capture of Process Monitor, a Windows Sysinternals program. Besides the 122, 171 events listed by Process Monitor in the screen capture, as the system continues to operate, more processes and changes will occur. So again, the decision not to interact with the system for fear of changing it, is actually a decision to allow the system to change regardless.

There are several factors to consider in the decision to choose a data acquisition method, each with risks and compromises. One of the most important factors to consider in approaching a live system is to decide to conduct a *Live Response* approach or shut down the system and directly image the evidence hard drive.

This is an important decision and cannot be taken lightly. You don't get a practice attempt or a do-over. Once the first steps have been taken, there is no starting over. To help make this decision, accept that unless the system was already shutdown upon your approach, the data will change regardless of the decisions you make.

There is also the consideration of the *"Order of Volatility"* when the choice to capture physical memory has been made. All data is considered volatile, in that, at a point in time, that data may not be available for recovery. This volatility of data can range from nanoseconds to an indefinite time period. As an example, certain data in RAM is susceptible to be destroyed by natural processes of the operating system or user intervention in nanoseconds, whereas other data stored on archival disks or backup tapes will exist indefinitely. Depending upon the needs of the investigation, the order of capturing different volatile has to be decided. Depending upon the case, all or some of the volatile data is required, and even the order of volatility has to be taken into account to capture data before it vanishes while you are capturing other data.

Specifically, if a system is shut down, physical memory will vanish. Physical memory, which is the most volatile data, resides in the Random Access Memory (RAM) and contains information from the programs that have been run and are running during the time the computer system has been on in the current session. Shutting down the computer system will cause that data being temporarily stored in RAM to vanish. Live Response involves collecting volatile data information, where live acquisition involves capturing memory as an image file.

Live Response and acquiring physical memory can be compared to acquiring a moving target. It is constantly in flux and volatile (non-persistent). One example of data contained in physical memory which is not written to the hard drive is chat messages using various social networking websites. These chats may only exist in the RAM and only for as long as the computer is running. If this data is not captured from the live system, the chats will not exist to be recovered from the hard drive, since they are not always written to the hard drive in the first place.

Table 1.3 lists examples of electronic evidence existing in physical memory. Each approach to a live system may or may not require acquiring the information in physical memory, depending upon the needs of each individual investigation.

Obtaining volatile physical memory may best be conducted with batch files or scripts to automate the process. Although there are multiple pre-configured volatile memory collection systems freely available, such as the Linux forensics live CDs, the investigator should be certain that the systems used fit the needs

Table 1.3 Examples of Physical Memory Data	
Mapped Drives	Shares
Contents of the clipboard	Network information and connections
Process information and memory	Service information
Logged on users	Routing tables
Kernel Statistics	Open files
Open ports	Address Resolution Protocol Cache

of the situation. Having the ability to create or modify which collection programs are run, and in which order, is an important option to have.

Table 1.4 lists several applications suited for physical memory acquisition. As any application may unexpectedly not operate on a given system, the examiner's ability to quickly transition from one non-working application to another, rather than troubleshoot a problematic program on a live system, should be done. Troubleshooting your software issue on an evidence will make many more changes to the system than using a different software.

Since the standard amount of RAM in personal computers now commonly ranges from 2 GB to 4 GB and higher, the amount of data contained therein is substantial. Given this amount of memory, it is also known that intruders have the ability to install rootkits or *malicious software* (malware) within RAM and that the code to these malware program will only execute in memory. By not capturing the physical memory, it is likely never to be known if a malware existed only in RAM and was never written to, or created files on, the disk.

If malware exists on the system, it is possible that this same malware will interfere with forensic applications used to examine and acquire memory. This interference, whether by design or chance, can cause the forensic applications to fail to work, fail to capture certain data, or even crash the system. The use of the suspect system to operate forensic applications is an unknown risk but in these cases, there aren't too many other choices.

One solution to minimize malware interference during a live acquisition of memory or hard drive is *acquiring the data remotely.* By connecting a forensic workstation to the suspect machine via a network or network cable, forensic applications can be run on the trusted forensic workstation rather than the suspect machine. Although typically, a small amount of code from the forensic program needs to be installed onto the suspect machine, the actual forensic applications will be run on the trusted machine, thereby reducing the amount of modifications to the suspect computer and risk of interference from the evidence system.

A unique and effective utility to facilitate this process is F-Response (http://www.f-response.com). F-Response allows examiners to connect their forensic

Table 1.4 Examples of Physical Memory Acquisition Tools

X-Ways Forensics	http://www.x-ways.net
X-Ways Capture	http://www.x-ways.net
ProDiscover	http://www.techpathways.net
FTK Imager	http://www.accessdata.com
Winen	http://www.guidancesoftware.com
mdd	http://www.sourceforge.net/projects/mdd/
Memoryze	http://www.mandiant.com

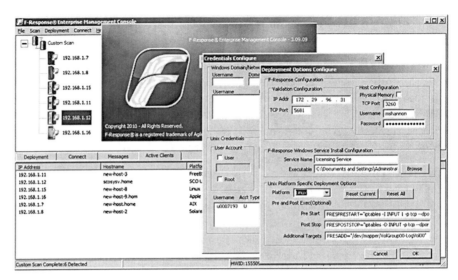

FIGURE 1.6 F-Response Enterprise, http://www.f-response.com.

workstations to suspect machines remotely. The connection to the suspect machine is Read-Only, in that the forensic examiner cannot modify the suspect machine's data (other than the changes that are made naturally by the suspect's operating system). Using F-Response, the hard drive(s) can be imaged as can the Physical memory.

As F-Response simply (yet ingeniously) provides a secure and Read-Only connection, it does not have the functionality to acquire data. This is an intentional feature not supplied as the forensic examiner can use virtually any application to acquire data through the F-Response connection. The ease of accessing systems remotely with F-Response can be seen in Figure 1.6.

Data encryption that is suspected or known to be employed can prevent acquisition of some or all of the data. Data encryption can encompass one or more files, folders, volumes, partitions, or even the entire hard drive. If an image is created of an encrypted file or hard drive, the decryption key will be needed to decrypt and analyze the encrypted data. Without the decryption key, the likelihood of recovering the encrypted data may be slim to none, depending upon the complexity of the encryption and decryption key.

Encryption programs, such as TrueCrypt seen in Figure 1.7, are plentiful and freely available on the Internet. TrueCrypt gives any computer user the option to encrypt their entire operating system or a specific container of files. Commercial products, such as the Microsoft Operating System, also offer full disk encryption as part of the operating system.

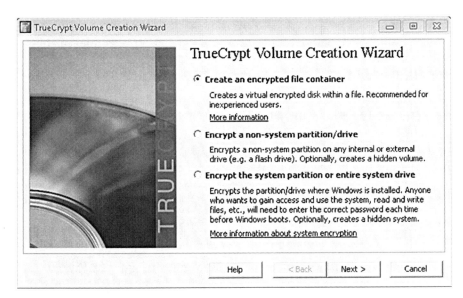

FIGURE 1.7 TrueCrypt, http://www.truecrypt.org.

Other operating systems, such as Linux, generally allow the computer user to encrypt their entire system or individual files as well. There are few operating systems that do not come with encryption programs by default. Any system that does not come with encryption programs by default most likely is able to have third party encryption programs to be used.

Ignoring encryption possibilities on a suspect computer will eventually lead to extremely short forensic examinations because when encrypted, there is little that can be done to examine an encrypted system without the decryption keys. You can assume that nearly any live system can be encrypted, either in whole or part, as many current operating systems include encryption as a system feature. There are also countless encryption programs that are freely available to accomplish encryption. So take some time to evaluate the encryption potential before pulling the plug from the computer.

Trusting the computer user to provide the key before or afterward, or even trust to be provided the correct key is a risk without resolution if the decryption keys do not work as promised. As current case law sways back and forth of demanding suspects to provide passwords, reliance on a court order risks not being able to access the information should a court order not be issued, or if the suspect conveniently forgets the password.

With full disk encryption, once the computer has been shut down, the decryption key will be needed, otherwise, it could take weeks or years to decrypt, with the possibility or being virtually unable to decrypt. Several forensic applications, such as X-Ways Capture seen in Figure 1.8, can be run on the suspect computer to not only determine if encryption is employed, but to also image the system's physical memory and subsequently, the evidence hard drive(s) should encryption be detected on the live system.

As described thus far, the clock continues to tick away when suspect computers are running and choices are being weighed. Yet another factor that can literally add hours to the process and modify the evidence even more are applications that may be running on the suspect machine. Commonly used programs, such as word processing programs, are not so much the concern as are other programs.

Data wiping programs that may be open are a serious concern and need to be addressed quickly to prevent evidence destruction. *Virtual machine applications also pose a problem*, if a virtual machine is running on your evidence system.

Virtual machine applications, such as developed by Vmware (http://www. vmware.com) and VirtualBox (http://www.virtualbox.org), allow for entire operating systems to be operated as guest systems within the host operating system. As an example, a computer with a physical hard drive running Microsoft Windows, can also run the VirtualBox application which can run a separate

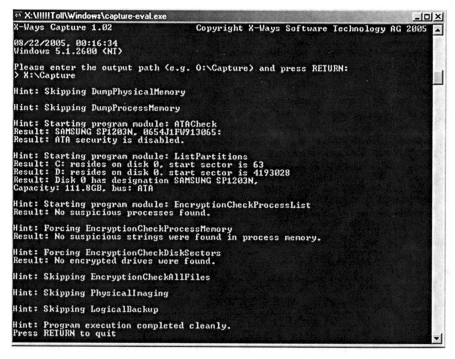

FIGURE 1.8 X-Ways Capture, http://www.x-ways.net.

operating system as a guest system, or several simultaneous guest systems. The guest operating system maintains its own data within its own files. In effect, an examiner that approaches a running suspect machine that is seen to have a running virtual machine on the desktop now has to decide acquisition methods of two systems.

The guest virtual machine will have many of the same considerations of data collection as the host machine. It is possible to temporarily suspend the virtual machine operating systems with some types of virtual machine applications such as vmware, storing the physical memory in file. This stored physical memory can be examined as if it were imaged. Other virtual machine applications do not suspend or store physical memory, which gives the investigator more difficult decisions on how to proceed.

Given the nature of a virtual machine containing all its data internally, it is conceivable that all evidence needed for the investigation could be contained solely within the virtual machine and not exist on the host system. This evidence could consist of Internet history, running processes, or email. The collection of a running virtual machine from a running suspect computer increases the risks of system crashes, lost data, and altered data.

However, this is expected and unavoidable and the investigator must make a decision based on the facts of that particular situation. Figure 1.9 shows a Windows host operating system with an Ubuntu guest virtual system. The approach to this one system is actually an approach to two individual systems.

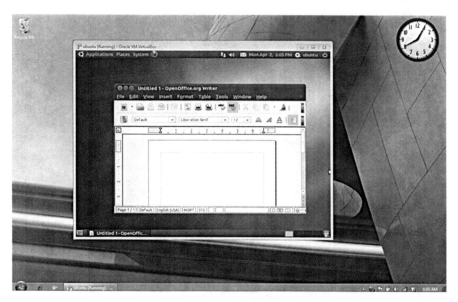

FIGURE 1.9 Windows 7 "host" and Ubuntu "virtual machine guest."

Other problematic programs and processes that will interfere in the collection of evidence include peer-to-peer networking applications, open remote connections, active file deletion or file copying, and active program installations. Closing some programs, such as Internet Explorer, may cause user created data to be written to the drive, which may be beneficial to the examination. Some applications may lose data when they are closed on a running system.

Each of these can contribute to a substantial loss of pertinent electronic evidence and create obstacles to the investigator's process of collection. All of the choices made will require explanations in reports and may be testimony for the choices made. Right or wrong, you have to make a decision based on what you know at the time.

As previously discussed processes can be seen in detail using Process Monitor, but indicators to active programs can also be seen in the task bar. A quick glance at the task bar can give information that might require immediate attention or direct you on how to move forward with data collections. Using Figure 1.10 as an example, an icon for "TrueCrypt" (http://www.truecrypt.org) is seen, indicating that encryption is probably certain.

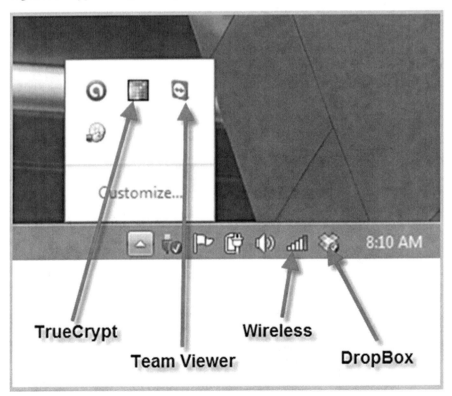

FIGURE 1.10 Windows Operating System, Task Bar Applications.

Knowing that encryption exists helps make choices of approaching live systems easier. The TeamViewer icon (http://www.teamviewer.com) shows that this computer can communicate with another system and it can be accessed remotely.

In this same example, there is a possibility of an active session with TeamViewer which the investigators at the scene may not be aware of. In effect, a suspect could listen and see with an attached webcam all that is happening around his system covertly, all the while, accessing and wiping files.

Another icon can be seen for "DropBox" (http://www.getdropbox.com). The Dropbox icon shows that files that exist on this computer and are stored online with Dropbox and are potentially shared with other computers. An online file sharing system such as Dropbox can be accessed by any Internet connected computer, and as this computer system remains connected, the files stored in the Dropbox folder can be modified remotely through any other computer. Examiners also cannot rely solely upon a lack of icons in the task bar since icons can be hidden by the computer user.

Even as a suspect may be away from his computer, he can easily access and delete files in his Dropbox using any other Internet connected computer. The online deletions will delete the files on his computer automatically, even as you stand and watch the screen. Of course, the files are probably recoverable with a forensic analysis, but the point is that the computer was being changed by the suspect remotely.

Observing active processes will give information to also base decisions on. Knowing which processes are important to the specific scenario depends upon the investigator's knowledge and skill level. And as mentioned, some processes deserve immediate attention to prevent the destruction of needed evidence while accepting the fact that destruction of other less relevant data is imminent.

DECISION-MAKING FLOWCHART

Since a great number of digital evidence seizure missions take place with unknown factors, such as the number of computer systems, types of operating systems, employed encryption, and other factors, having a plan developed beforehand helps the decision-making process. Experienced examiners are aware that no amount of planning and guessing will be absolutely correct when approaching computer systems. However, these examiners do know that by having some plans in place, the timeliness of making decisions is quicker and more apt to be reasonable decisions.

Case dependent, a certain flow of decision making can be developed that covers a range of situations. The time available to collect and analyze case data involving a missing or kidnapped person will be much shorter than the time frame to investigate a theft that was facilitated with a computer system weeks prior. Obviously, the risk of harm to persons causes decisions to be made quicker. Seizing computer systems without a plan is not only an ineffective method, but also places persons at a higher risk of harm if not identified or found due to overlooking or neglecting important data.

Search warrant raid briefings, where many persons are tasked with seizing digital evidence in different locations, can be significantly improved if a process has been discussed and agreed upon before examiners approach the suspect systems.

Such pre-planned decisions can be visually displayed using decision-making charts. These charts must be adjustable to each circumstance in each case. Since time may be the essence in person crimes, the perfect acquisition of all digital data may not be practical to obtain the most important information needed to prevent physical harm to victims. These can be considered a "Live Response" plan more than a data acquisition plan, although data acquisition most likely will occur afterward (see Figure 1.11).

PREVIEW/TRIAGE

The topic of previewing evidence has been an ongoing discussion for years. Even the terminology changes with definitions of the same processes being described as a "preview" or a "triage." In the context of this book, both previewing and triaging a computer system will have the same meaning as it relates to obtaining electronic evidence at the crime scene. Preview/triage can also occur at a lab with the goal to prioritize electronic evidence for examination. In the context of this book, the preview/triage goal is to obtain information to identify suspects and place them behind the keyboard.

The methodology of previewing and triaging computer systems can be viewed as nearly identical in processes, yet the goals may be completely different. In cases where gaining information must be timely due to critical circumstances, the objective in previewing multiple computers or a single computer is to quickly find the "low hanging fruit" and the most critical evidence. This evidence may consist of an email or a chat message stating the location of a planned kidnapping. Acquisition of the storage media is secondary compared to obtaining actionable intelligence to prevent a crime or save a life.

Practically, an examiner can triage a computer simply by poking around a live system looking for relevant evidence. This type of action obviously is not

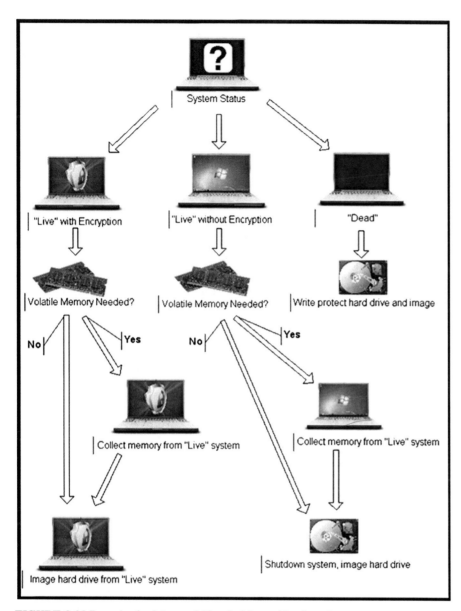

System Status

"Live" with Encryption

"Live" without Encryption

"Dead"

Volatile Memory Needed?

Volatile Memory Needed?

Write protect hard drive and image

No

Yes

No

Yes

Collect memory from "Live" system

Collect memory from "Live" system

Image hard drive from "Live" system

Shutdown system, image hard drive

FIGURE 1.11 Example of a data acquisition decision making flow chart.

recommended, since just as there are forensic software applications, there are also forensic triage software applications. Table 1.5 shows several examples of triage software, some of which is law enforcement (LE) only. The use of these applications will still alter data on the computer system, but will be a least intrusive method when triage is warranted.

Table 1.5 Examples of Pre-Configured Triage Tools

EnCase Portable	http://www.guidancesoftware.com
AD Triage	http://www.accessdata.com
SPEKTOR	http://www.evidencetalks.com
Triage Examiner	http://www.adfsolutions.com
Field Search (LE Only)	http://www.justnet.org
osTriage (LE Only)	http://feeble-industries.com/forums

The same principles of approaching systems apply when preview/triage is chosen as the first step. However, with live systems, triage/preview will cause data to be created on the system with other data potentially being overwritten during the process. Keyword searches, viewing images, and other aspects of a preview/triage on a live system will cause changes to both physical memory and the hard drive. Dependent upon the situation, this is probably completely acceptable and expected.

Perhaps the most important reason to preview/triage a computer system is to find information of immediate and actionable value. This may be to identify victims, suspects, or potential crimes. In the direst situations, such as a child being lured from home by an online sexual predator, the immediate objective concerning the victim's computer is to capture specific data.

In this type of scenario, where every minute counts, the option to create a forensic image of the hard drive, data carve files, index the drive for searching, and perform an analysis of the data would be the worst decision to make. Primarily, the goal would be to find items such as chat messages or emails related to the luring as fast as possible, even if that requires triaging the live system and changing data on the system.

An example of a preview/triage application available to law enforcement and military is Field Search. Field Search (seen in Figure 1.12) runs on the Windows operating System and the Apple Operating System. As a first responder utility, not a data collection application, its use is to obtain relevant and timely information based on a specific scenario.

One scenario where triaging a computer system is effective is with the computer owner's consent to search. Usually, this is done to determine if a crime exists, such as possession of child pornography, particularly for sex offenders under supervision. Triage utilities such as Field Search are able to quickly sort images, Internet history, and user activity to assist in determining if evidence exists on the system.

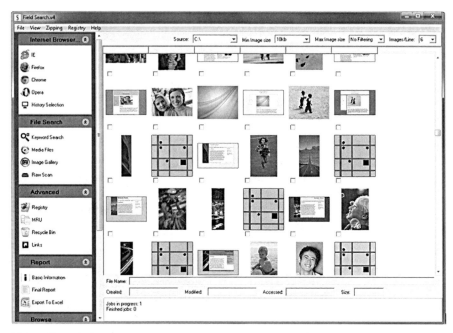

FIGURE 1.12 Field Search (courtesy of Jim Tanner, http://www.KBSolutions.com).

Conducting a preview/triage on a dead box can also be done without altering any information stored on a hard drive by write protecting the evidence drive through hardware write blockers or booting the suspect machine to a forensic boot environment. This would be the most forensically sound method, however, it does require the computer being shut down. This would eliminate physical memory unless the physical memory was captured before shutdown.

Conducting a preview/triage with suspects present or in close proximity can be an effective method of obtaining admissions through evidence immediately collected to aid in questioning suspects. Crime scenes in which a computer has been left unattended and running are particularly important to respond with both a preview/triage method and live response. The information stored in RAM may be the best source of information as to the most recent activity that had taken place which may identify the most recent user or users. Locations where computer systems are accessible by many persons, such as an Internet café or business, also require that a live response and triage be conducted. Activity on a public computer that has been stored on the hard drive in the past could reach several years in the past whereas potentially, only the information existing in RAM during the most current and active session will be of importance.

SMARTPHONES AND CELLULAR DEVICES

Many of the commonly accepted practices for seizing electronic evidence as it pertains to computer desktops and laptops do not fit nicely within the practices of seizing smartphones and cell phones. Regardless of differences, these devices also need collection for examination as at times, a smartphone may be the primary means of identifying a suspect.

A consideration for cellular devices includes data on the device being accessible by the suspect remotely. If the phone is capable of remote access, a suspect can send a 'wipe' command to the phone, destroying much or all of the data contained in the device. Precautions to prevent the device accessing a cellular network, such as placing the device in "airplane mode" or storing in a container blocking cellular reception, may be the first priority.

In addition to the device's internal memory, many of these devices will contain removable flash memory and a SIM card. A singular cellular device can easily contain 30GB or more of data, stored in various media locations on the phone, which can store data such as text messages, GPS information, call logs, photos, videos, documents, and voice recordings, any of which may help pinpoint a suspect's activity or location.

GPS

Cellular devices currently provide a GPS feature. Coupled with cell phone tower records and internal GPS data, tracking the past mobility of a cellular device can lead to information necessary to corroborate a witness's or suspect's story. Other GPS devices, that include devices installed in vehicles and mobile GPS devices, are also of much value to prove or disprove alibis. The collection of these devices can allow for a forensic examination to recover the data and make presentable as evidence.

GPS devices contain a goldmine of information to be used in creating a timeline of activity of a person or persons that were in control of the GPS:

- "Trackpoints" (location stored by the GPS as a record of where it has been),
- "Track Logs" (complete list of trackpoints),
- "Waypoints" (user stored location, where the GPS was physically present, and
- "Routes" (serious of waypoints taken by the GPS).

The combination of analyzing GPS data, crimes committed data, and other digital evidence can effectively allow for creation of a timeline of activity of a suspect. Dates and times of locations traveled with the devices used will show the historical movements of a suspect, easily displayed visually on a map or chart.

SUMMARY

Electronic evidence cannot be ignored. Nearly any device that contains storage of electronic data to include the temporary storage of data such as RAM must be considered for examination. Any one device or a combination of devices may contain the key piece of information that can effectively tie a suspect to a crime or to the device used.

The methods to approach computer systems will vary in degree based upon the needs of the investigation, the skill of the investigator, and the configuration of the systems encountered. No approach will be able to collect all data without loss or modification of some data. The forensic imaging of a write protected hard drive will allow for the collection of the entire hard drive data, but not of RAM that existed before the system was shut down.

The collection of volatile data also does not allow for the collection of all pristine data, as merely touching the computer (or not touching the computer) will create data and cause data to be lost through normal operating processes. The examiner has to choose which data is more important, knowing that some data will be lost or changed.

The goal of "first do no harm" in regard to collecting electronic data may more appropriately be described as "do as little harm as possible". As long as the investigator performs the least intrusive means possible, which may vary depending upon the immediacy of the situation, then that means it will be a reasonable choice to have been made. The least intrusive means in one particular case may be different compared to another. Again, where the threat of bodily harm exists, the threshold of acceptable changes to data will need to be adjusted to obtain timely information. Even with each decision made, the examiner may feel that the choice made was not the best choice upon later reflection. Given any scenario placed before an investigator, such as a running computer system, where time is clearly the essence, any decision made is certainly better than no decision at all.

Bibliography

Apple Operating System, Apple. <http://www.apple.com>.
Backtrack. <http://www.backtrack-linux.com>.
CAINE. <http://www.caine-live.net>.
DEFT. <http://www.deftlinux.com>.
DropBox. <http://www.getdropbox.com>.
Farmer's Boot CD. <http://www.forensicbootcd.com>.
Field Search, KBSolutions. <http://www.kbsolutions.com>.
Forward Discovery. <http://www.raptorforensics.com>.

F-Response. <http://www.f-response.com>.

Guymager. <http://www.guymager.sourceforget.net>.

Maresware. <http://www.dmares.com>.

mdd. <http://www.sourceforge.net/projects/mdd/>.

Microsoft. <http://www.technet.microsoft.com>.

osTriage. (LE Only) <http://feeble-industries.com/forums>.

Tableau SATA/IDE Bridge, image courtesy of Forensic Computers, Inc.
    <http://www.forensiccomputers.com>.

TeamViewer. <http://www.teamviewer.com>.

TrueCrypt. <http://www.truecrypt.org>.

VirtualBox <http://www.virtualbox.com>.

Vmware. <http://www.vmware.com>.

Windows Forensic Environment. <http://winfe.wordpress.com>.

High Tech Interview

INFORMATION IN THIS CHAPTER:

- A main goal of questioning a suspect
- The line of questioning for suspects
- Questions for victims
- Questions for network administrators
- Summary

INTRODUCTION

There are investigators with an uncanny knack for obtaining admissions and confessions during their interrogations. Other investigators avoid interrogations because of a pattern of only being able to get requests for an attorney from suspects. Reading books on interview techniques, taking course work in interviews and interrogations, and experience can each contribute to becoming a more effective interrogator. This chapter is not designed to teach interrogations. It will give you the questions needed for interrogations that are related to computer-related investigations. Each investigator must choose the timing and the delivery of the questions to elicit the truth from the suspect based on her own training, experience, and specific knowledge of the investigation.

Some of the most successful interrogations appear more like interviews or conversations, which many times could be the best description of the activity when speaking to suspects. Although an interview is an exchange of information and an interrogation is mainly a one-way road of information, the use of the terms "interrogation" and "interview" are used interchangeably throughout this chapter. The intention, regardless of definition, is eliciting truthful statements from suspects.

In cases where a suspect has been identified and arrested with enough evidence to charge them with a crime, the interview phase can solidify details, but only if the right questions are asked which elicit truthful answers. As with any suspect interview, some questions are asked to which the investigator already knows the answer, intermingled with questions to which answers are sought. Although not a foolproof method of guaranteeing all answers are truthful, it does provide a means of corroborating known and truthful information.

THE MAIN GOAL OF QUESTIONING A SUSPECT

The timing of contact with a suspect in any given case is not entirely dependent on the investigator. Sometimes, a suspect may not be identified until late in the case and the interview may only be used to corroborate evidence discovered previously. Other times, suspects may be contacted early in the case, during which time the evidence may be minimal.

Either situation still requires specific questions to be asked concerning technology involved. The listing of questions in this chapter gives the interviewer a foundation of evidence-gathering questions related to technology involved in the investigation. The questions do not depend upon whether or not the suspect is interviewed early in the case or prior to submitting charges.

The best case scenario is where the suspect freely admits guilt and confesses all details of the act. The sooner, the better for everyone involved. Sometimes that happens. Most times, it does not. For these investigations, it takes a person (the interrogator) to ask another person (the suspect) questions that elicit the truth. Unlike technology, there are no physical buttons to push, no debug program to determine why a question doesn't work. It is purely human-to-human interaction.

Non-criminal cases employ many of the same interviewing techniques as criminal investigations, although confessions and admissions won't necessarily result in criminal convictions more so than civil penalties or internal employee discipline. With many investigations, a computer system is only a part of the crime, either by use to facilitate a crime or maybe containing evidence of a crime. Therefore, not every crime has a digital forensics examiner assigned as the lead case agent. Additionally, since the digital forensics examiner in many organizations may be a rare breed, the non-digital forensics investigator conducts high-tech interviews, sometimes to the detriment of the case when necessary questions are not asked.

The information obtained by a suspect willing to be interviewed will be beneficial whether the suspect lies, tells the truth, stretches the truth, or omits facts. Everything admitted by the suspect needs independent verification to confirm the veracity of the statements. If the statements were true, then verification goes to show credibility. Conversely, if any statements were false or misleading and further investigation can show the inconsistencies and untruthfulness, those statements then lead to the suspect's lack of credibility. Either way, statements made are statements that, if possible, need to be fact checked through independent means.

The suggested questions listed in this chapter can be used as a guide of questioning, in any order best suited to the investigator, the suspect, and the case. The particular manner of speaking, specific words used, and interviewing methods are up to the investigator to use with these. Technical information, for which the interrogator does not understand during the questioning, may even sometimes be best left to elaborate by the suspect. This not only educates the interrogator of the suspect's mindset, but also allows the suspect to give even more information about the alleged crime.

To assist in the corroboration of suspect statements, any alleged suspect activity on computer devices should be detailed in order for forensic examiners to more quickly prove or disprove the statements. As an example, if a suspect denies ever using a peer-to-peer networking program or downloading files with such a program, a forensic examination may find information on the system that could counter the denial, thereby, discrediting that statement and suspect's credibility. Other information given by a suspect, especially those statements made against a penal interest, could save hours or days of an examiner's time in looking for electronic evidence that could have been identified by the suspect.

Investigators should keep an open mind as to the number and type of electronic devices that any suspect may have access at home, work, or public locations. For practical experience, an investigator can conduct a simple walkthrough of her own home and workplace, taking note of electronic devices and the interconnectivity to each other as well as to the Internet. Even with experienced investigators, conducting an informal visual survey of the home will most times be a surprise realization of the high number of devices used by family members on a regular basis. The actual devices used by cybercriminals will not be much different than the average computer user.

As can be seen in Figure 2.1, a multitude of devices exists outside the basic desktop computer. Some of the devices have specific uses but interconnected with each other. Modems, wireless routers, external storage devices, multiple computers, multiple cellular devices, and even Internet connected game stations may contain electronic evidence as

FIGURE 2.1 Commonly used electronic devices, any or all, may be interconnected through wired or wireless networks at home or the workplace.

single points of analysis or as obtaining corroborating evidence for a whole picture of user activity across a spectrum of devices.

THE LINE OF QUESTIONS FOR SUSPECTS

The rule of not asking any question for which you don't know the answer works, but only if you knew the answer beforehand. In every other instance, you are asking questions to get answers. As the interviewer, it really doesn't matter if the answers are true, half true, or lies. The goal is to corroborate the answers with other facts, regardless of what you hear in an interview.

The sets of questions in this chapter are divided by topic and purpose. Not every question needs to be asked in every interview, but having a list of possible questions will help you guide the interview with a goal to accomplish.

Computer skills, ability, and knowledge

Obtaining a foundation of computer knowledge of the suspect helps counter arguments of ignorance of technology skills at some point in the case. Most questions are benign and innocent without any inference of guilt; yet could be vitally important to the investigation. Depending upon the position of the interviewer (whether the interviewer is the forensic examiner or the case agent), certain questions may seem unimportant. It is vital for the interviewer to understand that an unimportant question asked now may be extremely important for her counterpart in the investigation later.

Questions an interviewer may not understand can still be asked, as long as the interviewer is aware of the types of answers expected from each question. The assistance of a forensic examiner, or someone more versed in technology than the interviewer, would benefit the interviewer in obtaining accurate information from the suspect. Of course, one of the best questions to ask is simply, "Did you do it and how did you do it?" and take notes!

- Do you have any computer training or education?
  - When and where?
  - What did the training and education consist of?
- Have you ever taught computer subjects? When and where?
- Have you ever written software?
- Have you ever built a computer?
- Have you ever replaced parts of a computer?
  - What parts?
- Have you ever installed software?
  - What kind of software?
- What operating systems have you used?

- Are you comfortable using computers for basic tasks, such as Internet and word processing?
- How often do you use computers each week? How many hours per day?
- Do you have antivirus programs installed on your devices?
    - Is it kept up to date?
    - What is the program?
- Have you ever had a virus on your device?
    - Did you clean the virus with any software?
    - Do you still have a virus?
    - Do you know what a virus or Trojan is? Do you have any on your devices?
- Have you ever defragmented your hard drives?
    - How often?
    - When was the last time?
- Have you ever reformatted your hard drives?
    - How often?
    - When was the last time?
    - Why did you reformat your hard drives?
- Do you maintain or own any websites? Blogs? Forums? Lists?
    - What are the website Internet addresses?
    - When did you start maintaining or create the websites?
- What content is on the websites? Blogs? Forums? Lists?
- Do you own any computer-related books?
    - What kind of books are they?
    - Where are they?
- Have you written technology books, papers, or guides?

Password, encryption, steganography, and deletion

The presence of *encryption* plays an important aspect of any digital forensics examination. Considering that many current operating systems include encryption features by default and Internet users can easily download any one of dozens of encryption programs, the odds of approaching encrypted systems or encrypted data increase. Depending upon the encryption scheme used coupled with a complex passphrase, it may be literally impossible to access certain files, folders, or entire storage devices that have been encrypted. The quickest method to obtain passphrases is usually just politely "ask" to be given the password by the suspect. And many times, it may be the only method to gain access.

As many electronic devices also have encryption or password protection features, such as smartphones and USB flash drives, interviewers should remember to obtain passphrase information to all devices. Assuming computer users have ill intent using encryption would be a risky assumption to make, especially as many devices and programs require a password to log into the system or program. Rather than assume data has been encrypted for nefarious purposes, let the suspect describe the intentions behind using encryption. Perhaps the use is innocent and unavoidable, but perhaps the suspect will detail intentional attempts to hide criminal evidence through the means of encryption.

An uncommon use of computers involves *steganography*. Steganography as it relates to electronic data simply means that data is hidden from view as to not be seen. The presence of data hidden using applications designed for steganography is significant to show intention of the suspect in knowingly concealing evidence. Forensic examiners will never know how many times they encounter steganography, other than the times they actually discovered steganography.

Given the high likelihood that properly hidden electronic evidence may never be found, it is crucial to obtain this information from the suspects through interrogations. Figure 2.2 shows a freeware utility capable of easily hiding files within files through a few clicks of the mouse. As the ease of hiding data increases, the odds that data will be hidden by suspects also increase.

- Do you use encryption for files or computers?
  - What kind of encryption?
  - What software do you use to encrypt?
  - Why have you used encryption?
- What are your current passwords?
- What are past passwords you have used in the past?
- Do you have hidden files? How are they hidden?
- Do you have hidden partitions or volumes? How are they hidden?
- Do you have any hidden volumes or partitions hidden within encrypted containers?

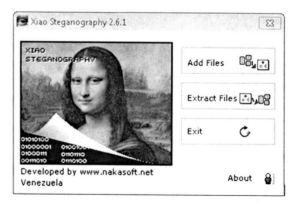

FIGURE 2.2 Steganography programs can easily hide electronic data within electronic data. Xiao Steganography, http://www.nakasoft.net.

- Does anyone else know or use any of your passwords?
  - Who?
  - Which passwords?
  - When do others use your passwords?
- Do you have a written or printed list of your passwords?
- What is your login information to each of your devices?
- How do you delete files?
- Do you empty the Recycle Bin/Recycler/Trash Bin? How often?
- Do you use wiping programs?
  - What kind?
  - How often?
  - When was the last time used?
- Have you ever wiped an entire hard drive?
  - When?
  - Why?
  - How did you wipe the hard drive?
- Do you use steganography or data hiding programs?
  - What kind?
  - How often?
  - How do you use it?
  - On what files do you use it?
  - Why do you use data hiding programs?
  - Who do you want to hide data from?

Control of the device(s) in question

A claim from a suspect that no other person had *access to the computer device used in a crime* is a powerful statement. However, specific questions asked about the control of the devices should still be asked to ensure no details, alibis, or failure to recollect details accurately occur later by the suspect. These specific questions clarify any doubts as to the person or persons that had access or control of an evidence device.

- Is this device (computer, phone, etc.) yours?
- Do you own it?
  - Did you purchase it?
  - When did you obtain it?
  - From where?
- Who owns it?
  - Why do you have it?
  - When did you obtain it?
  - Do you have the owner's permission?
- Does anyone else have permission to use it?
  - Who?

- When did they use it last?
- How often do they use it?
- Does anyone else have access to it?
  - Who?
  - How?
- Does anyone else have the login information?
  - Who?
  - What is the name of their account?
  - Does anyone else use your account? Who? Why? When?
- Do you have other devices?
  - Where are they currently?
  - Did you ever have other devices?
- Does anyone else have access to them? Who?
- When was the last time you used the device?
- When was the last time someone else used the device?
  - Who was it?
  - What did they use it for?
  - Did they have your permission?
- What do you use the device for?
- Where do you normally use the device?
- Where else have you used the device? Home? Work? Public places?
- Is the room secured where the device is stored?
  - Is there a key to enter the room/office/home?
  - Who has access to the key or spare keys?
  - Is there a keycard access to the room/building/office?
  - Have you allowed use of your keycard to anyone?
    - Who used it?
    - Why did you allow someone to use your keycard?
    - When did they use it?
- Do you have remote access configured for any computer?
  - How is it configured?
  - What software do you use?
  - From where do you remotely access your computer?
  - What activity do you usually conduct when connected remotely?
  - Does anyone else connect to your computer remotely?
    - Who do you allow to do this?
    - Why do you allow others to connect remotely to your computer?

Other devices used by suspect

- What other devices do you own? (Laptops, PDA, smartphones, external hard drives, etc.)

- How many cell phones do you have?
  - Where are they?
  - Which carriers do you use?
  - Have you taken photos or videos with the cell phones?
  - Where are the photos and videos saved?
  - How many desktop and laptop computers do you have?
  - Do you have other types of computer systems?
- Where are the other devices?
- When did you last use each device?
- What did you use the devices for?
- Does anyone else have access to them?
  - Who else has access?
  - When were the devices used by someone else?
- Do you use your computers at your work for personal use?
  - How many work computers have you used for personal use?
  - Do you have an assigned computer?
  - Have you downloaded personal files with work computers?
  - How else do you use work computers for personal business?
- Do any of these devices require passwords to use?
  - What are the passphrases?
- Do you use your personal computers for business?

Software used by suspect

- What operating systems do you use?
- What types of programs do you use?
- Do you use any password or encryption programs?
- Do you use any programs that hide your identity?
- Do you install the programs yourself?
- Do you download programs from the Internet?
  - What kind of programs have you downloaded?
- Have you ever written any programs or code?
- Have you modified the code of any programs?
- Have you ever used cracked or pirated software?
  - Which software?
  - How did you crack it?
  - Where did you obtain it?
  - Have you ever shared a copy of it?
- Did you install "name of software?"
  - When did you last use this software?
  - How did you use this software?
  - Where did you obtain this software?
  - Have you changed the default settings?

Internet use by suspect

- Do you have Internet access at home?
    - What is your Internet Service Provider (ISP)?
    - Do you have wireless Internet in your home?
    - How long have you had this ISP?
    - What was your previous ISP?
    - Is your wireless encrypted or open access?
    - What is the login?
    - Does anyone else have access to your Internet account?
    - Does anyone else have access to your Internet?
    - Who else has access? When was the last time used by someone else?
    - Do you have other means to access the Internet?
        - What are they?
        - How often do you use it?
        - Why do you have other Internet access accounts?
- Which Internet browsers do you use?
- Do you clear your Internet history?
    - How?
    - How often do you clear the history?
    - Why do you clear the history?
- Do you use any method of concealing your IP address?
    - What method?
    - How often do you use it?
    - Why do you use it?
- Which search engines do you use?
- Do you bookmark favorite websites?
    - Which websites have your bookmarked as favorites?
    - How often do you revisit these websites?
    - What are some of your favorite bookmarked websites?
- What search terms do you usually search?
    - How often do you search for these terms?
    - When was the last time you searched for these terms?
    - What were the most recent words you searched?
    - Do you use any method to clear your search history?
        - Why do you clear your search history?
        - When was the last time you cleared your search history?
- Do you search for pictures on the Internet?
    - What words do you search for pictures?
    - What kinds of pictures show in the search results?
    - Do you download these pictures? When? How many? How often?
    - Do you view pornography on the Internet?

- What kind of pornography?
- Do you download pornography? How much? How often?
- Have you written stories?
  - Are they posted online or shared with anyone?
  - What are the stories about?
- Do you search for movies or videos on the Internet?
  - What kind of movies or videos?
  - What search terms have you used?
  - When was the last time you searched for movies or videos?
  - Did you download the movies or videos?
  - Did you watch any of the movies or videos?
  - Did you share any movies or videos with anyone?
  - Have you sold any of the videos or movies you downloaded?
    - Who did you sell them to?
    - Did you sell them online or in person?
- Have you ever used Virtual Private Networks?
  - What VPN did you use?
  - When did you last use it?
  - What did you use it for? Why?
  - What is your login information?
- Have you ever used Tor or other anonymity software?
  - When did you last use it?
  - What did you use it for? Why?
  - Where did you use it?
- Do you make purchases online?
  - What type of purchases
  - What have you purchased?

Online chat, email, forums, boards, online social networking

Few persons are not connected through any number of social networking Internet services. Information posted in these accounts by the users can assist in obtaining investigative leads or evidence from the services directly. Most social networking services keep logs of a user's access to their websites which can include Internet protocol (IP) addresses, date/time of login, and information posted.

Alibis may be proven or disproven depending upon the totality of the alibi with other corroborating information, such as obtaining the IP address of specific logins to place a person at a location during a specific time. Also, other related victims and suspects may be identified through the review of information obtained from these online services.

- Do you chat online?
  - What program do you use to chat?
  - What are your nicknames/user names/screen names?
    - How did you pick these names?
    - Do you use these names on multiple chat system?
    - What are your passwords to access chat?
  - How often do you chat online?
  - Who do you chat with?
  - When was the last time you chatted online?
  - What did you/do you chat about?
  - Have you ever transferred files while chatting?
    - What types of files?
    - Who did you transfer the files to/who did you receive files from?
- Do you play games in chat rooms?
  - What kind of games?
  - How often do you play these games?
  - Do you play games online to meet children?
- Have you ever met anyone in person that you met online?
  - Who did you met?
  - When did you meet?
  - Where did you meet?
  - Have you met more than once?
  - Have you met more than one person?
  - Who were these people you met?
- What type of email do you use?
- What are your email addresses?
- Do you download your email?
  - What program do you use?
  - Do you save or delete your email?
- Does anyone have access to your email accounts or passwords?
  - Who else has access?
  - Why do you allow access to your email?
  - Do you send attachments in emails?
    - What kinds of attachments do you send?
    - Who do you send attachment to?
  - When was the last time you used your email accounts?
  - What are other email accounts you have used in the past?
    - Are these accounts closed?
    - When did you last use them?
    - Did anyone else have access to these accounts?
- Do you visit forums or Internet boards?
  - Which forums/boards?
  - Have you commented or shared files on these forums/boards?

- What comments did you make?
- What files did you share?
- Have you received files from any of these forums/boards?
- How often do you visit these forums/boards?
- What are your user names/screen names/login for these forums/boards?

- What user groups do you belong?
  - What is your screen name?
- Who is on your "buddy" or "friend" lists?
  - Do you know them personally?
  - Have you met any face to face?
- Do you have a Facebook account?
  - What is your user name and login information?
  - Does anyone else have access to your account?
  - How often do you log into the account?
    - From where do you log in?
    - Do you chat with Facebook?
    - Do you play games on Facebook?
- What other social websites do you visit or have accounts?
  - Do you use dating websites? What is your user information?
  - Do you use game websites? What is your user information?
  - Others? What are your logins?
  - How often do you use these social networking sites?

Suspects that browse the Internet with applications configured to allow for anonymity on the Internet have the ability to interact with others, such as victims of their harassment without being tracked by their true IP address. Some methods of anonymous browsing configurations include using virtual private networks (VPN) and The Tor Project (Tor) browser. With each of these methods, the IP address of the suspect is hidden through a series of random global nodes.

Figure 2.3 shows the Tor Network Map, in which the suspect's originating IP address is hidden behind dozens of anonymous relays, preventing detection. The IP address will only be from a Tor exit node, not the actual IP address of the suspect. Although these methods of remaining anonymous online are not illegal, questioning the intentions of use of these applications by suspects builds evidence in their knowledge of attempting to thwart investigative efforts.

Identifying each uncommon use of a computer system gives the investigator insight into the mindset of the suspect. The average computer user does not typically hide data under other data, encrypt data, wipe data, and cloak IP addresses while surfing the Internet on a regular basis. The combination of all of these types of activity gives the impression that not only was the suspect

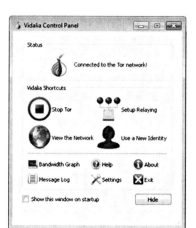
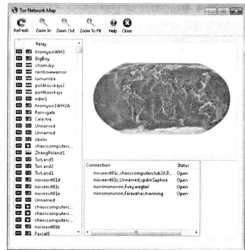

FIGURE 2.3 The Tor Project (Tor) application allows for anonymous Internet surfing. http://www.torproject.org.

well versed in computer technology, but also took advantage of uncommonly used technology to facilitate crimes. This is not to say use of these applications is illegal, but coupled with criminal activity, their use can show facilitation of the criminal activity.

Another key component in questioning suspects about their use of programs includes discovering their intention and knowledge of using *file sharing programs*. File sharing programs, such as Frostwire seen in Figure 2.4, allow for files to be downloaded from many sources, globally. Several file sharing applications can be configured to search and download files automatically and be left virtually unattended by a computer user.

Claiming ignorance as to the types of files downloaded may be plausible if enough information is not obtained to prove or disprove knowledge and intention. Digital forensics most likely will show the use of file sharing programs to include the files searched, downloaded, and shared. For example, downloaded files that have been renamed, placed into a folder other than the default download folder, or copied onto removable media show the suspect's intent to view and save the files.

Peer-to-Peer Networking

- Do you use Peer-to-Peer Networking software?
  - What is the name of the software?
  - How often do you use it?
  - Do you search for files with the software?

FIGURE 2.4 Frostwire is one of many "Peer-to-Peer" file sharing applications. http://www. frostwire.com.

- Have you downloaded files with the P2P programs?
  - Have you shared files or folders with the software?
  - What kind of files have you downloaded?
  - What kind of files have you shared?
- Is your software installed by default or did you make changes?
  - Is file sharing on or off?
  - What other changes did you make?
  - Why did you make those changes?
- Have you used other file sharing software applications?
  - Which applications?
  - How often?
  - When was the last time used?
  - Have you changed any of the default settings? Why?

Duplicating and storing data on a local media, such as desktops, laptops, and external storage devices, has quickly become common practice in homes and businesses. Forensic examinations of storage media can find all files that have been backed up or copied and sometimes deleted. However, forensic examinations of storage media will not be able to recover data that has been stored online. Finding traces of information leading to believe data may be stored online is important, but more important is being able to access that data.

Online data storage services, otherwise known as the "*Cloud*," range from freely available to paid services. Configurations of online storage can be set to backup specific folders or an entire system, automatically and incrementally. Online data storage services usually encrypt the customer's data and may not be able to decrypt the data that exists on their storage servers without the customer's credentials. Without having access to any notes containing login credentials, it is critical to obtain them from the suspect through the interview process.

Investigators should also be aware that data stored in the Cloud may be shared with other users. Having shared access allows for the users to upload and delete files as well as potentially cancel accounts. If electronic evidence is suspected of being stored in the Cloud, precautions need to be taken immediately, such as sending preservation orders to the providers in preparation of obtaining search warrants to prevent destruction of the evidence.

There are a number of services currently available at no charge, such as ADrive seen in Figure 2.5. ADrive offers a free online storage capacity of 50 GB for every account. Paid accounts allow for even more online storage. Those investigators tasked with investigating child pornography cases may want to remember the potential evidence cache of online storage. Offenders using these types of freely available systems can share illicit images directly with other offenders, without the need of peer-to-peer networking applications.

File storage

- Do you store files on your computer hard drive?
  - Where do you store them on your hard drive?
  - Do you organize your saved files?
  - How do you organize files?
  - What kind of files do you save?
- Do you make backups of your computer hard drive?
  - What software do you use?
  - What do you store the backups on?
  - Where are the backups?
  - Are they encrypted? What are the passwords?
  - Does anyone else have access to your backups?
- Do you use flash drives?
  - Where are they?
  - How many flash drives do you own?
  - What is stored on the flash drives?

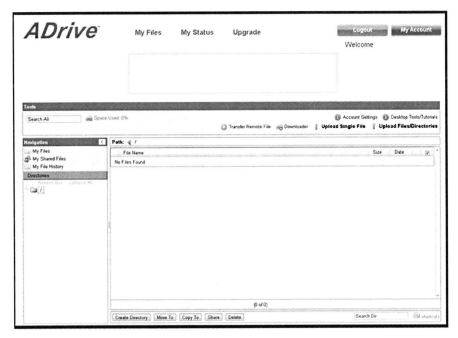

FIGURE 2.5 ADrive online storage, http://www.adrive.com.

- Do you use external hard drives?
    - Where are they?
    - How many external hard drives do you own?
    - What is stored on the external hard drives?
    - Do you encrypt these hard drives?
        - What are the passwords?
- Have you ever replaced a hard drive on your computer/s?
    - Why was it replaced?
    - What did you do with the previous hard drive?
- Do you use online storage?
- What service do you use to store files online?
    - How often do you use online storage?
    - What is you login information?
    - Are the online files encrypted?
    - Are the files accessible by anyone else? Who else? Why?
- Do you share files with others with these services?
    - Who do you share with?
    - What files do you share?
- Does anyone else have access to your online storage?
    - Who? Why?

- When did they last access your files?
- Has anyone else uploaded files to your storage? Who? When? What files?

Crime specific—child pornography

Child pornography investigations sometimes involve hundreds of thousands of images with most of the images leaving no question that the subjects in the images are children. Other times, the subjects may not be clearly identified as children. As the mere possession of child pornography is a crime, these investigations could be considered easier than other computer-related crime.

However, that would be an incorrect assumption. If not simply for the benefit of other past and future victims, questioning suspects involved in this crime could not be more important, to not only prove a case, but to also find unreported cases of exploited and missing children. The following list of questions for Child Pornography is not all inclusive but is specific to computer use. Other questions, such as asking specific details related to the crime and victims, should also be asked.

- Can you tell me what you believe child pornography to be?
- Have you ever seen it before?
  - When did you see it?
  - How did you see it?
  - How do you know it was child porn?
  - Did you save it?
  - Did you share it with anyone?
- Have you searched online for child pornography?
  - What search engine did you use?
  - What search terms did you use?
  - Did you find child porn through searching online?
  - Did you download any child porn from searches?
- Have you ever uploaded child porn to the Internet?
- Have you used Peer-to-Peer Networking programs to access child porn?
  - Have you downloaded child porn using P2P?
  - Have you shared child porn using P2P?
- Have you ever encountered child porn on the Internet unintentionally?
  - Did you download any?
  - Did you delete any?
  - Did you share any?
- Is there child pornography on your computer/s?
  - Where is it saved?
  - How did it get there?

- When did it get saved?
- Describe the child pornography on the computer.
- What file formats do you use? JPG? AVI?
- Did you rename any child porn files?
- Did you organize any child porn files? By age group? By sex? By act?
- Did you copy any child porn to compact disks or other devices or media?
- Have you ever deleted child pornography from your computer?
- How many images and videos of child porn do you estimate to have?
- Have you ever sent or received child porn in an email?
  - To/from whom?
  - When did this happen?
  - How else do you trade/buy/sell child porn?
- Have you ever received spam that was child porn?
- Have you printed child pornography from your computers?
  - Where are those printed photos?
  - When did you print them?
  - What printer or printers did you use?
  - Where are those printers?
  - Have you shared those printed photos with anyone?
  - Who have you shared them with?
- Have you ever copied printed pages of child porn?
  - What copy machine did you use?
  - When did you make the copies?
  - What did you do with the copies?
- Do you keep any photos of children?
  - Why do you keep these photos?
  - Where do you keep them?
- Do you search for "pre-teen" images or "Lolita" websites?
  - Have you saved these images?
  - Where are they saved?
- Do any of your friends or family know you have child pornography?
  - Who else knows?
  - Do they also have child pornography?
  - Have you shared child pornography with them?
- How old do you think the children are in the images?
- Are you sexually aroused by the child porn images?
- Have you taken photos of children…
  - …with clothes on?
  - …without clothes?
  - …in sex acts?
  - Where did you meet these children?
  - Where are they now?

- How did you meet these children?
- Did you touch the children?
- Have you communicated with minors online?
  - With email? With chat?
  - Have you sent photos to the minor? What kind of photos?
  - What were the screen names of the minors?
- Have you ever meet a minor face-to-face that you met online?
  - Where did you meet?
  - What was the minor's name?
  - How old was the minor?
  - What took place during the meeting and any subsequent meetings?
  - How far did you have to travel?
  - Did you bring any gifts?
  - Did you have sex with the minor?
  - Did you touch the minor?
- What percentage of your pornography collection are minors?
- Do you know anyone that has taken photos of minors engaged in sex acts?
  - Do you have or have you seen those photos or videos?
  - Who took the photos or videos?
  - How were they distributed?
  - Where the children were first met?
  - Where are the children now?
- Have you had sexual fantasies about children you have seen in photos/videos?
- Do you know what NAMBLA refers to?
- Do you know what Lolita refers to?
- Do you know what "pre-teen" refers to?
- What percentage of your pornography collection are adults only?

Crime specific—identity theft

- Have you ever made ID cards?
- Have you ever purchased ID cards fraudulently?
- Have you ever used a stolen ID to purchase items or obtain credit?
- Have you ever sold a person's personal information?
  - Did you sell it online?
  - How did you sell it?
- Have you used scanners to scan stolen ID cards or ID cards you created?
  - What scanner?
  - Where is the scanner now?
- Have you ever portrayed yourself with another's personal information to obtain items or credit?

- Have you ever searched for methods of obtaining personal information to create fraudulent ID card?
  - What search engine did you use?
  - What search terms did you use?
  - What websites did you find?
- Have you used software programs to create and alter ID cards?
  - Which programs?
- What are the names you have used that were obtained through theft or fraud?
- What items have you purchased using fraudulent ID and credit cards?
- Do you know any persons that create fraudulent ID cards and credit cards?
  - Have you provided them with someone's personal information?
  - Have you paid for services from them? When?
- Where did you get personal information used to obtain credit in someone else's name?
- Do you have personal information about other persons on your device?
  - What information do you have on other people?
  - Where did you get this information?
  - Have any of the names been used to create credit cards or ID cards?
  - Have any of the names been used in any manner by you or others?

Other alleged crimes

Creating an atmosphere where suspects admit their guilt with graphicaly details helps any investigation. But it may be also helpful for other investigations to not only obtain information about their involvement in the criminal acts under investigation, but also about other yet to be detected crimes.

At times, asking questions about criminal activity, other than the crime in question, can lead to information beneficial to other cases. Suspects may also be more apt to give information on others and their crimes rather than personally admit guilt.

- Do you know why you are arrested/investigated/questioned?
- Have you ever been questioned about this sort of thing before? When? By whom?
- Have you ever been charged or arrested for this type of crime before? When? Where?
- Do you know what this alleged act consists of?
- Do you know why someone would accuse you of any crime or this crime? Who?
- Do you know the identity of anyone that may have committed this crime?

- Do you know of any others that may be involved in any aspect of this crime?
    - Who are they?
    - How do you know them?
    - How do you know they are involved?
    - Where are they now?
- Do you know any others involved in any other crimes?
    - What types of crimes?
    - Who are they?
    - How do you know them?
    - How do you know they are involved?
    - Where are they now?
    - Do you know the victims?

QUESTIONS FOR VICTIMS

Computer-related questions for victims are not intended to prove or disprove their knowledge of computer systems, but rather to help determine the role of those systems in a crime. Victims may not be as well versed with computer systems as their victimizers, which can make them easy prey to scammers, phishing attacks, and hacking.

The questions posed to the victims will hopefully lead to information as to how they were victimized in order to determine the identity of the suspect. The questions also will help prevent overlooking physical evidence to be collected, such as recorded voicemails or printed pages of emails and websites.

Computer crime victim questions—identity theft

- How often do you use your computer?
- Do you have anti-virus software installed? Is it up to date?
- Have you had viruses on your computer before?
- Have you given your name, date of birth, social security number to anyone in any email?
    - Do you still have the email?
    - Did you speak to anyone on the telephone too?
    - Do you have any contact information or name of the person?
    - Did you fax or mail any information?
- Have you received emails from a bank or other institution asking to provide your account information?

- ▦ Did you provide any information?
- ▦ Do you still have the emails?

- Have any friends told you that they received spam from your email account?
  - ▦ When did this happen?
  - ▦ Did you change your password?
  - ▦ Has this happened before?
- Have you seen unauthorized banking activity in any of your accounts?
  - ▦ Have you contacted the banks?
  - ▦ Does anyone else have access to your online banking information?
    - Who else?
    - Why would they access your account?
    - Do they have permission to access your account?
- Do you have a Facebook (or other) page?
  - ▦ Have you "friended" any strangers?
  - ▦ Have you posted personal information online, such as your date of birth?
- Have you applied for credit cards online?
  - ▦ Did you bookmark the website address?
  - ▦ Did you receive any credit cards for which you applied?
  - ▦ Did you receive a denial if not a credit card?

Computer crime victim questions—harassment via email/text/online postings

- Did you save all emails that you consider harassing?
- Do you know the person that may have sent the emails?
- Did you reply to any of the emails?
- Did you give permission to post your personal photos online?
- Did you share these photos with anyone?
- Were any photos manipulated?
- How often are you receiving harassing emails/texts?
- Have you printed or saved harassing webpages that have been uploaded by others?
- Has anyone posted information online using your name?
- Why do you think someone is harassing you?
- Have you received phone calls that are harassing?
  - ▦ Do you have Caller ID?
  - ▦ Do you know the person(s)?
  - ▦ Do you have voicemails from the person(s)?
- How long has this been happening?

QUESTIONS FOR NETWORK ADMINISTRATORS

Network administrators are needed many times to obtain information necessary for search warrants when they are third-party hosts to electronic evidence stored by their customers. These questions will help the investigator draft affidavits that specifically request information sought in support of their investigations. The customer referenced in these questions refers to the alleged suspect in a crime. Any computer-related crime requires sensitivity to timeliness of evidence identification and collection. The Order of Volatility applies to data that naturally becomes unavailable in time due to natural processes such as shutting off a computer. It also applies to data that is intentionally deleted through normal business operations or computer use.

Document retention policies are not written with the purpose of preserving evidence as it is more so written to support business operations. Questioning network administrators as soon as each is identified will reduce the risk that relevant evidence will be destroyed through normal business operations.

Customer accounts—Internet Service Provider, online data hosting, other online services

- Who is the system administrator or contact?
- What log files are kept of customer logins?
    - How far in the past are they kept?
    - What information is contained in the log file?
    - Are incorrect attempts logged?
    - Are IP addresses logged?
- Are backup copies made of customer data?
    - Are backups available?
    - How far back in time do backups exist?
- Does customer "x" currently have an account?
- What is the email address of customer "x?"
- Is communication tracked with customers?
    - Is this communication able to be produced?
    - Does it include phone calls and emails?
- Where does the data physically reside for customer "x?"
- Is any customer identifying information needed for verification to create an account?
- What customer information is maintained?
- What Internet addresses do customers use to access their accounts?
- Can customers share files with their accounts?
- Is information maintained by all users included shared users, on accounts?
- Can you describe how data is saved onto customer accounts?

- What is the document retention policy of cancelled accounts?
- Is encryption employed on customer accounts?
- Are payment records maintained? For how long?
- Can you immediately preserve the account of customer "x" in preparation of a search warrant?

SUMMARY

The suggested questions are crucial in a computer-related criminal investigation. Answers may be truthful, untruthful, or portions of answers willfully omitted. Having the suspect commit to answers in one or more interviews will benefit the case regardless if the suspect was entirely truthful. Either the suspect tells the truth, providing incriminating statements, or the suspect is untruthful, which potentially discredits statements of innocence.

The investigator should intermingle questions with known answers to help determine the truthfulness of the questioning and to lead to additional questions. The suspect should not know which answers to questions are known as control questions. As the investigator, it is not only the confession that is sought, but also the admissions that will bolster physical and circumstantial evidence.

Confessions and admissions are only part of the investigative process and cannot solely be relied upon. Statements can be retracted, restated, or disproven. If evidence is weak in other areas of the investigation, the case can begin to be disrupted and torn apart, even if the suspect is guilty. Yet, confessions can be the most powerful evidence as the statements are made against the suspect's penal interest.

Bibliography

ADrive. <http://www.adrive.com>.
Frostwire. <http://www.frostwire.com>.
The Onion Router (Tor). <http://www.torproject.org>.
Xiao Steganography. <http://www.nakasoft.net>.

Physical Investigations

INTRODUCTION

In the world of digital forensics, getting lost in the data happens quickly and easily. This chapter focuses on physical investigations, detailing only those points useful in supporting currently available electronic evidence, or finding additional sources of electronic evidence.

The physical investigation and surveillance of a computer related crime perhaps best places the suspect behind a keyboard. The physical investigation should not be overlooked in any case where doubt exists to the actual suspect tied to activity with a computer. The forensic analysis to uncover the criminal activity is equally as important as finding the person responsible for the crime, as finding evidence of a crime does not complete an investigation by itself. The culprit needs to be identified and brought to justice with a complete and thorough investigation.

Understandably, not all digital forensic examiners will conduct physical investigations in addition to their forensic duties. For the forensic examiners having the luxury of solely working in a forensic lab, this chapter simply provides an overview of physical evidence collection techniques outside the lab and encourages forensic examiners to communicate with case investigators.

Equally important, investigators not tasked with forensic analysis should communicate their investigative findings to their forensic analysts. An ongoing theme in any investigation is that the small and unimportant details are unimportant, until they are not. The point at which a small detail becomes most important is when connections between collected data are made, and usually these previously unimportant details become most important. The key is to share information; every piece of the investigative puzzle is needed to complete it.

The investigative methods in this chapter are geared toward those techniques to physically place a person at a location, at a specific time, using a variety of measures. The importance of knowing where a suspect was located at any specific place and time cannot be understated. The objective of establishing a physical nexus between persons and places is what makes or breaks an alibi. Since a suspect's presence at a specific location during a specific time is of utmost importance, all information related to time and place must be documented thoroughly. This includes information given by the suspect during interviews, witness statements, and physical surveillance conducted.

Not every method can be used in every investigation for a multitude of reasons. Some of these reasons include not having the legal authority or that the method may be ineffective in collecting the evidence sought. An example of having a lack of legal authority would be civil litigation investigation where a wiretap approval would not be possible. With suspects that are not mobile, wherein the suspect may never leave their residence, aerial or mobile surveillance would be ineffective.

As you read through the methods of physical surveillance, keep in your mind that the ultimate goal here is that you are building a *timeline of the suspect's activity*. During the digital forensics analysis of electronic media, in which a timeline of user activity may be created, the timeline of the suspect's locations (and activities?) will similarly be needed to paint a complete picture of the investigation.

With any investigation undertaken by an investigator or forensic examiner, one of the most important questions to ask is, "Is this legal?" When in doubt, ask for legal guidance. This not only includes the private sector investigator or forensic examiner, but also law enforcement. Of serious legal ramifications are violations of intercepting electronic communications. As jurisdictions differ in authority and case law fluxes over time, no two cases will be alike.

HAZARDS OF ACTING UPON MINIMAL INFORMATION

Acting upon information based solely derived from a computer system can have disastrous effects to the investigation and persons if additional steps are not taken to corroborate and confirm investigative findings. In some instances, acting upon minimal information can be unsafe for investigators responding to a scene, whereas in other cases, innocent persons can be affected and inaccurately labeled and arrested as offenders.

Obviously, many situations demand action with time being precious and gathering additional information may not be practical. However, when there is time to corroborate information and test assumptions, you should take the time. Otherwise, you may cause certain personal and professional disasters to both investigators and innocent persons with a poor investigation. No law enforcement professional wants an innocent person to be arrested or charged because such an incident damages both the innocent person and investigators, personal and professional reputations. Not to mention, few of us want a news crew on our lawn asking about mistakes that may have been made.

One example of an unintended consequence due to not taking extra necessary steps for corroboration started on July 3, 2007, with a tip from the Washington's Missing and Exploited Children Task Force to the Washington State Patrol. This tip originated from the web-hosting company, Yahoo!, which had found images of child pornography on a hosted website. The tip was accurate as child pornography images did exist on the website and undoubtedly deserved law enforcement attention.

During the investigation, detectives from the Washington State Patrol obtained search warrants for subscriber information on the websites, which included IP addresses and billing information. Billing records showed that Nicole Chism had paid for the hosting through a credit card, with her correct residence address, phone number, and credit card number.

Several IP addresses used to log in to the website were traced back to physical addresses, however, the addresses were not the Chism's residence. Even as the IP addresses used were traced back to locations across the state and out of state and none traced to the Chism residence, a search warrant was served at the Chism residence and the workplace of Todd Chism, a Lieutenant at the Spokane Fire Department.

After a forensic analysis of computers from both the Chism home and workplace, no evidence of child pornography was found. No charges were filed. Todd and Nicole Chism endured the stress of being targeted in a felony investigation along with the negative public attention that usually accompanies the arrests of pedophiles. Yet, both were apparently not only innocent of the charges, but oblivious to any suspected criminal activity.

The point to be made is that corroborating information through other means is imperative on many levels. If for no other reasons than to physically place a suspect at a crime scene, consider the extra steps to also prevent innocent citizens from being wrongfully targeted or placed under suspicion/investigation.

Even in this case, certain facts were not making sense, such as IP addresses being traced across the state and none tracing back to the Chism residence.

Other facts such as previously reported stolen credit cards and nonsensical information obtained in the subscriber records should give investigators pause to gather more information. Some of the nonsensical information included incorrect personal information in the subscriber records obtained by the Washington State Patrol.

As any investigator that has been party to any situation such as this knows, the fact that a wrongfully charged criminal case based upon an inadequate or negligent investigation will end quickly is not much of a consoling factor. The imminent civil litigation that usually ensues afterward is much longer lasting. Such is the case of Chism v Washington (2011).

PHYSICAL SURVEILLANCE

Investigators must keep an open mind when conducting physical surveillance of a suspect. The intention may be to identify locations the suspect frequents and commits crimes using various computer systems and network access, but it may also provide a legitimate alibi should a crime be committed while the alleged suspect was under surveillance.

Although the best method of placing a suspect behind a keyboard at a specific date and time is visually watching the suspect at a keyboard, it is also the most difficult to accomplish. A simple obstacle such as the computer existing within an enclosed and secure building is more than enough to prevent actually observing a person sitting behind any computer. Physical surveillance also requires intensive manpower and equipment spread across several hours, days, or weeks for a single surveillance operation.

Many times, the result of hours of surveillance is not successful causing frustration. Skill, timing, and luck play important roles in surveillance, but having a plan with surveillance options and contingencies reduces wasted time and increases the odds of completing a successful operation.

This chapter gives the investigator options to consider when planning surveillance operations. The goals of surveillance may be to observe computer user activity at various locations in order to identify potential evidence collection points. Other objectives may include documenting the suspect's location in order to prove or disprove future claimed alibis or even to apprehend the suspect if seen to be committing a serious violation such as downloading child pornography.

Surveillance operations may be overt or covert, depending upon the desired outcome. Overt surveillance, sometimes known as "bumper locking", allows the suspect to know he is being followed with an intention to prevent criminal activity. Bumper locking may also be conducted to induce a response from the suspect, such as making phone calls, sending emails, or attempting to dispose of evidence with the goal to collect the disposed evidence.

Covert surveillance, which is the main focus of this chapter, has the goal of watching and/or listening to the undisturbed activities of a suspect to gather intelligence and evidence.

Before initiating any of the options for surveillance, goals and objectives need to be identified. Work schedules, equipment, available personnel, and documented planning take considerable amount of effort before the first operation begins. A thorough background of the suspect allows for a more effective operation. Knowledge of the suspect's residence, work, associates, and activities beforehand will allow for better planning and successful operations. This information will help the start of the surveillance by knowing where the suspect could be at any given time and may help find the suspect should surveillance lose sight of the suspect.

Mobile surveillance

Mobile surveillance is one of the more commonly used methods of physical surveillance. A mobile surveillance team, riding solo or in pairs in inconspicuous vehicles, simply follow a suspect as he or she travels in a vehicle. However simple it sounds, conducting a mobile surveillance operation that does not alert the suspect requires skill and coordination within the team, relying upon radio communication. The need for fluidity, coordination, and detailed planning increases as the number of surveillance operators is involved.

A single vehicle surveillance operation creates a high risk that the operation will be compromised, or "burned" as a single vehicle will not be able to be out of the line of sight of the suspect. Having more vehicles involved in mobile surveillance allows for the lead vehicle, known as the "eye" to be switched randomly at various locations or turns. The altering of the lead vehicle prevents the suspect from seeing the same vehicle often enough to recognize it during the surveillance operation.

The lead vehicle will also have primarily control of radio communications during mobile surveillance. When the "eye" has been transferred to another surveillance vehicle, the replacement lead vehicle will take primary for radio communications. As long as the lead vehicle has the suspect in a visual line of sight, other surveillance vehicles should not be in view of the suspect to prevent being compromised.

A visual line of sight does not mean the lead vehicle is directly behind the suspect, but rather in a position to have constant and rarely interrupted visual

FIGURE 3.1 The lead surveillance (the "eye") vehicle does not need to be directly behind the suspect for effective surveillance and is covered with normal traffic.

contact, such as seen in Figure 3.1. Normal traffic is used as cover cars, in that other vehicles on the roads are used to cover, or hide, the lead surveillance vehicle.

Intelligence derived from mobile surveillance should answer questions such as; with whom did the suspect interact, what did the suspect do, where did the suspect travel, which routes were taken, and what are the obvious reasons for each location visited. Having a suspect's normal activities documented will assist in identifying associates, obtaining sources of information, corroborating information from sources, future suspect interviews, and search warrant planning.

The environment and suspect actions affect specific methods of mobile surveillance. Crowded urban areas with high traffic decrease the ability for the lead vehicle to frequently change as other surveillance vehicles cannot weave through traffic without potentially drawing attention. Rural areas pose a problem of surveillance team vehicles outnumbering the average amount of vehicles on the road, or even being the only vehicles in the area. Suspects that park and enter buildings require that surveillance operators consider leaving their vehicles and conduct surveillance on foot.

To obtain the identity of suspects during surveillance, check the ownership of the suspect vehicle through the Department of Motor Vehicles. This information may be accurate only if the vehicle being driven is owned by the suspect. Another avenue of potentially identifying the suspect is through recovering fingerprints. Should the suspect touch items during the surveillance through eating in a restaurant, it may be possible to recover a glass from the suspect's table for fingerprinting or possibly from a credit card used to pay for the meal depending upon the environment and potential cooperation of the business.

Internet cafés or businesses that provide access to computer systems are a source of suspect fingerprint identification. Suspects that are seen using a publicly accessed computer system may be checked for the possibility of recovering fingerprints from the keyboard or other items the suspect may have touched and left identifiable fingerprints.

Fingerprints could also be recovered from discarded property in garbage from the suspect's property after having been collected by the waste management company. Electronic devices used by the suspect and examined covertly or after seizure with arrest or search warrants should be dusted for fingerprints. If for no other reason than to show the suspect actually touched that evidence item, but also to fully identify other potential suspects that may have touched or used the electronic devices.

Potentially, items that the suspect may have used in a crime, such as a hacking incident or sending harassing emails, may be tossed in a public trash receptacle. Surveillance operators that are in the position to observe this activity and recover the items most likely will have collected some of the best evidence in the investigation.

Mobile surveillance may seem to be an overly exhaustive effort for a cybercrime investigation. However, when an investigation requires placing a cybercriminal at a computer, this type of surveillance may be necessary. The benefits of the resources spent on surveillance with expected outcomes as compared with other investigative methods should be considered.

Aerial surveillance
Aerial surveillance affords a near invisibility of investigators for suspect mobile surveillance. Most persons never look up as they travel which makes aerial surveillance one of the best methods to track a suspect's movements. Depending upon

FIGURE 3.2 A greater land area is visible from the air reducing the risk of losing the suspect in traffic.

the type of aircraft, ranging from small drones, helicopters, or fixed wing aircraft, the flying height can be virtually invisible to persons on the ground. As can been in Figure 3.2, aerial surveillance covers a larger area with ease as compared to mobile surveillance alone seen in Figure 3.1.

Aerial surveillance also brings the ability to video record the surveillance. Using infrared (night) vision and thermal imaging cameras, nearly any time of day or night is effective. However, aerial surveillance is rarely even an option for most agencies. Unless the investigation is high profile, the odds of obtaining aerial surveillance support will be low. Even with a high profile investigation, the financial cost per flying hour along with the few aircraft available make aerial surveillance a luxury to which few may have access.

Without supporting ground surveillance, suspect activities occurring within public buildings, such as a coffee shop or shopping mall, will be unobserved from the air. Aerial surveillance in combination with mobile surveillance brings coordination efforts to a new level. Just the communication between air and ground surveillance between different agencies may require a re-configuration or sharing of radios and radio frequencies. Though not to be discounted as a viable means of surveillance, the use of aerial assets does require intensive coordination and resources.

Video surveillance

In an Orwellian surveillance world, all public places would be monitored with video surveillance, documenting every person and all activities. At least the goal of such a Big Brother World of an all-encompassing surveillance system could be so much. Most likely, should any government place such a system into operation monitoring all citizens, public outcry would most likely demand the systems removed.

However, certain systems are already in place by various government jurisdictions. Some of the most common systems currently employed are Department of Transportation cameras along freeways, red-light cameras at intersections, and real-time cameras placed at either high crime or high traffic areas.

Figure 3.3 shows an example of a real-time (live feed) video camera at a controlled intersection which can capture all traffic. Red-light cameras, that is,

FIGURE 3.3 Many controlled intersections are equipped with real-time video and still photo cameras.

FIGURE 3.4 The video feed from the traffic camera seen in Figure 3.3 (http://www.cityofbellevue.org/trafficcam/).

those cameras that just take still photos should a vehicle run a red-light, will only capture those vehicles violating a traffic law. The view from the camera in Figure 3.3 can be seen in Figure 3.4. Many of these cameras can pan, tilt, and zoom (PTZ) for more targeted detail.

Government agencies maintaining traffic cameras may allow for public viewing on the Internet, although live streaming video may not be available. Since many of these cameras allow for panning/tilting/zooming, investigators should seek the agency responsible for the cameras in order to gain access to internal viewing, control, and recording.

Although photos taken with the red-light camera most likely are maintained for any period of time, the camera feed for live videos may not be recorded or even constantly monitored. Having internal access to multiple cameras can increase the effectiveness of suspect surveillance with an additional video recording.

To corroborate a suspect's alleged alibi, obtaining recorded video or photos that might exist should be undertaken quickly. Some systems may retain recordings

FIGURE 3.5 Surveillance camera typically used in businesses.

for weeks where others may only maintain previous day's recordings. During a suspect interview, locations that the suspect claimed to have been (or not been) may have security cameras to prove or disprove an alibi. This would also include locations where the suspect may have made purchases at gas stations, used an ATM, or other locations with security cameras present.

In addition to cameras in use by government agencies, private companies employ the same technology in more locations for the security of businesses. These locations include security cameras in department stores, gas stations, banks, and even coffee shops. Figure 3.5 shows a commonly used security camera used in many business locations. Businesses with high value property at risk, such as casinos and banks, will not only maintain recordings of the videos, but may also employ full-time monitoring of live feeds to detect criminal activity. As these systems are fairly inexpensive, many businesses employ the security cameras. As an example to the normalcy of security cameras, patrons of most coffee shops hardly pay a glance to the numerous cameras mounted on the ceiling.

The combination of government placed security cameras with private business cameras affords a great amount of coverage of public areas. During mobile surveillance operations, investigators should take note of cameras seen during the surveillance. These would include government cameras on freeways and at intersections as well as private business cameras that surround the perimeter or a business or within the business. A subsequent follow-up to each entity having control of these cameras may recover recorded still images or video of the suspect. These photos and videos would be pertinent documentation of the location, time, and visual identification of the suspect.

Suspects that exhibit a pattern of travel or visits to specific businesses allow for investigators to take full advantage of security camera systems. Given a specific location where a suspect frequents, in which a security system with cameras exist, may present an opportunity for close surveillance without fear of being compromised. Security cameras that are monitored in real-time usually allow control of the individual cameras in varying the angle and magnification.

In some situations, it may be possible to view a computer monitor through a security camera in a public area, such as a coffee shop, as well as record that activity. Figure 3.6 shows an example of a business lobby captured by a ceiling installed security camera. Although the ceiling mounted camera is clearly visible, patrons rarely are concerned or aware of these types of cameras.

Businesses cooperating with law enforcement or conducting their own internal investigations can take full advantage of a range of security camera systems. Installation can take place afterhours and be installed specific to monitor a single person or multiple persons. However, there most certainly are limitations as to the extent of surveillance that can be conducted in regard to a person's privacy, even in the workplace.

FIGURE 3.6 Surveillance video frame of a business lobby (intentionally blurred).

Covertly installed cameras

Even as there are private and government owned security cameras through-out public areas in most cities, not every location is covered by a camera. For those areas, investigators may choose to install a security camera specific to the needs of the surveillance. These cameras can be real-time live feeds, monitored constantly or recorded constantly, or configured to take still photos based on programmed schedule or motion detection.

Self-installed systems can be directed at a specific area for a specific purpose. If the suspect activity is suspected to occur at a certain location, such as an Internet Café or a residence, by a specific individual, recording the suspect arriving and departing that location can be matched to later identified acts. A covert surveillance camera can practically eliminate investigators organizing surveil-lance teams and only requires periodically reviewing the recordings.

Covert surveillance cameras offer more flexibility than overtly exposed cameras. These cameras can be installed in vehicles, such as the classic Hollywood surveillance van, or can be attached to buildings and outdoor fixtures. As one example, Figure 3.7 shows where a covert camera can be installed on a tele-phone pole or near a power transformer without detection. Issues of personal privacy still need to be considered, even in public areas, as to the legality of placing any device capable of capturing video or photos.

Some criminal investigations require the covert installation of audio and/or video in a suspect residence or vehicle. These instances require court approved

FIGURE 3.7 A covert surveillance camera can be installed on telephone poles, hidden among standard equipment, without being detected as a camera.

search warrants and highly skilled professionals. Covertly entering a residence, business, or vehicle without activating alarms and without leaving traces of having entered is a risky activity. Additionally, nearly any covertly installed device can be discovered either visually or with electronic countermeasures.

Other sources of surveillance records

Rather than using keys to unlock doors, many businesses employ access-control systems. Access-control systems assist in tracking employee access to any location of a business location that has an access-device installed. Few are foolproof, but some systems are more accurate and less able to be defeated than others.

One of these security devices is the keycard access system. This system utilizes a Radio Frequency Identification (RFID) to control access to secure areas. An RFID chip, about the size of a grain of rice, is usually embedded in a credit card shaped item, a key fob, or other easily carried container. The RFID chip is programmed with the employee's information and specific security authorization for different access points. The RFID is placed near a receiver that reads the RFID chip. If access authority has been programmed, the door will be unlocked and the action logged by date, time, and user. Without additional evidence, it can only be assumed that the suspect was using the card and not another employee using the suspect's card. Figure 3.8 is an example of an RFID chip in a handheld, credit card size container.

Businesses with heightened security may usually have additional security measures that not only log employee access, but prevent unauthorized access by those that attempt to portray themselves as an employee. These additional security measures, known as biometrics, can be physical biometrics or

FIGURE 3.8 RFID keycard security system.

behavioral biometrics. Physical biometrics recognition devices rely upon a person's physical features and include retinal scanners, fingerprint scanners, and facial recognition.

Behavioral biometrics relies upon an individual's behavior for identification. These include signature recognition, speech recognition, and even keystroke dynamics, where a computer user's timing of using the keyboard is an identifying factor. Any of these methods contributes to the identification of the suspect and timeline of activity.

Surveillance notes and timelines

Throughout any type of investigation, notes are taken to memorialize events with written documentation. Investigators later transcribe handwritten notes to formalized documents, such as reports, declarations, and affidavits. In addition to these forms of documentation, importing handwritten notes of events into timelines has become a more common method of visualizing a series of events.

An example of handwritten notes taken from a physical surveillance is shown in Figure 3.9. The format for handwritten notes is usually any form available at the time that an event is observed, even on a scrap of paper if necessary. It is not the appearance as much as it is documenting activity observed to later be transcribed into useful information.

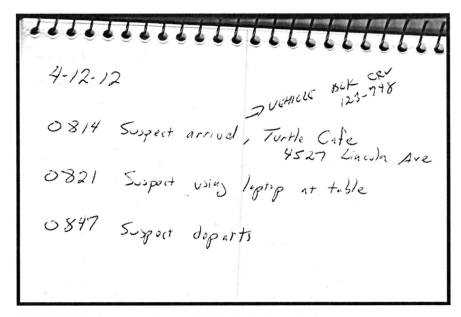

FIGURE 3.9 Typical handwritten surveillance notes on a notepad.

All persons involved in a surveillance operation are responsible for their own notes. Notes recorded electronically, such as using a digital recorder, should be transcribed to paper. All notes from every person need to be transferred to the case investigator as a central repository of information. In criminal cases, these notes, even the haphazardly written notes on a napkin, are evidence and depending upon agency policy, need to be preserved as such.

The transcription of notes taken throughout surveillance can be entered into an ongoing timeline of events. Investigators are intimately aware of all information in their cases, so much so, that they may assume everyone else is also fully aware of all information in the cases. The creation of an activity timeline, created specifically to show event, helps to visually describe related activity of an investigation. The transcription of handwritten notes into an investigation timeline is shown in Figure 3.10.

A spreadsheet is perhaps one of the easiest methods to store events. A database will have more capability to store more information but the ease to which a spreadsheet can be more quickly created and shared with other persons. A spreadsheet timeline can be sorted by any sorting column to find information or view specific information. Events can be entered in the order received, not necessarily as they occurred, yet the timeline can be sorted by time of event quickly.

A visual representation using the sample information from Figure 3.10 is seen in Figure 3.11. Case presentation methods involving massive amounts of data from forensic analysis and physical surveillance operations will be detailed in

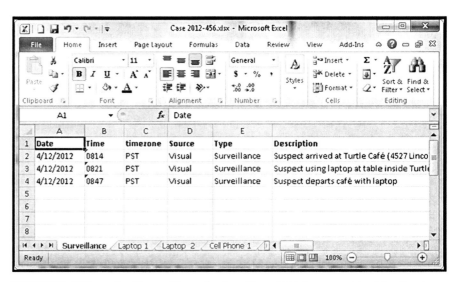

FIGURE 3.10 Example of transcribing notes from Figure 3.9 into a spreadsheet timeline.

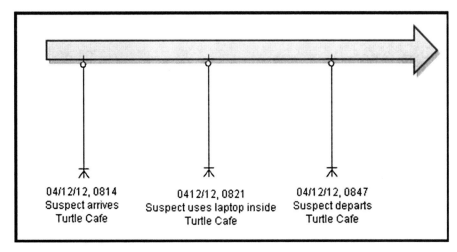

04/12/12, 0814
Suspect arrives
Turtle Cafe

0412/12, 0821
Suspect uses laptop inside
Turtle Cafe

04/12/12, 0847
Suspect departs
Turtle Cafe

FIGURE 3.11 Simple example of creating a visual timeline of activity.

a later chapter. But, it will be helpful to keep in mind the reason for keeping track of all events, even events that may seem inconsequential, for later analysis and case presentation. One of the end results of constantly working on a timeline is the visual representation of physical suspect activity and computer activity across a multitude of devices and locations.

Complex cases will have complex visual representations. Copious notes and voluminous phone records will add to this complexity. Organization skills are a valued trait in these types of investigations, especially when event information from multiple electronic devices is merged with surveillance activity notes.

ELECTRONIC SURVEILLANCE

Nearly all surveillance methods noted in this book are available without legal authority such as a search warrant. Both licensed private investigators and law enforcement can follow persons in public without hindrance in furtherance of their investigations. Businesses can place cameras in openly public areas of their property for security purposes. However, electronic surveillance, as it pertains to obtaining private information, is conducted only by government agencies with the appropriate legal authority granted to them for each circumstance. This type of electronic surveillance includes technology such as wiretaps to covertly capture the spoken word of any and all parties of a phone or electronic communication conversation.

Several of the electronic surveillance methods detailed in this section require authority granted by a court order, search warrant, or subpoena (administrative, grand jury, or trial). Depending upon the state, certain methods may not be approved at all. The investigator needs to be aware of local, state, and federal laws when considering employing electronic surveillance due to the possibility of carelessly committing a criminal offense in the process. Other methods are clearly available to any entity as long as the personal privacy of individuals is not violated. When in doubt, ask for legal advice. Even if not in doubt, asking never hurts.

Oral intercepts

The most publicly well-known type of electronic surveillance authority is the wiretap, also referred to as Title III (Federal Wiretap Act). The Title III is not found in the United States Code under "Title 3." It is actually under Title 18. Title III refers to the title number in Omnibus Crime Control and Safe Streets Act of 1968 which is Title III. Some states, such as California, also allow for wiretaps conducted by local law enforcement. The wiretap of oral communications requires a high burden of necessity for approval, usually because other investigative means are shown ineffective or expected to be ineffective. Some states, such as California, approve wiretaps only as the last resort.

Wiretap authority applies not only to the interception of telephones and cell phones, but also real-time capture of text messages, email communication, and Internet Relay Chat through network monitoring and use of Sniffer software. Sniffer software are programs that intercept routed data and examine each packet for information such as passwords and other data transmitted in clear text. Sniffer software can be configured to capture specified data or targeted data, depending upon the needs of the investigation.

Wiretaps are an extremely effective means to collect evidence in real-time, capturing the actual spoken words of suspects. Wiretaps also require intensive resources, both in personnel and finances, but as mentioned, may be the last resort in some investigations. An important note with wiretaps is that it is usually the suspect and all the communication devices used that are authorized for a wiretap. As it is common for criminals to use disposable phones, roving oral interceptions are approved to cover for the devices used.

Dialed number recorders

Pen Registers and Trap and Trace devices are electronic devices that record all outgoing and incoming information from telephone calls and Internet communications. Practically, a Pen Register records outgoing numbers with the Trap and Trace device recording incoming numbers. More accurately, the devices can be called Dialed Number Recorders (DNR). The type of information captured is in the form of dialed telephone numbers, the length of calls, and the identities of an email message's sender and recipient. Although the

TARGET NAME	TARGET NUMBER	DATE	TIME	DURATION	RECORD TYPE	DIRECTION	NUMBER DIALED	SUBSCRIBER
CASEY ANTHONY	(407) 619-9286	6/19/2008	12:12:00	0:34:00	Unknown	OUTGOING	(954) 328-9214	AMY HUIZENGA
CASEY ANTHONY	(407) 619-9286	6/19/2008	13:20:00	0:01:00	Unknown	OUTGOING	(954) 328-9214	AMY HUIZENGA
CASEY ANTHONY	(407) 619-9286	6/19/2008	13:20:00	0:05:00	Unknown	OUTGOING	(954) 328-9214	AMY HUIZENGA
CASEY ANTHONY	(407) 619-9286	6/19/2008	13:20:00	0:01:00	Unknown	OUTGOING	(954) 328-9214	AMY HUIZENGA
CASEY ANTHONY	(407) 619-9286	6/19/2008	14:09:00	0:01:00	Unknown	OUTGOING	(407) 701-7965	ANDY FRANCE
CASEY ANTHONY	(407) 619-9286	6/19/2008	14:10:00	0:02:00	Unknown	INCOMING	(407) 701-7965	ANDY FRANCE
CASEY ANTHONY	(407) 619-9286	6/19/2008	14:58:00	0:01:00	Unknown	OUTGOING	(407) 619-9286	CASEY ANTHONY
CASEY ANTHONY	(407) 619-9286	6/19/2008	16:20:00	0:03:00	Unknown	OUTGOING	(407) 629-7992	GENTIVA HEALTH
CASEY ANTHONY	(407) 619-9286	6/19/2008	16:23:00	0:04:00	Unknown	OUTGOING	(954) 328-9214	AMY HUIZENGA
CASEY ANTHONY	(407) 619-9286	6/19/2008	17:52:00	0:00:00	Text Message	OUTGOING	(954) 214-1187	SEAN HICKEY
CASEY ANTHONY	(407) 619-9286	6/19/2008	21:13:00	0:06:00	Unknown	OUTGOING	(407) 275-4909	CYNTHIA ANTHONY
CASEY ANTHONY	(407) 619-9286	6/19/2008	21:18:00	0:01:00	Unknown	OUTGOING	(407) 619-9286	CASEY ANTHONY
CASEY ANTHONY	(407) 619-9286	6/20/2008	11:38:00	0:00:00	Text Message	OUTGOING	(407) 929-7509	JEFFREY HOPKINS
CASEY ANTHONY	(407) 619-9286	6/20/2008	13:03:00	0:04:00	Unknown	OUTGOING	(407) 701-7965	ANDY FRANCE
CASEY ANTHONY	(407) 619-9286	6/20/2008	13:16:00	0:01:00	Unknown	OUTGOING	(407) 928-0982	ALEX RYAN GREEN
CASEY ANTHONY	(407) 619-9286	6/20/2008	13:17:00	0:02:00	Unknown	OUTGOING	(407) 421-9700	TROY BROWN
CASEY ANTHONY	(407) 619-9286	6/20/2008	13:19:00	0:05:00	Unknown	INCOMING	(407) 421-9700	TROY BROWN
CASEY ANTHONY	(407) 619-9286	6/20/2008	13:23:00	0:02:00	Unknown	OUTGOING	(407) 712-3665	STEPHANIE KOSTAKIS
CASEY ANTHONY	(407) 619-9286	6/20/2008	13:25:00	0:02:00	Unknown	OUTGOING	(407) 462-9293	DEBORAH GRUND
CASEY ANTHONY	(407) 619-9286	6/20/2008	13:28:00	0:02:00	Unknown	OUTGOING	(850) 368-2027	ROBERT WESTENBARGER
CASEY ANTHONY	(407) 619-9286	6/20/2008	13:29:00	0:01:00	Unknown	OUTGOING	(850) 368-2027	ROBERT WESTENBARGER
CASEY ANTHONY	(407) 619-9286	6/20/2008	13:30:00	0:03:00	Unknown	OUTGOING	(631) 902-5443	ANTHONY LAZZARO
CASEY ANTHONY	(407) 619-9286	6/20/2008	13:53:00	0:01:00	Unknown	OUTGOING	(407) 629-7992	GENTIVA HEALTH
CASEY ANTHONY	(407) 619-9286	6/20/2008	14:54:00	0:06:00	Unknown	OUTGOING	(407) 629-7992	GENTIVA HEALTH
CASEY ANTHONY	(407) 619-9286	6/20/2008	15:00:00	0:01:00	Unknown	OUTGOING	(407) 619-9286	CASEY ANTHONY
CASEY ANTHONY	(407) 619-9286	6/20/2008	19:25:00	0:00:00	Text Message	OUTGOING	(850) 368-2027	ROBERT WESTENBARGER
CASEY ANTHONY	(407) 619-9286	6/20/2008	19:34:00	0:01:00	Unknown	OUTGOING	(407) 252-3633	CHRISTOPHER STUTZ
CASEY ANTHONY	(407) 619-9286	6/20/2008	20:01:00	0:02:00	Unknown	INCOMING	(407) 252-3633	CHRISTOPHER STUTZ
CASEY ANTHONY	(407) 619-9286	6/20/2008	20:03:00	0:04:00	Unknown	INCOMING	(850) 368-2027	ROBERT WESTENBARGER
CASEY ANTHONY	(407) 619-9286	6/20/2008	20:33:00	0:02:00	Unknown	INCOMING	(407) 275-4909	CYNTHIA ANTHONY
CASEY ANTHONY	(407) 619-9286	6/20/2008	21:27:00	0:01:00	Unknown	INCOMING	(850) 368-2027	ROBERT WESTENBARGER
CASEY ANTHONY	(407) 619-9286	6/20/2008	21:32:00	0:00:00	Text Message	OUTGOING	(904) 614-3687	MARIA
CASEY ANTHONY	(407) 619-9286	6/20/2008	22:15:00	0:01:00	Unknown	OUTGOING	(407) 923-2353	IASSEN DONOV
CASEY ANTHONY	(407) 619-9286	6/20/2008	22:16:00	0:02:00	Unknown	OUTGOING	(407) 754-4058	JENNA PRENTICE
CASEY ANTHONY	(407) 619-9286	6/20/2008	23:23:00	0:05:00	Unknown	OUTGOING	(407) 923-2353	IASSEN DONOV

FIGURE 3.12 Phone tolls from the Casey Anthony murder investigation.

content of phone calls and emails is not captured, intelligence can be derived by the capture of this information and merged into a case timeline.

An example of phone records, also known as "phone tolls," is seen in Figure 3.12, from State of Florida v. Casey Marie Anthony (2011). Cell phone records, showing calls/text made and received, combined with cell tower analysis, can give indications of suspect location. Further investigation of phone records, such as interviewing those listed communicating with the suspect phone, may confirm that the suspect possessed the phone, discrediting a suspect's claim that someone else possessed the phone.

Identifying a suspect's cell phone is problematic unless the cellular number is publicly available. When the cellular is not publicly available, or the suspect frequently changes cell phones, law enforcement can obtain the numbers through use of a device known as the "Triggerfish." The Triggerfish device mimics a cell phone tower. By being seen as a cell phone tower by cell phones in the area, or an area targeted by the Triggerfish, the cell phones will reveal their phone numbers, serial numbers, and location to the Triggerfish device. Neither the cell phone nor cell phone tower is alerted to the use of the Triggerfish.

A Triggerfish was used in the capture of one of the world's most well-known hackers, Kevin Mitnick (Shimormura, 1996). Mitnick's hacking career started when he was 16 in 1979 and continued until 1995, where he was arrested and convicted and served over 4 years in prison.

The Triggerfish also assists in obtaining cell phone information for Dialed Number Recorder (DNR) applications and wiretaps. The need for a DNR in an investigation can be determined in the same manner as any investigative method. Will it be beneficial to the investigation? Are there other more effective methods? Does this method pertain to the suspect's use of cellular phones? What legal authority is needed?

Residence landlines are a source of information that can also corroborate a suspect's location. Retrieving records from the phone service provider will show calls made and received by the home landline. Interviews with the owners of numbers listed in the records may be able to confirm that the suspect used the phone in question on a specified day. Claims that a suspect was not at home during an incident, such as the downloading of contraband on a home computer, may be able to be disproven through phone records, even though no physical surveillance was conducted. A partial listing of home phone records from State of Florida v. Casey Marie Anthony (2011) can be seen in Figure 3.13.

Trash runs

The legality of collecting another person's trash from the curb varies state to state, and federally. If legal authority exists in which investigators can collect the suspect's trash, evidence obtained from the trash may be able to place the suspect at various locations. Examples would be finding receipts from locations that provide access to wireless networks such as a café. An example of such a fantastic find is seen in Figure 3.14.

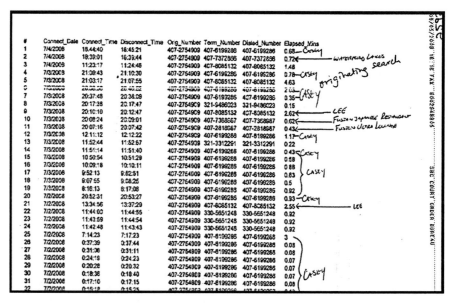

FIGURE 3.13 Home phone records from the Casey Anthony murder investigation.

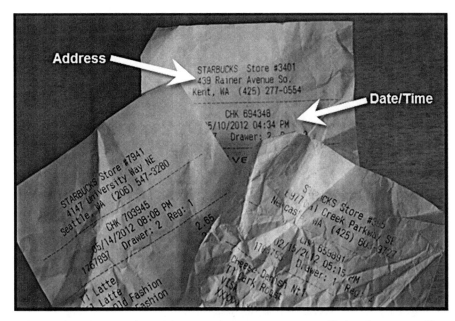

FIGURE 3.14 Example of "trash" that can place a suspect at a specific location at a specific date and time.

The significance of evidence that can be recovered from trash is that purchases made in cash, in which the suspect kept the receipt only to throw it away, would not be found through a search of bank records or credit card purchases. Even with multiple persons living at a single residence, receipts and other items placing a person at a location will be beneficial to the investigation. Many investigations are solved through pure luck. Timing plays a part. Skill plays a part. Suspect mistakes also play a part. But in many cases, it seems as if pure luck breaks a case.

In the example of finding receipts with dates, times, and locations that provided wireless access, if there were IP addresses previously obtained that were identified used in criminal activity result that matched, then luck in finding these receipts could break the case. Potentially, store video could be obtained based on thrown away receipts. The term "luck" is used loosely as good investigators seem to be lucky all the time when in fact, it is just hard work and tenacity.

Tracking cell phones

For a cell phone to be able to make and receive calls, it must communicate with cell phone towers. As a cell communicates with cell phone towers, the provider of the cell phone service generates a log of the connections. The phone service provider maintains those logs of communication with the cell towers for a length of time. The retention of data varies with providers, but most times will be available for at least one or more billing cycles.

Cell phones with Global Positioning System (GPS) enabled can be tracked remotely, in real-time. Currently, there are few, if any cell phones being manufactured without GPS capability. Corporate owned cell phones can be tracked by GPS and monitored online by the owner, just as a corporation can employ GPS on its fleet vehicles. The corporate monitoring of physical assets is conducted without the need of court approved search warrants.

Obtaining and analyzing cell tower records allow the investigator to track the movements of the phone through a given time period, nearly like a Global Positioning Device would. Investigators can plot the communication with cell towers on a map, and if the device can be tied to the suspect, it can be assumed that the travel of the cell phone was similarly that of the suspect.

Cell tower information accuracy depends upon various factors. The type of tower, number of towers in the area, terrain, buildings, weather, and even the time of day will affect the accuracy of location. There are numerous online sources to find locations of towers based on location. One such website is

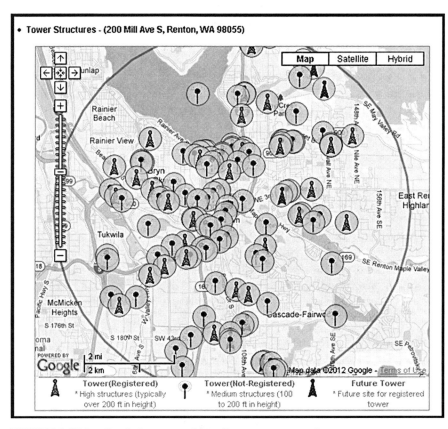

FIGURE 3.15 Results of a tower search http://www.antennasearch.com.

http://www.antennasearch.com. The results for cell towers for 200 Mill Ave S, Renton, Washington returned the following visual representation of cell phone towers seen in Figure 3.15. As can been seen in the visual, there are many towers for which the suspect cell phone could communicate with better accuracy than locations with fewer cell towers.

Cell tower analysis contributes to physical surveillance efforts. Relying solely upon cell tower analysis does not confirm the suspect possessed the phone, only the location of the phone itself. Potentially, any cell phone may be shared or even inadvertently forgotten in another person's vehicle and recovered at a later time by the suspect. Combined with other surveillance methods, a cell tower analysis can corroborate intelligence gathered throughout the investigation as to the whereabouts of the suspect.

Vehicle tracking

Installing a GPS device on a suspect vehicle allows for constant monitoring without fear of losing sight of the vehicle with mobile surveillance. Combined with an identified cell phone belonging to a suspect, movements can be tracked using cell tower analysis of the cell phone which can result in surveillance resources able to be curtailed.

As with any electronic surveillance method, investigators must abide by the current law in their jurisdiction, which will change as technology changes. There are different methods to employ GPS on vehicles. Attaching a GPS device can be either magnetic ("slap on") or hardwired to a power source on the vehicle. The use of the GPS and ease of covertly installing the device usually determines the type of installation.

Depending upon the GPS device, information can be stored and not transmitted or data can be transmitted wirelessly for real-time review. For regularly transmitted GPS data, which can be once every second to any time afterward, the power needs for the GPS will be higher. Wireless transmission configuration is best when the GPS is hardwired to a power source from the vehicle.

GPS units that do not transmit data usually require the investigator to manually recover the data by either connecting to a computer or be within a close distance to connect with a short-range wireless connection. If a suspect is identified as renting a vehicle that has GPS installed, obtaining the data after the vehicle is returned could lead to pertinent location information.

As newer vehicles have options for factory installed GPS systems, the ability to remotely activate (if not already activated) the vehicle's onboard GPS system exists. However, having access to the suspect's GPS system could potentially be compromised due to factors such as the suspect activating or deactivating the GPS through the provider of the service.

GPS devices are also becoming common for home detention, where a person convicted of a crime such as drunk driving, may opt to serve their jail sentence at home, and agree to wear a GPS device. This allows for the person to travel between work and home while under electronic supervision. These GPS devices most always transmit real-time data, accessible by the agency responsible for monitoring the persons.

Automated toll collection devices are a source of location information for a suspect's vehicle. These toll collection devices will log the vehicle's date, time, and location for billing purposes. Automated toll collection data collection can be in the form of scanning license plates using cameras or through Radio Frequency Identifying devices (RFID) attached to vehicles. This information is available from the billing third party and can add to the suspect's location.

Another method to determine historical locations of a suspect and vehicle is through a check of the suspect's driving record. Traffic stops by any law enforcement agency that issues a citation will be entered into the suspect's driving record. Even if a citation was not entered, should the traffic officer check the driver's name for wants and warrants, this information may be available for some time. Traffic stops have placed suspects in close proximity to crimes for many years. A classic example of a common traffic stop resulting in the arrest of a suspect is the case of United States America v. Timothy James McVeigh (1997), bombing of the Alfred P. Murrah Federal Building Oklahoma City, where one McVeigh was identified through a traffic stop shortly after the bombing.

Keystroke logging

The installation of keyloggers will almost always require the authority of an approved search warrant. A keylogger may be a software program that covertly logs selected or all keystrokes or it may be a hardware device connected to a computer system to collect keystrokes. Either system requires installation on the suspect computer system in a covert manner. Hardware keyloggers, disguised as a keyboard connection adaptor, must be physically installed by attaching the adaptor to the computer.

A software keylogger program must be installed as any other software program. Both of these methods inherently cause a risk of compromise with the initial installation since physical access to the computer system is needed. Software keyloggers can be installed remotely through an email or other network connected means.

Hardware keyloggers pose a risk of discovery only if the computer user inspects the connection of the device, such as when replacing a keyboard or mouse. The computer operating system is not able to detect a hardware keylogger as the device does not interact with the system. Software keyloggers may be detected by anti-virus software, which would immediately disclose to the suspect compromise of the computer system.

Sophisticated computer user logging software not only captures keystrokes, but also captures screenshots, all of which may be covertly sent to investigators for remote viewing. It is also possible to remotely access the entire system of the suspect computer, at the operating system level and physical level without alerting the suspect. This access allows for forensic capabilities to search for specific data or recover deleted files remotely. However, to gain remote access, the system needs to be compromised through the installation of these programs through an email or having physical access to the suspect machine.

With the use of the on-screen keyboard, where a keyboard is literally displayed on a computer monitor, keystrokes are actually mouse clicks on this virtual keyboard. Keystroke monitoring software may log the mouse clicks, but not the letters or numbers clicked on the virtual keyboard with the mouse. The use of a virtual keyboard to log in to password protected accounts renders a keystroke logging software useless.

Several cases have been successful with the use of keyloggers. One such example is case, United States of America v. Nicodemo S Scarfo and Frank Paolerico (2001). In this particular case, the suspects were employing encryption programs to protect their electronic communications. The FBI obtained approval to install a keylogger to log passphrases used in encrypting communication. Through the use of this program, the FBI had access to passphrases needed for email accounts and encrypted files.

Consumer purchase records

Once a suspect's activities have been detailed to some extent through surveillance and other information, locations which are frequented may be of a great resource. Shopping clubs, gyms, hotels, grocery stores, and other locations where the suspect may make purchases when using a membership card can yield historical information that may be of value.

Obtaining and analyzing credit card purchases quickly lead to past suspect locations for each purchase. Many locations, such as gas stations, will maintain video surveillance records for a time period. To place a suspect in an area of activity, the use of a credit card combined with a video surveillance of the purchase will be best evidence. This type of information can be used to corroborate an alibi if a suspect denies having physical access to a computer system if it can be shown through purchase records or video surveillance records.

Real-time monitoring of a suspect's credit card purchases may also provide investigators with potential leads to a crime in progress. Should a known cybercriminal regularly visit a location to use an open wireless connection, any purchases made could be indicative of using that wireless connection again for a crime.

OBTAINING PERSONAL INFORMATION

Aside from government maintained personal information on suspects, which is in the form of criminal history and arrest data, publicly available information is well suited in increasing surveillance operations. With the Internet becoming an integral part of our lives, personal information has become widely available online. Surveillance of suspects via the Internet is not only easier on resources, but is effective.

Perhaps the most important reason to gather suspect information from online (public) sources is to determine current suspect activities, behaviors, associates, and physical locations. By having a list of frequented locations, surveillance can be enhanced. Routes from the suspect residence to known locations can be scouted as can the actual locations. Surveillance operators can be inserted into known locations prior to suspect arrival and greatly decrease risks of surveillance being compromised.

As an example, with social networking websites, notices of events are posted and shared openly. Should a suspect be known to attend any event, surveillance operations can plan to begin surveillance at the expected location rather than starting from the suspect home. This decreases the odds of surveillance compromise as the suspect will not be followed from his residence. Additionally, if a surveillance operator has been positioned in the location, even as an attendee, the suspect's awareness should be lower than having had been followed.

Information gained online may be used to discredit claims by the suspect at some point. Membership and attendance at computer-related clubs would help discredit claims of being computer illiterate. Claims of not having access to a laptop or portable device would be discredited should the suspect be seen carrying or using a device to a meeting or conference previously identified.

Other information gleaned from online sources may be actual evidence to be used in the investigation. Forums, blogs, and comments attributed to the suspect that detail criminal activities should be preserved immediately before disappearing from the Internet. A number of motives may be able to be found among suspect postings on the Internet, such as displeasure with the government, business, or particular person. Suspects may even reveal information concerning sources of evidence such as detailing purchases and use of computer systems.

Placing the suspect behind a keyboard is possible through an online search for that user's Internet activity. Postings to blogs and forums are usually tagged with the date and time of the posting. Attributing a user account to the suspect, or any number of user accounts to any number of blogs or forums, can lead to a timeline of computer activity by the suspect without the investigator having physical access to the actual suspect computer. Although it is possible for a suspect to arrange for postings to be made in his behalf, the general assumption is that the suspect is making the online postings.

For any websites or blogs with suspect comments or posts, search warrants or subpoenas would be a good investigative method to use in order to obtain the originating IP addresses of the postings. Tying the suspect to an IP address, which may even be corroborated with physical surveillance, puts the investigator that much closer to placing the suspect behind a particular keyboard.

Most social networking sites allow users to upload photos. There are also a number of websites that are specifically designed to solely upload user created photos. As digital photos may contain embedded geographical location ("geotagging") metadata, investigators may be able to determine not only the date and time a photo was taken, but also the location. This feature is turned on by default in many cell phones and users are sometimes blissfully unaware of the embedded locations.

In 2012, the FBI identified and arrested a notorious criminal hacker, Higinio O. Ochoa, through a photo posted online that contained geographical location in the metadata. The photo of Ochoa's girlfriend was taken using a cell phone camera, with GPS indicating a location in Melbourne, Australia. Through an investigation of other related photos found online, Ochoa was identified through his girlfriend's GPS location and posts on the Internet. The main point of this example would be that even the most experienced cybercriminals will make mistakes allowing for their capture.

UNDERCOVER AND INFORMANT OPERATIONS

Undercover operations in cybercrime investigations obviously will include use of electronic communication. Undercover (UC) agents email, text, and chat with suspects online to communicate. This can be in the form of the UC assuming the identity of a child to investigate child molestation cases or perhaps the UC will assume an identity of a high-tech criminal to investigate a hacker. Either method can require face-to-face interaction between the UC and criminal suspect. This interaction and investigative method will apply similarly to civil investigations.

A great example of a successful undercover operation began in 1999 with the Internet Service Provider (ISP), Speakeasy Network, in Seattle, Washington. The Speakeasy Network was hacked from Russian IP addresses. The suspects contacted Speakeasy, identified themselves, and offered to not disclose Speakeasy's flaws if Speakeasy would pay or hire them. The hackers also claimed to now possess thousands of passwords and credit card numbers from Speakeasy customers. These hackers, Alexey Ivanov and Vasily Gorshkov, continued to hack and extort businesses in this manner.

The FBI conducted an intensive undercover operation, in which both Ivanov and Gorhkov agreed to enter the United States to discuss their hacking skills with FBI undercover agents. Through audio and video recorded conversations, keyloggers, sniffers, search warrants, undercover business fronts, and even setting up an undercover computer network for them to hack into, both were convicted on federal felony counts of computer fraud, mail fraud, and conspiracy.

All undercover operations carry an inherent risk to personal safety. As an investigative method, it also carries a need for intensive resources and skilled UC operators. The effectiveness of a successful undercover operation cannot be overstated. A benefit to being able to speak openly to a suspect while assuming the role of a criminal or conspirator allows for intelligence to be gathered exponentially faster than physical surveillance. Confessions made to an undercover are just as valid as a confession made to a uniformed officer. Future suspect activities, something not easily obtainable otherwise, can be spoken directly to the UC to which future operations can be planned.

Less extreme undercover activities can be conducted requiring no more than a phone call. If a specific time and place has been identified as a source of criminal activity, a simple phone call to the suspect will place the suspect at the location at a given time. The phone call need be no more than false pretenses in which the suspect is identified by voice or name. The phone call may not definitely place the suspect at a keyboard; however, tying the suspect to the location by voice is a strong indication. For criminal activity in progress, such as a victim receiving harassing emails from a previously identified location through an IP address trace, a call can be made while the activity is occurring to identify the suspect by voice.

If a suspect email address has been identified, emails can be sent to the suspect with a tracking code that obtains the local IP address of the suspect, and then sends the date and time of the email being accessed along with the IP address of the suspect computer. These tracking codes are invisible to most users and email programs, but pose risk of compromise should the code be identified by the suspect through a warning from anti-virus software.

Undercover operations coupled with surveillance may also be necessary in order to obtain evidence not able to be obtained otherwise. If a suspect obscures his IP address through any means, without having physical access to the system used in crimes, close contact with the suspect may be required. This contact could be in the form of befriending the suspect in hopes of having information disclosed to the UC. Even only if the manner of hiding the IP address was disclosed, investigative methods to counter the IP address hiding method could be conducted.

Informant operations pose the same risks to safety and compromise of the investigation with the added danger of informants being untrained. Informants have varied reasons for cooperating with law enforcement and not every reason is trustworthy. In many cases, informants are developed from cases, in which the arrested suspects agree to cooperate in consideration for lesser charges. Such was the case of Hector Xavier Monsegur, in June 2011, when he was arrested by the FBI. Monsegur agreed to work for the FBI as an informant, and in doing so, helped the FBI successfully investigate multiple hackers as conspirators. Although Monsegur did agree to cooperate, he also pleaded guilty to a multitude of computer crime charges.

Probably the biggest benefit to using informants in a cybercrime investigation is being able to take advantage of this past history and contacts with other cyber-criminals. Their reputations may be known and few, if any associates would suspect their long-time partner-in-crime to be working for law enforcement. Undercover officers enter without a history or known accomplices, unless an informant is used to vouch for the undercover officer.

WITNESSES

A witness may be a rare find, depending upon how you define what makes a witness to cybercrime activity. Practically, a witness would not only have access to viewing a computer monitor, but would have to identify the activity on the monitor as nefarious. Still, with a witness placing a person at a particular computer at a particular time, the investigator's determination that a crime had occurred negates the witness having knowledge of witnessing a crime.

Witness identification has drawbacks and potential dangers. Essentially, a witness can wrongly identify a person. Wrongly identifying any person that cannot provide a legitimate alibi has resulted in persons being convicted for crimes and later absolved. A single witness may be the most important evidence factor in the identification of a suspect in an investigation, and as such, investigators need to be aware of the potential of falsely identifying someone. The selection of a suspect by a witness when presented a montage of photos or a lineup has the potential of outside influences affecting the selection. The verbiage and tone spoken to the witness by investigators, the selection of individuals used in the lineup or photo montage, and even the mannerisms that are subconsciously exhibited by investigators can influence the witness.

At a minimum, when using lineups or photo montages, the person presenting these to the witness should not know which individual is the suspect. The persons chosen in a lineup or photo montage should be of similar appearance to each other and the certainty to which the witness decides should be documented in detail. Outside factors that affect the witness which cannot be controlled include the duration and conditions to which the witness observed the suspect.

In the corporate environment, witness identification is more certain and rarely requires the need for photo montages or lineups. This is due mostly to witnesses personally knowing or observing the suspect in their workplace. A corporate witness can testify to the number of different persons that have been seen accessing a specific computer system and probably identify each of them by name. As the witness may not have been knowingly observing criminal activity or policy violations, the witness may be able to at least place a person at a computer system at a given date and time.

Neighbors as Surveillance Agents

Depending upon the surrounding environment, surveillance of a suspect's residence is typically not a difficult task. But, there are instances where surveillance may be impossible due to a multitude of factors, such as existing in remote location. The investigator can consider contacting a neighbor of the suspect to assist in surveillance. The risk of using any citizen is that the surveillance and investigation may be intentionally or accidently disclosed by the neighbor.

Depending upon the severity of the investigation, in which violent offenders may be involved, neighbors may be placed at risk when asked by investigators to watch their neighbor. Confrontations between the suspect and witness neighbors also increase the risk of compromise especially for any neighbor now believing to have police powers.

At times, a neighbor may be the most reasonable, or only, option, but rarely is it the first option to consider. Usually, neighbors are best contacted afterward in search for historical information they may have observed about the suspect. Having citizens engage in active investigations without constant supervision incurs a risk of the investigation becoming compromised inadvertently.

DECONFLICTION

Law enforcement officers regularly "deconflict" with other law enforcement officers to avoid compromising investigations and increasing officer safety. Deconfliction is conducted by contacting a central repository of criminal investigations. Nearly all cases are naturally deconflicted internally within an agency simply due to have a centrally used reporting system within the agency. Informally, the investigating agency may contact surrounding agencies for information on suspects and investigations on those suspects.

The most effective and widely used law enforcement deconfliction method is provided by the High Intensity Drug Trafficking Area (HIDTA). Figure 3.16 shows the HIDTA website where law enforcement can contact for more information and access to the Watch Center. HIDTA operates the "Watch Center,"

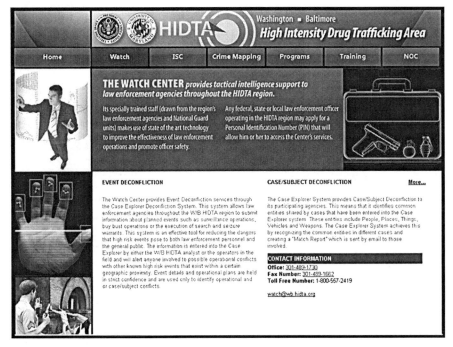

FIGURE 3.16 The HIDTA Watch Center website, http://www.hidta.org.

a central repository for all law enforcement agencies to submit case or event information. This information includes specific suspect details, case details, and current operations, which is used to cross check against other law enforcement agency submittals. If the Watch Center discovers a match on any event, person, or case between any agencies, those agencies are notified by the Watch Center to coordinate the exchange of information.

In this manner, law enforcement agencies can either pool resources together for related investigations or the agencies can share the information for more effective law enforcement cases. Having access to past investigations, to include surveillance notes of suspects, may not only save time on subsequent surveillance operations, but also could help determine the methods used by suspects more quickly. The benefit is mostly because the work may have already been verified, corroborated, and documented by another agency for you.

SUMMARY

Physical surveillance, including electronic surveillance, can be an extremely labor-intensive and risky investigative method and requires training for safety and success of the operations. In many cases, it is also required to compile a thorough investigation. Investigators must constantly be aware of the digital crime scene as it interacts with the physical crime scene. Although law enforcement has options not available to non-law enforcement, the abundance of techniques possible should suffice for the majority of investigations.

The process to build a timeline of activity for a case, whether criminal or civil, should take into account the activity of suspects while they are not only behind a computer, but when they are not near any computer systems. As the goal of all investigations is to find the truth, as much intelligence gathering as possible should be completed to accurately identify the suspect.

The culmination of information gathered during the surveillance phase of investigations can be integrated with information collected during the forensic analysis of electronic media to create a complete picture of events.

Bibliography

Shimormura, T. (1996). *Takedown*. New York: Hyperion.

State of Florida v. Casey Marie Anthony (Ninth Judicial Circuit of Florida. 2001).

Todd M. Chism, individually and as husband and wife, Nicole C. Chism, individually and as wife and husband v. Washington State; Washington State Patrol; Rachel Gardner individually; John Sager, individually. (Court of Appeals for the Ninth Cir. 2011).

United States of America v. Nicodemo S Scarfo and Frank Paolerico (US District Court 2001).

United States of America v. Timothy James McVeigh (US District Court 1997).

Further reading

Title III of the Omnibus Crime and Control and Safe Streets Act of 1968 (Pub. L. 90-351: 6/19/1968).

Technical Investigations

INFORMATION IN THIS CHAPTER:

- Digital investigative techniques
- Who? What? When? Why? Where? and How?
- "Other" device forensics
- Online social networking
- User activity
- Digital authorship
- Profiling
- Biological forensic evidence
- Triage and previews

INTRODUCTION

This chapter gives principles of extracting and interpreting digital evidence that can help place the suspect behind the keyboard. Although the information described will be based on the Windows Operating System, it will be the principles and concepts that are most beneficial to the investigator. Keep in mind that this single chapter cannot replace entire texts on forensic analysis, nor will this chapter go into great detail on any one specific topic.

A continuing concept, as with the preceding chapters, is building a timeline of the suspect's activity. So far, we have collected information through interviews and conducting physical surveillance. Now we will dive into the electronic crime scene to create a timeline of data with the end goal to merge both into a comprehensive investigation.

As you read through this chapter, keep in mind you are not only building a timeline of the suspect's activity, but also looking for evidence that shows *intention* and *knowledge* of the incident under investigation. An incident discovered without having evidence proving guilt is simply just a discovered incident and not a resolved investigation. All incidents still have a basic foundation that a person or persons cause the incidents or commit the crimes, no matter how the high, or low, tech method they may use.

This chapter is not a 'how to do forensics' chapter. There are plenty of resources that go much further in detail in specific areas than can be fit into one chapter. This chapter gathers various troves of digital evidence relating to suspect attribution with the expectation the examiner can either conduct the forensic analysis work already or learn methods using available resources.

All references to specific software are solely for demonstrative purposes, not instructive in the use of any software. Whether commercial, open source, freeware, or personally developed software is used depends upon the individual situation of each examiner. That also includes personal validation of the tools and appropriate use of software licenses.

Furthermore, not all aspects of recovering digital artifacts are described in this chapter, only a selection of those artifacts used to tying a specific person or persons to a specific device and activity. The verbiage of using the terms 'suspect' and 'crime' not only pertains to criminal investigations but also civil or internal investigations. Substitute 'suspect' with 'custodian' and 'crime' with 'allegation' as it fits your situation.

DIGITAL INVESTIGATIVE TECHNIQUES

An investigator may be an expert in a physical crime scene, just as a forensic examiner may be an expert in an electronic crime scene, but both need to be aware of how the physical and electronic crime scenes interact with each other. A basic premise of any crime scene is that evidence exists. Dr. Edmond Locard surmised that every contact between objects leaves some trace of that contact, usually as material exchanged between the objects (Bisbing R., 2006). Whether it is a strand hair, a drop of blood, tool mark, or even DNA, there is some trace of evidence to be found when two objects touch. This is what became to be known as Locard's Exchange Principle.

In the electronic world, the traces of evidence may include modification or creation of files, or logs that document other user activity. Merely turning on a computer leaves traces that not only was the computer turned on, but the exact files that were changed while the computer was on. Locard's Exchange Principle also applies to the electronic world as electronic files are touched when accessed, modified, or created.

Most forensic examiners have been asked at least once if they can prove a specific person was at the keyboard at a specific time. The common, and correct, answer is that without corroborating evidence, it is virtually impossible to place a person at the keyboard. Corroborating evidence may be a single item, such as security camera footage of the suspect and computer together. Or it may be a multitude of circumstantial evidence that, when examined in a totality of the circumstances, shows that no one but the suspect could have been at the keyboard.

What is a person?

An *IP address* is not a person. An IP address is simply a numerical designation of a device that uses the Internet Protocol. This IP address can usually be traced to a physical location; however, sometimes, it may not even be tied to an accurate location. An IP address is a clue as to where a device may have physically existed while connected to the Internet. There are also other problems associated with IP addresses such as dynamic addressing where at a given point, the IP address may be reassigned after the commission of an incident.

As an IP address can be used by any person with access rights, such as a home wireless network, identifying an IP address does not identify an individual person. Using a home wireless as an example, persons outside the home can access the wireless network either by permission of the owner or through bypassing security measures for access. Therefore, even the physical location to which an IP address is listed may not be the physical location where a person accessed the network. Potentially, a person can access an open and unprotected wireless network or even bypass security of the wireless network from the street or hundreds of feet away from the physical location. An IP address by itself means that additional investigative methods are necessary to ensure proper identification of the suspect.

Even more troublesome when solely focusing on an IP address to identify an address is the existence of methods to obscure IP addresses. Examples include virtual private networks (VPN) and the The Onion Router, also known as Tor Project. A suspect using any one of these methods may not only be effectively hiding their actual IP address but also placing other persons at risk of being wrongfully identified. Relying upon IP addresses in which a VPN or Tor was used will most likely result in following inaccurate investigative leads.

A MAC address, on the other hand, is the number assignment given to network interface cards which usually can be traced back to a physical machine. The MAC address is much like a serial number imprinted on a physical device, but like IP addresses, it is also possible to change MAC addresses to obscure tracking methods. So, *a MAC address is also not a person.*

Tor is free software that uses a network of virtual tunnels by which a Tor user's IP address is effectively hidden through many anonymous relays. Figure 4.1 shows a visual example of how Tor works. As can been seen, relying upon an IP address that is a Tor exit relay will not be the suspect's IP address but only the last relay that was used.

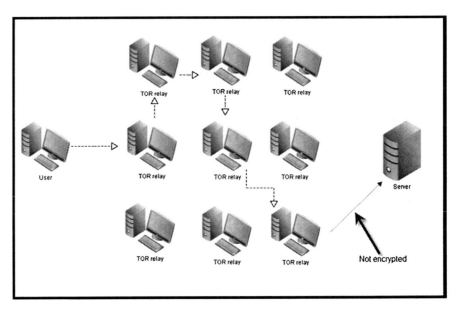

FIGURE 4.1 Tor exit relays, last exit relay is not encrypted.

An unfortunate Tor exit relay case example occurred during the spring of 2011. Immigration and Customs Enforcement agents served a search warrant and seized six computers in a child pornography investigation in which the suspect and location was identified by an IP address (Hofmann, 2011). The IP address was a Tor exit relay, which as can be seen in Figure 4.1, is just the last computer in which traffic goes through before reaching its destination. In this case, the alleged suspect allowed his computers to be used as a Tor exit relay for other Tor users. However, the alleged suspect had no knowledge or control of the data exiting his Tor relay and accordingly, was not involved in child pornography.

Investigators relying upon IP addresses are advised to check the Tor Project website (http://www.torproject.org) to compare a suspect's IP addresses with a list of known Tor exit relays. This will reduce the risk of focusing on an IP address and person that is of no relation to the actual suspect, other than being the last exit relay in a long chain of relays.

A *computer user account is also not a person*. User accounts are simply a convenient method where multiple users can have their data confined and protected from other users of the same computer. Or it may be to give different users of a system different access rights. Either way, it is only a convenience and not a surefire method to allow only authorized users to access their own account.

In a residence where multiple persons have access to a computer, it is possible that all residents use a single user account or that they may share all of the accounts.

In a business location, users may inadvertently leave their computer open to access by any passerby. Any of these situations allows for a user account to be considered a clue as to the actual computer user, but not affirmatively tied to any person without corroborating evidence.

So what is a person? A person is a human, not a number such as an IP address, MAC address, or name on a user account. As an investigator, remember that you are working toward identifying the person that committed violations in question and placing that person at the keyboard.

WHO? WHAT? WHEN? WHY? WHERE? AND HOW?

A key factor in placing any person at the scene of a crime is obtaining evidence that can place an identified suspect as it relates to the scene of the crime. Previously discussed methods of physical surveillance and obtaining records are usually the best evidence of placing a suspect at a specific place and at a specific time, but as most investigations involve reacting to incidents, this may not be always possible.

Second best evidence is the examination of an electronic device that had been possessed by a suspect. The only reason why this is not as good as physically placing a person at a scene is because unless there is additional corroborating information, a forensic examination of electronic media by itself cannot place a person to that device.

Investigations need to establish where the electronic device has existed by date, time, and location based on the device's activity. As there will be a multitude of dates and locations collected, our ever-growing timeline of suspect activity comes into play to keep track of the evidence chronologically. In a case where several electronic devices have been used by a suspect, the amount of data expands exponentially.

With our goal of placing devices in the hands of the suspect, the more devices we have to examine, the more likely we will be able to accomplish this task using all available information. By obtaining the likely physical location of an electronic device through forensic analysis and also obtaining the physical locations of a suspect through means other than a forensic analysis, inferences can be made as to the likelihood the suspect controlled the device. Not a certainty, but definitely a piece of circumstantial evidence to build upon.

Location

Physical surveillance methods easily determine physical locations by visually watching suspects travel to different locations. Dates, times, and the physical addresses are documented for each instance of surveillance observing the suspect. In addition to physical surveillance of persons, geolocation is used to track electronic devices, not persons. Through the means of GPS coordinates, Radio Frequency Identification (RFID) scanning, Wi-Fi connections, and a myriad of other electronically stored location information, geolocation refers to either the process of assessing a location or the actual physical location.

More electronic devices are being outfitted with geolocation capability which pinpoints the location of the device through GPS or cell tower triangulation. Triangulation uses two known geolocation points to identify a third unknown location. Wi-Fi network connections can also be used to provide geolocation to a device. In particular, smartphones may rely on a combination of geolocation sources to provide accurate location identification. Geotagged information can be embedded in photos, videos, text messages, emails, and even websites.

Forensic analysis of electronic devices can result in extensive historical records of geolocation points along with the dates and times of each point. Tying these locations of devices to specific persons gives a clear picture of activity and the identity of the suspect in control of the device.

Time

All forensic examinations commonly include determining the date and time of the evidence system. Dates and times play one of the most critical parts of a forensic analysis as it is the basis of a timeline analysis. Extracting data and activity is also important, but the activity needs to be attributed to specific and accurate dates and times. Where numerous persons may have access to a specific computer, a process of elimination of suspects helps to narrow the potential number of suspects. This elimination hinges on having accurate information on the dates and times of the evidence system.

Determining the time zone of the evidence system aids in location in that at least the evidence system is configured for a time zone relevant to an investigation. Obtaining the date and time from the physical system can be done by accessing the BIOS, as seen in Figure 4.2. In this example, the time zone is not available, only the date and time. If this information matches the local time, then you can assume the time zone to be the same as the local time zone.

Many computer users are aware of their computer clock since it is usually displayed on the task bar unless intentionally hidden. Adjusting the computer date and time has been made extremely simple for even the most beginning

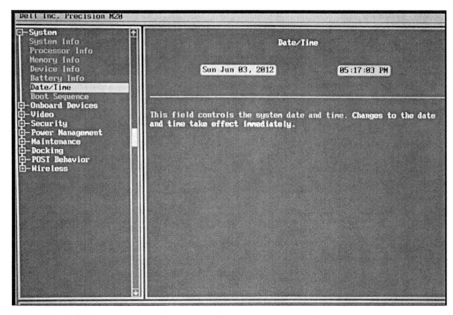

FIGURE 4.2 BIOS.

computer user by easily double-clicking the displayed time and changing the date and time with a popup dialog box as seen in Figure 4.3.

Since the ability to change the date and time is easily made, examination of the other information from the system to corroborate dates and times is necessary. As Locard's Exchange Principle shows, every contact leaves a trace. By changing the system date and time, traces of this activity may be found through analysis of the UserAssist key and possibly the Windows Event Log. This further corroboration can include examining the headers of emails as the headers will have server dates listed which can be compared to the received dates in the email programs. Internet records, such as cookies, can be checked as some cookies may also have server time listed in the cookies.

FIGURE 4.3 Windows date and time dialog.

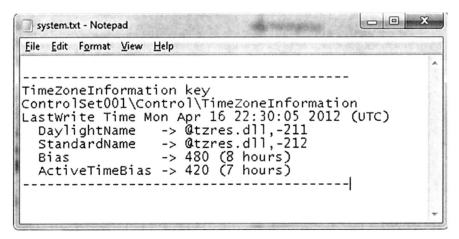

FIGURE 4.4 RegRipper output of time zone information from the registry key, ControlSet001\Control\TimeZoneInformation.

Recovering the Windows clock settings forensically involves extracting this information from the registry using any number of forensic software applications. RegRipper is an open source application aptly suited for extracting this information. As seen in Figure 4.4, the output of RegRipper is a text file which shows the TimeZoneInformation key. The information extracted is in UTC/GMT time, but can be converted to a time zone by adding the ActiveTimeBias to the displayed UTC time.

Other applications may not use UTC/GMT time, so it is solely up to the examiner to make sure any references to dates and times are consistent and correct based on the tool used. There are many unintentional methods to completely confuse a courtroom when explaining computer technology, but do not let the confusion of time be one of those unintentional methods. Sometimes the simplest method to communicate complicated technology is to show the validated output of an application that clearly shows the court that which may be obvious to the examiner but not to a layperson. An example of showing the time zone setting of a computer system can be seen in Figure 4.5.

Obviously, having shown that a suspect computer is configured to the same time zone compared to an incident may not be much in the way of clear evidence, but the point is gathering tidbits of evidence to paint an entire picture. Once a precise basis of time has been established on the electronic systems, an accurate timeline can be created. An excellent utility to help maintain consistent time values throughout an investigation is the Time Lord Utility by Paul Tew, as seen in Figure 4.6.

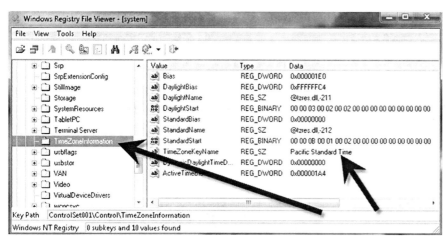

FIGURE 4.5 Windows Registry File Viewer, http://www.mitec.cz/.

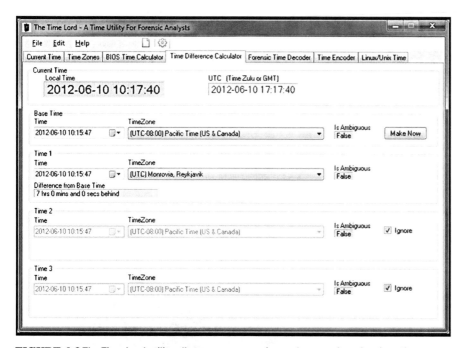

FIGURE 4.6 The Time Lord utility allows easy comparing and conversion of various time related tasks. http://computerforensics.parsonage.co.uk/timelord/timelord.htm.

FIGURE 4.7 Windows wireless connections as seen by the computer user.

Wireless connections

Computer users having wireless capabilities in their systems can selectively choose the wireless networks of choice, given they have access rights to the network. This is done simply through an interface in Windows. An example of a computer user's view of wireless and wired networks through an icon in the task is shown in Figure 4.7.

Recovering this information from the registry can be accomplished through most forensic application suites or standalone registry applications such as RegRipper.

In Windows 7, the following registry keys are relevant to network connections. The first contains the networks accessed with timestamps. The second maintains the MAC addresses, SSID name, and additional information for each accessed network. The remainder keys store duplicative network settings of specific connections. This information can be used in geolocation efforts to physical place the system at a specific place.

1. HKLM\SOFTWARE\Microsoft\WindowsNT\CurrentVersion\NetworkList\Profiles\(GUID)

2. HKLM\SOFTWARE\Microsoft\WindowsNT\CurrentVersion\NetworkList\Signatures\Unmanaged

3. HKLM\SYSTEM\ControlSet001\services\Tcpip\Parameters\Interfaces\(GUID)

4. HKLM\SYSTEM\ControlSet002\services\Tcpip\Parameters\Interfaces\(GUID)

5. HKLM\SYSTEM\CurrentControlSet\services\Tcpip\Parameters\Interfaces\(GUID)

Figure 4.8 shows extracted registry information from wireless connections which includes the dates and times of last connections using the open source program Registry Decoder. Obtaining this type of information showing wireless connections greatly enhances placing your suspect at different locations.

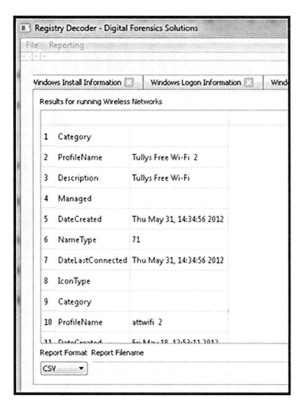

FIGURE 4.8 Registry Decoder display of wireless networks from a software registry hive; http://www.digitalforensicssolutions.com/registrydecoder/.

Network (cloud) connections

An abundant source of evidence documenting the location, date, and time of an electronic device is from third parties, such as from the suspect's Internet Service Provider. Third parties typically will maintain records of customer logins and connection information for a certain period of time. With court orders or administrative subpoenas, this information can be had with a simple fax to the provider where a listing of IP addresses from which the customer used will be available.

One example of a cloud connection that may go unnoticed by a computer user is that of automated online backup services. A service such as Dropbox provides free and paid accounts of automated, full backups of folders without requiring user intervention. Other online storage providers offer similar free and paid storage amounts and almost all are set by default installation of the programs to automatically backup complete folders or make incremental

THE AUTHORITATIVE REFERENCE ON REGISTRY FORENSICS

Windows Registry Forensics

Windows Registry Forensics: The Advanced Digital Forensic Analysis of the Windows Registry by Harlan Carvey describes these settings and the analysis of the Windows registry in greater detail.

uploads as files are created or modified on the local machine. Many of these automated online cloud storage systems are also mobile phone capable.

Even without a subpoena, logging into a Dropbox account shows the number of linked systems and the information regarding the last connection of each device with the relevant IP address. Linked systems displayed by in the user's Dropbox account refer to individual computer systems with access to the account, which may be additional sources of electronic evidence to seek for examination. Figure 4.9 shows a screen capture of a Dropbox user's view of this record. In this example, there are three computers listed that have the Dropbox application installed and linked to this one Dropbox account.

Providers of these online services will most likely maintain more than just the last connection. Suspects that use Internet connections in public locations to commit any acts using their computer or other mobile device will be logged by any automated online file backup service. The examiner can place the suspect's computer at a location, date, and time with the inference that the suspect controlled the device given the service provider's connection logs. Secondary evidence may be obtained from the security video footage from those locations to affirmatively identify the suspect.

Obtaining server provider logs of all existing connections may be able to offer investigators locations where the laptop is commonly used outside the home

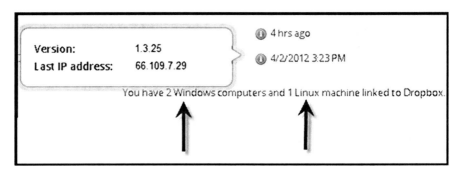

FIGURE 4.9 Dropbox most recent computer connections as seen by the account owner. http://www.getdropbox.com.

or work environment through obtaining IP address subscriber information. A side benefit of this automated connection is in the assistance of stolen device recovery. If the thief starts the device and connects in any manner to the Internet, the IP address will be logged by the service provider under the owner's account.

Photos and videos

Photos and videos can be both evidence of an incident, such as the photo being a crime in and of itself, or photos evidence. Photos of child pornography would be actual physical evidence and photos of suspects posing with the proceeds of a crime would be an example of photos taken of evidence. Photos and videos can corroborate evidence that places a suspect at an exact location at an exact time, which may not be relevant to an incident, but could be important in placing the suspect in the area of an incident close to the time of the incident.

Automated file search software programs can help identify objects in photos based on comparisons of other known photos. A great example of such a program is the Google program, "Bedspread Detector", which detects elements in photos to different photos having the same elements. This program was created in response to a child pornography analyst who recognized a similar bedspread in different child pornography photos. The recognition of one object, the bedspread, resulted in the identification of more victims and offenders and subsequently, the name of the program, "Bedspread Detector" (Allen, 2010).

Beyond the content of a photo or video, there exists additional information about the actual electronic files known as EXIF data (Exchangeable Image File Format). This additional information, or metadata, provides evidence to investigators that is specific to each file. The type of camera used, date and time the photo was taken, and in some circumstances, even the location of where the photo was taken through embedded GPS coordinates.

An example seen in Figure 4.10 shows a photo of a bedroom and some of the EXIF data of the photo. As can be seen in the EXIF data, the image illustrated in Figure 4.10 was probably taken with a Blackberry smartphone. If the location was identifiable by the content of the photo and the Blackberry was identified, this photo would place the device at the location at a specific date and time. This would be a simpler task if the photo is geotagged, that is, GPS coordinates embedded within the EXIF data of the photo.

Mobile devices, such as smartphones and tablets, contain a wealth of information. It was not so long ago where the analysis of a mobile phone consisted of jotting the numbers that were seen in the display. The current advances in mobile device technology coupled with forensic software and hardware applications have

FIGURE 4.10 EXIF data example, using program PhotoME, http://.www.photome.de.

practically made an entirely separate discipline in mobile device forensics, yet information from mobile devices can directly affect the information in computer systems through interconnectivity between the devices and systems.

Extracting data from mobile devices such as any cellular phone or tablet requires a wider variety of tools and skillsets than those needed with computer hard drives. Mostly, this is due to the difficulty in being able to access and extract the memory physically or logically from the devices while reducing the amount of file modification. The methods and software used for extracting data from these devices vary almost as much as the number of different devices.

Examining the mobile device data is similar to examining almost any electronic data, but getting to the data may not always be as easy or possible due to current limitations in acquisition software. For that reason, this section will only discuss the type of data contained in mobile devices that is directly relevant to the suspect's activity for your investigative timeline analysis.

There are several reasons in which mobile devices greatly enhance investigations. Other than containing obvious direct evidence such as a photo taken during the commission of a crime or logged phone calls to victims or conspirators, mobile devices are practically an attached GPS device on the user. Considering that in today's society and culture, having one or more cellular devices is the norm, and that almost every device has GPS capability, mobile device users are literally carrying around a GPS system, logging their daily movements, 24 h a day. In addition to the geolocation logging that occurs, users will self-report their location through a variety of consumer services, such as posting their whereabouts on social networking websites.

GPS enabled mobile devices are certainly convenient for their owners because of the third party applications that rely on knowing the location of the device to provide information to the owner. Some applications include navigation, social networks, weather, travel services, banking, Internet searching, and an ever–growing list of applications that can be instantly downloaded to the devices. The more a user depends upon the mobile device for these services, the more data that will be available in tracking the user's historical locations.

The suspect's mobile device which logs geolocation aids investigations by documenting the travels a device makes by date, time, and location. Tying that device to a person or persons can corroborate information obtained on an evidence computer system should the device and computer system exist at the same place, at the same time.

A feature for users and their use of social networking websites is informing their friends, or the entire public, of their daily whereabouts and activities. This is done intentionally with messages posted on their personal social networking sites and sometimes unintentionally with photos taken by cellular devices which are posted online. Many cellular devices embed within photos taken by the device, the GPS location along with other metadata such as the date, time, and device information.

The photo stored in the device will have this information available and if the photo is uploaded to a website, anyone with access to the photo will also be able to access the GPS location of that photo. Figure 4.11 is an example of a Geo-tagged photo taken with and stored on a mobile device.

Additional information is generated when users update their status on social networking sites through uploading photos or posting comments. Figure 4.12 shows an example of Geotagged Facebook activity by the mobile device user.

Devices that are wireless enabled, in that the device can connect to an available wireless network most likely will have connection activity logged. Figure 4.13 shows an example of Wireless connections from a device, which also includes the date and time stamps of the connections.

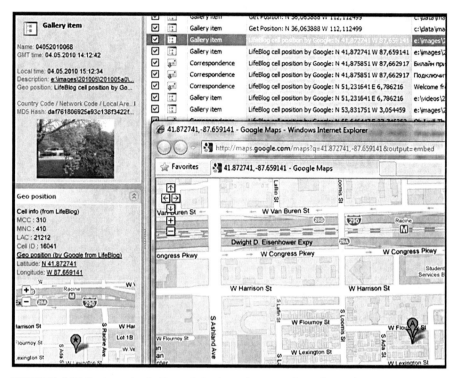

FIGURE 4.11 Geotagged cell phone photo shown in oxygen-forensics analyst.

Mobile devices with Skype capability can connect to wireless networks, which, not surprisingly, are also logged for your recovery by the device. Figure 4.14 shows an example of extracted Skype calls and connection information. Skype (http://www.skype.com) is an Internet video conferencing application that can be run on computer systems and some smartphones.

Call data records (CDR), available from the cellular service provider, give detailed records of call activity, more so than just calls made or received. The CDR includes the call duration, billing number for the call, disposition of the call (failed call, busy, etc.), the type of call (text, voice), and cell site accessed. An analysis of the geolocation information from accessed cell sites from the CDR is a contributing source of a suspect's history location points and travels.

The compilation of geolocations obtained from connections to wireless networks, geotagged photos, and cellular tower connections can give a thorough picture of locations the device traveled. Even locations saved by the device user of map locations, such as searching for locations using Google

FIGURE 4.12 Geotagged Facebook update. Courtesy of Oxygen Forensics
http://www.oxygen-forensic.com.

Maps, can be effective at obtaining leads of possible historical locations. All of these device locations may be instrumental in showing a suspect's location at or near a crime scene or incident or corroborating an alibi away from the scene.

Geolocation warning

An important aspect of relying on geolocation information extracted from mobile devices is that you cannot always rely on geolocation information extracted from the mobile devices. Sometimes it is just another lead, or clue, as to where to search for corroborating information. This is especially important information when geolocation is based on cellular towers. The intention of geolocation in mobile devices is not so much to track the user's movement. This service is to give the owner of the device-specific location information as desired, such as navigation or nearby locations for personal services.

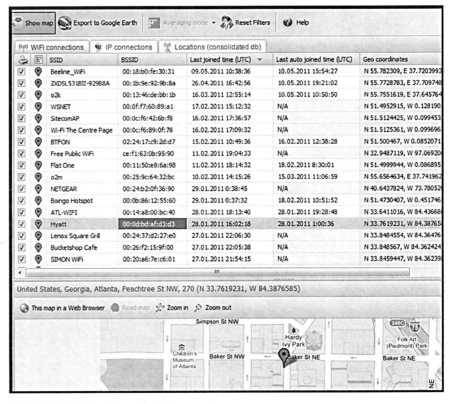

FIGURE 4.13 Smartphone Wi-Fi log records.

As discussed, cellular devices connect with cellular towers in order to function properly and these connections are logged by date, time, and location. However, this location may not be as accurate as it appears. In fact, especially in rural areas, the location can be within a range of miles.

Depending upon the number of cellular towers available, the surrounding environment, and even the type of cellular tower, it may be impossible to determine the exact location of the device. Also, geolocation based on wireless connections may be even more inaccurate. Devices that connect to an open wireless connection may appear to be located in New York, when the wireless spot accessed was actually in an airport in California.

The analysis of geolocation goes beyond an exported spreadsheet of locations since it is important to determine the source reliability of the extracted coordinates. Although connections to the suspect's own network or GPS data will be more accurate than other connections, all connections most likely will have evidentiary value or give investigative leads.

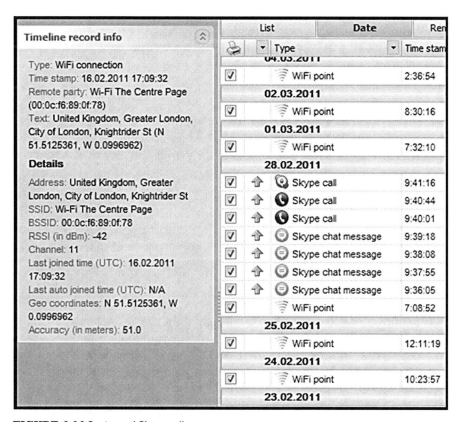

FIGURE 4.14 Geotagged Skype calls.

Internet evidence (mobile devices, computers, and game systems)

Today's computing systems with Internet connectivity are not restricted strictly to personal computers. More electronic devices have the ability to connect to the Internet by design. This includes mobile devices and game consoles. Each of these devices should be considered as prime sources of information in your investigations.

Notes on device interconnectivity

Most current consumer computing devices, from cell phones to desktop computers, have not only Internet connectivity, but also connectivity between devices to share information. Examiners need to be aware that any electronic device belonging to a suspect that has some aspect of connecting to a network or the Internet may also hold key evidence. Also, as these devices may be connected in some fashion, the destruction of evidence through remote commands is a possibility. Even with many smartphones, a delete or wipe command can be sent via a text message which can make data recovery practically impossible in some cases.

Therefore, rather than focusing on a single electronic evidence item, examiners may want to take a step back from the one device to make sure the totality of a suspect's network contributes to the analysis. This network does not have to be a user configured computer network by intentional design, but rather a network of interconnected user devices through automated file sharing and user accessed devices.

Since these devices are commonly interconnected, each device may also be able to prove or disprove allegations based on the contained information. At a minimum, just knowing that device interconnectivity can affect a forensic examination may save frustration. A simple example of the effect of suspect-created data can be seen with the Internet-capable and camera-equipped smartphone. Not only can this smartphone take a geotagged photo and upload it instantly to a social networking website, but it can also be synced through a wireless connection to a home computer.

Photos and videos that are taken by the smartphone can be transmitted and saved onto the unattended home computer or multiple computers. In an instance such as this, there would be activity on the home unattended computer with new files being created as well as activity on the smartphone, showing the suspect to be at two locations at the same time.

Digital cameras are another potential source of evidence that can be connected wirelessly to a suspect's network and devices. A non-Internet capable camera is easily given Wi-Fi access with memory cards with a Wi-Fi feature. The Wi-Fi enabled memory cards connect to wireless networks and uploads to storage locations chosen by the user, to include smartphones, computers, and file sharing websites. As with geotagged smartphone photos, these photos may also be geotagged, giving the investigator more suspect locations based on the EXIF data embedded in the photos.

Conversely, just as easy as it is to create files remotely through file sharing via a smartphone, files can be deleted remotely. Computer tablets or mobile laptops with remote connections to home computers can allow the suspect to control multiple computers remotely, giving an initial impression of an actual person being at a keyboard unless the forensic examiner discovers the remote connections having taken place.

Internet history

Some of the best evidence to find on any examined computer is that of Internet history. Of the billions of websites available, with an immense number of generalized topics and themes, the computer user will most always visit those websites of personal or professional interest. Favorite websites may be bookmarked or saved and revisited regularly. If for no other reason but to gain a glimpse into the mindset of the suspect, Internet history is a goldmine of information.

To place a suspect behind a particular computer using Internet history adds more credibility given certain actions having taken place. The most common method is logging into webmail through the Internet rather than an email client. Suspects that have logged into their webmail account verified their identity, or at least verified ownership, of the email account by entering the username and password. It is possible that a person other than the suspect may have the login credentials, but this may not be likely based on other factors, such as the other person needing access to the computer, perhaps login credentials for the operating system, and permission from the suspect to even use the computer.

If an explanation that it was not the suspect that had control of the computer but another person logged onto the suspect's computer, then logged into the suspect's email, a further analysis is warranted. Along the same lines of a suspect logging into webmail is that of logging into any website requiring login credentials. This can be social networking websites, shopping websites, blogs, forums, or company intranet websites. The more websites that require suspect credentials to access, the more unlikely that another person would have access. The likelihood that the suspect's mobile phone was used for Internet surfing and account access by another person can be considered slim, or at least the suspect most probably was within arm's reach of the smartphone at all times if that was the case.

The analysis of Internet history has become more automated with current forensic applications specific to Internet forensics. One example of an intensive Internet analysis tool is Internet Examiner from SiQuest. As can be seen in Figure 4.15, Internet history can be parsed from the major browsers, sorted by URL address, host name, or dates. Webpages can also be automatically rebuilt through reconstruction of Internet history files.

The questioning of a suspect should also include confirmation on all persons that had access or control of any evidence device, not just the suspect. In some homes, multiple persons may have access to a single computer, but these same persons probably do not have the login credentials to the webmail accounts of other persons in the home. In the instances where multiple persons can access the Internet on a common computer, the only evidence that the suspect was the person behind the keyboard may rest on the accessing of protected accounts known only to the suspect.

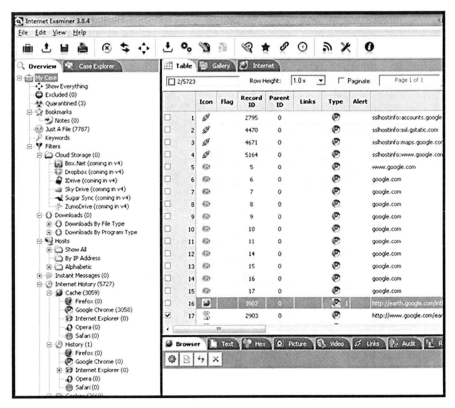

FIGURE 4.15 Internet Examiner, http://www.siquest.com.

Online groups

Message boards, listservs, forums, blogs, and newsgroups are examples of online services allowing the communication of persons online by either posting comments to websites or sending email messages to a group of persons. Both comments and group emails can be made private where only the group members have access or made public where anyone on the Internet can access and view.

For all online groups where settings are private, user login credentials are needed, which is attributing evidence to a specific person due to having to use a private password. Public boards may not require any login credential and also allow for anonymous posting. Anonymous posting does not mean that the IP address used by the commenter will be anonymous, only that no credentials are needed. Owners and moderators of blogs and websites generally will have immediate access to any comments made along with the date and time stamps, as can be seen in Figure 4.16.

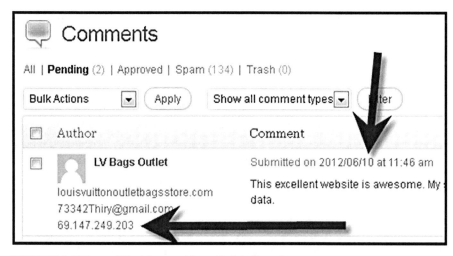

FIGURE 4.16 Logged IP address on blog with date/time stamp.

Suspects that post or comment to any of these online groups create a trail of geolocation data on the servers of these third party providers. The recovery of membership or access to any online group from examined systems should be an indication to the investigator that additional geolocation may exist. This is particularly important when a suspect accesses the online groups using different computers at different locations, resulting in a bread trail of geolocations.

Game consoles

Conducting forensics on electronic game consoles, such as the X-Box (http://www.xbox.com) or the Playstation (http://us.playstation.com/), is not new, nor is the criminal use of these devices. The mere appearance of an electronic game console in a residence usually does not automatically raise a warning flag containing evidence and may be easily overlooked. In the most basic description, these game machines are computers, capable of many of the features available in the common desktop computer. This includes Internet connectivity, video and photo creation, file transfer, file storage, and electronic communication through voice, video, and typed chat. Hard drives of varying sizes are common as is the ability to attach external storage devices such as USB hard drives and flash media cards.

A game console may have been the instrument of a crime or contain electronic evidence of a crime. Even if the game console was not used as an instrument of a criminal act, the historic evidentiary value of user activity may be helpful in corroborating a suspect's alibi. Since a game console is a computer system, the user activity is logged as such. For example, the Internet history on the Playstation is maintained in a directory containing Internet history files (\PSP\SYSTEM\browser). This directory stores URLs that were entered in the browser address bar and bookmarks chosen by the user. Websites that are discovered may be directly linked to the suspect through supplied login credentials.

Game console activity, or inactivity, may be a very important piece of evidence concerning an alibi. An alibi of playing games all night on the night of a crime can be discredited if an analysis shows the game console not being used at all on that night. Even if the game console did show activity for a date in question, the location of the game console may be available and important for the investigation.

Through the interconnectivity between online players, IP addresses, server addresses, and daily connection logs are stored locally on the consoles and by third parties that provide online services. These third parties that provide peer-to-peer gaming or group gaming most likely will maintain the IP addresses of the game consoles only for a certain period of time. The locally stored information includes the connection name, such as home network or broadcasted wireless network.

HTTP extraction

In May 2012, a technical report published from the University of California detailed a method of extracting geolocation data from a seized hard drive based on HTTP header information. The method discussed involved analyzing HTTP header content from websites existing on the hard drive. This intriguing method, using data from cookies and Internet files stored on the system, was shown to identify IP addresses and dates. The paper states that additional corroborating information is needed to verify the identified geolocation, but of course, that is also one of the themes of this book.

IP address and relationships to devices

In nearly every investigation type, from civil electronic discovery cases to a global hacking case, electronic devices are most always connected to third party commercial or government providers through Internet connections at some point. A forensic analysis of a device identifies many of these third parties, such as a wireless access point discovered from the registry leading to the identification of a previously connected network or networks. Internet history showing a user's webmail history identifies third party webmail providers.

A visual seen in Figure 4.17 shows how most devices may directly identify a single third party, online service provider. The reasons for device connections to third party providers range from communication to storing data such as digital photos on the third party data storage systems. A single third party provider could provide a single user account's information related to more than one device.

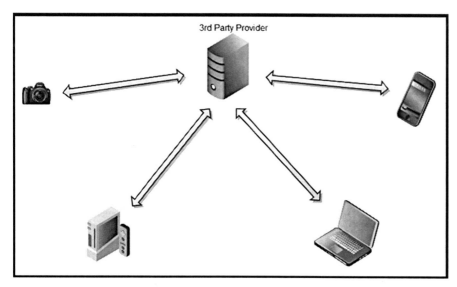

FIGURE 4.17 Third party online service provider example.

As these third parties regularly maintain records of customer logins and attempted logins, neglecting to review their logs could result in missing additional avenues of suspect location identification and additional electronic evidence. Through the third party connection logs of user IP addresses, investigators may be able to trace back to a physical location to where a device was used.

Reviewing a webmail provider's records will usually show multiple IP addresses of access by the user. This is due to the user accessing the webmail account using computers at home, work, and school, or through mobile devices and game consoles. Each of these points of access potentially identifies the location of access through the logged IP addresses, which could lead to additional sources of electronic media.

Figure 4.18 shows a visual example of a third party service provider identifying multiple locations of user account access. Each of the access points may or may not be from the same device, but can be assumed that the owner of the online service account is probably the same person as the owner should be the only person with authorized access.

Identifying third party service providers through analysis of each device may result in identifying more electronic devices and suspect locations. Corroborating these locations and suspect account logins with other methods, such as call data records, will build circumstantial evidence to help place the suspect at that particular keyboard, at a particular date and time.

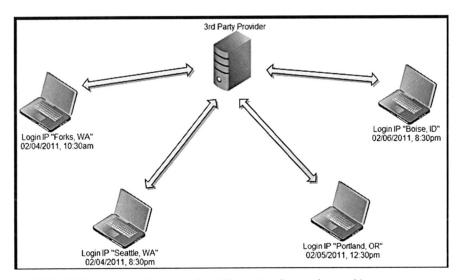

FIGURE 4.18 Customer login records from third party online service provider

Texts and emails

The spoken, or written, word of a suspect is powerful, particularly when the statement is against the suspect's penal interest. Text messages or emails that state time and location from a suspect are helpful to verify verbal statements that may be in contrast with physical evidence. The content of a text message may not always contribute evidence to an investigation. However, if any messages are tied to the user, then the GPS, Cell Site, and Wi-Fi coordinates obtained from the device or from call detail records place that suspect at a location with that device.

Text messages shown in Figure 4.19 are examples of a mobile device user stating his future time and location, again placing the device in suspect's hands at a specific location and time.

Emails can also be good sources of geolocation data based both on content of the emails as well as the email headers. Content based, in that the suspect may state dates and location in his own words, or header based information. Header based information includes the IP addresses or the sender and receiver in which the physical addresses of subscribers can be obtained, whether it is at a residence, workplace, or public location. Figure 4.20 shows an example of an email header with the originating IP address noted.

The location of the suspect based on the IP address of emails authored and sent from the suspect's account can be supported through email header analysis. As discussed, methods to obscure the true IP address, such as proxy servers

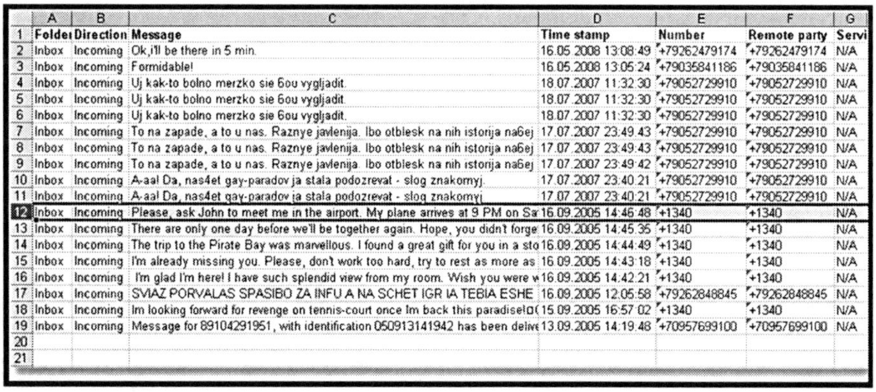

	A	B	C	D	E	F	G
1	Folder	Direction	Message	Time stamp	Number	Remote party	Servi
2	Inbox	Incoming	Ok,i'll be there in 5 min.	16.05.2008 13:08:49	+79262479174	+79262479174	N/A
3	Inbox	Incoming	Formidable!	16.05.2008 13:05:24	+79035841186	+79035841186	N/A
4	Inbox	Incoming	Uj kak-to bolno merzko sie 6ou vygljadit.	18.07.2007 11:32:30	+79052729910	+79052729910	N/A
5	Inbox	Incoming	Uj kak-to bolno merzko sie 6ou vygljadit.	18.07.2007 11:32:30	+79052729910	+79052729910	N/A
6	Inbox	Incoming	Uj kak-to bolno merzko sie 6ou vygljadit.	18.07.2007 11:32:30	+79052729910	+79052729910	N/A
7	Inbox	Incoming	To na zapade, a to u nas. Raznye javlenija. Ibo otblesk na nih istorija na6ej	17.07.2007 23:49:43	+79052729910	+79052729910	N/A
8	Inbox	Incoming	To na zapade, a to u nas. Raznye javlenija. Ibo otblesk na nih istorija na6ej	17.07.2007 23:49:43	+79052729910	+79052729910	N/A
9	Inbox	Incoming	To na zapade, a to u nas. Raznye javlenija. Ibo otblesk na nih istorija na6ej	17.07.2007 23:49:42	+79052729910	+79052729910	N/A
10	Inbox	Incoming	A-aa! Da, nas4et gay-paradov ja stala podozrevat - slog znakomyj.	17.07.2007 23:40:21	+79052729910	+79052729910	N/A
11	Inbox	Incoming	A-aa! Da, nas4et gay-paradov ja stala podozrevat - slog znakomyj.	17.07.2007 23:40:21	+79052729910	+79052729910	N/A
12	Inbox	Incoming	Please, ask John to meet me in the airport. My plane arrives at 9 PM on Sa	16.09.2005 14:46:48	+1340	+1340	N/A
13	Inbox	Incoming	There are only one day before we'll be together again. Hope, you didn't forge	16.09.2005 14:45:35	+1340	+1340	N/A
14	Inbox	Incoming	The trip to the Pirate Bay was marvellous. I found a great gift for you in a sto	16.09.2005 14:44:49	+1340	+1340	N/A
15	Inbox	Incoming	I'm already missing you. Please, don't work too hard, try to rest as more as	16.09.2005 14:43:18	+1340	+1340	N/A
16	Inbox	Incoming	I'm glad I'm here! I have such splendid view from my room. Wish you were w	16.09.2005 14:42:21	+1340	+1340	N/A
17	Inbox	Incoming	SVIAZ PORVALAS SPASIBO ZA INFU A NA SCHET IGR IA TEBIA ESHE	16.09.2005 12:05:58	+79262848845	+79262848845	N/A
18	Inbox	Incoming	Im looking forward for revenge on tennis-court once Im back this paradise!□(	15.09.2005 16:57:02	+1340	+1340	N/A
19	Inbox	Incoming	Message for 89104291951, with identification 050913141942 has been delive	13.09.2005 14:19:48	+70957699100	+70957699100	N/A
20							
21							

FIGURE 4.19 Extracted text messages from mobile device. Courtesy of Oxygen Forensics http://www.oxygen-forensic.com.

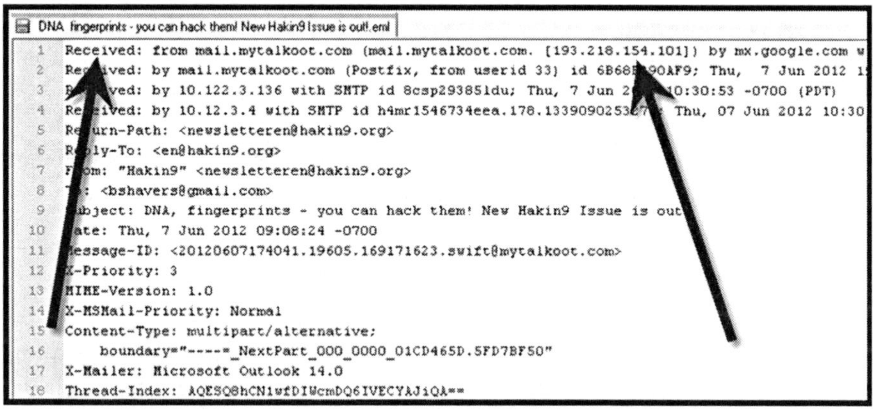

FIGURE 4.20 Example of email header showing originating IP address.

or anonymizing services, may render the use of IP addresses useless in determining the physical location. Email providers may also cause difficulty by not providing the original IP address in the email headers, which would require court or administrative authority to demand originating IP addresses.

Calendar evidence

Many email programs have an incorporated calendar function which could contain a suspect's historical location information. Smartphones with an appointment and calendar function, if in use by the suspect, can also identify past and future meetings locations. Smartphone calendars may or may not be synched with their personal or work computers.

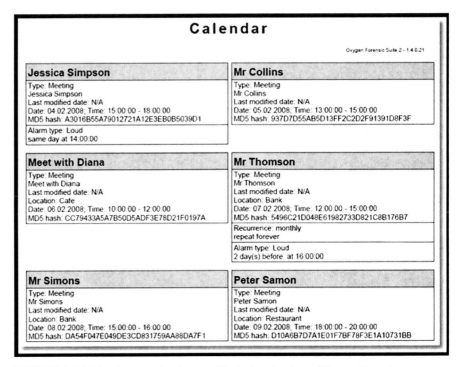

FIGURE 4.21 Calendar extraction from mobile device. Courtesy of Oxygen Forensics http://www.oxygen-forensic.com.

Although any calendar appointment is not absolute confirmation that the suspect may have completed any listed appointment, it still can provide leads for further investigation to verify the whereabouts of a suspect. Figure 4.21 is an example of a calendar displayed in Oxygen-Forensics Analyst existing on a smartphone. Since appointments are made with people, investigators can develop a set of persons to interview in order to corroborate relevant dates discovered in a calendar.

"OTHER" DEVICE FORENSICS

If a computer system cannot be tied to a suspect, perhaps a computer accessory may be used instead. Devices that a suspect controls or admits to controlling may be physically tied to one or more computers through a forensic analysis of the computers. All devices plugged into a system are logged by that system, by date, time, and type of device. Smart cards, USB storage devices, media players, digital cameras, and smartphones are examples of these devices.

If the suspect's smartphone has been connected to a computer system, even if the suspect does not admit ownership of the computer system, it can

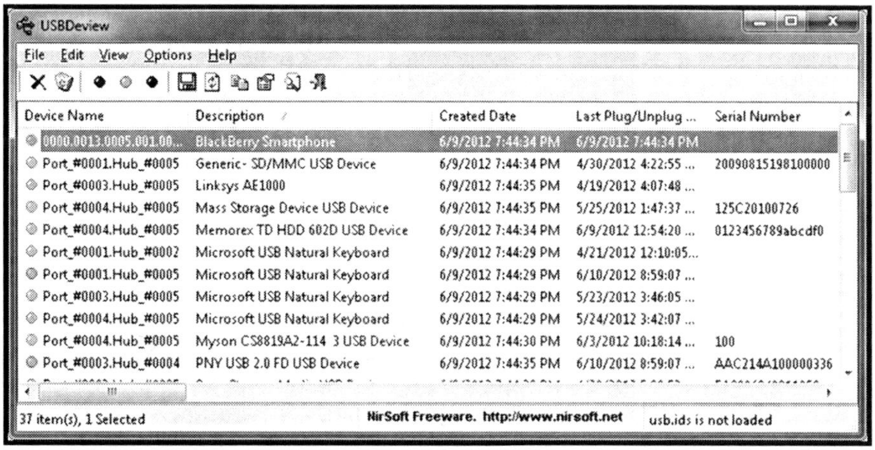

FIGURE 4.22 Connected devices, USBDeview, http://www.nirsoft.net.

be assumed that the suspect accessed that computer, on the date and time logged with the smartphone. Additional devices attributed to the suspect that have been connected over a period of time to any computer system contribute to tying the suspect to those systems on those occasions. Depending upon the device, an automated backup may occur with each connection. Media players can back up music and video while smartphones may back up the entire phone's data, including text messages, videos, and geotagged photos.

Figure 4.22 shows a list of connected devices by description, created date, last plug/unplug date, and serial number (if available) using USBDeview from Nirsoft (http://www.nirsoft.net). Most forensic software suites and registry specific utilities are able to extract the same information as seen in this figure.

Every electronic device identified should be considered as a source of information that can place a suspect at a location at a specific time. Even some printers store historical information on printing, including storing complete digital copies of documents that have been printed. It is the concepts and principles applied across the spectrum of electronic evidence that makes the difference in an investigation.

ONLINE SOCIAL NETWORKING

Online social networking provides a wealth of information and evidence well beyond could ever be dreamed years ago. Public and government databases containing information on persons, such as credit histories and criminal histories, have always been relevant to investigations. But the mass public appeal to social networking websites adds an entirely new dimension in obtaining personal information.

All social networking websites allow the customer to create their own information using a computer or mobile device to upload photos, post comments, and engage others from any location that has access to the Internet. Each of these connections creates the breadcrumb trail of geolocation based on IP address connections, geotagged photos, and self-admitted comments which state physical locations.

When examining social network website activity, examiners need to be aware that one suspect may control multiple personas. The reasoning may be to restrict the amount of personal data with each online identity or to create confusion and anonymity. Also, one online identity can easily be controlled by more than one person, in that several may share the online identity. Again, the reasons may be to throw suspicion off a suspect, such as providing an alibi of being online from one physical location at the time of a crime committed in another.

It is also plausible that a suspect could create an automated, updated, electronic identity through software applications that do not require human intervention. This method could create data on multiple connected devices giving the appearance a person was at the system, when in fact; the suspect may be committing a crime at a different location.

It is unfortunate that criminals victimize legitimate users of social networking sites through stalking and harassment; however, the same methods can be used by investigators to obtain evidence on the criminals. The words submitted to any social networking website by the suspect may or may not be important or even pertinent to an investigation, but the geolocation at the time of the comment most likely will be.

USER ACTIVITY

Apart from a forensic analysis to recover electronic evidence, such as stolen intellectual property or child pornography, this section on user activity will detail only that activity to help place a specific suspect behind the keyboard, not the actual evidence of the incident under investigation. The recovery and analysis of electronic evidence is best discussed with books dedicated to the science of digital forensics, where this book supplements evidentiary findings by placing an identified suspect at the keyboard.

User logins

The easiest method of suspect identification is that when the suspect self-identifies through supplying login credentials to access a computer system or online accounts owned by the suspect. When these credentials include fingerprint identification or facial recognition, identification is that much more accurate.

Claims that another person other than the suspect logged into a particular account by password guessing can be made irrelevant depending upon the password. Complex passwords consisting of varied uppercase, lowercase, numbers, and characters would be nearly virtually impossible to guess.

Each additional security measure required to log into a system diminishes the possibility that any person other than the suspect logged into the account or system. This can include physical security measures, even locked doors, to access the computer system. The more layers needed to gain ultimate access results in more credibility in placing an identified suspect behind the keyboard.

User-specific computer activity

Attempting to attribute user activity to a specific person may involve examining the content of data created as it relates to a person. Using a word processing document as an example, the context of the document may be more accurate of owner identification than the metadata contained in the document. Metadata of a document, as seen in an example document in Figure 4.23, shows the author as "James Smith" and last saved by "acer".

Based solely on this information, James Smith would be considered the creator of this document. However, looking at the content of the document may go against what the metadata shows. Figure 4.24 shows the content of the same file with a signature name of Jessica Bell. Whether or not the author is James Smith or Jessica Bell is not so much the issue as to not rely upon one piece of information for suspect identification. However, the more specific the content applies to a person, especially with personal information known only to one person, the more likely the identification of the author will be certain.

Typed URLs and Internet history can be extracted from computer from registry key HKCU\Software\Microsoft\Internet Explorer\TypedURLs key, as well as from the cache and Internet history files of web browsers. This includes typed searches made with Internet search engines and social

FIGURE 4.23 Example of metadata in document.

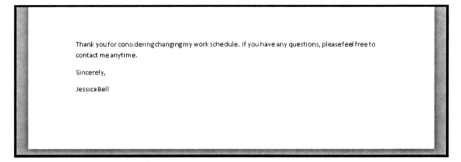

Thank you for considering changing my work schedule. If you have any questions, please feel free to contact me anytime.

Sincerely,

Jessica Bell

FIGURE 4.24 Content of document inferring identity.

networking websites. As the content of a word processing document can point to a specific person, search terms may also point to a specific person. Examples of search terms to attribute to a user could be terms related to the planning or commission of a crime or even search terms of complete sentences with context of an incident under investigation.

DIGITAL AUTHORSHIP

Digital authorship may be compared to a handwriting exemplar, which is the forensic examination of handwritten samples for comparison of documents. This requires a high degree of skill to compare unique handwritten notes, but cannot be applied in the same manner with documents created using computers. Electronic writings must focus on the words, grammar, and context as typed, not the words as written on a paper document.

One method to identify an author is through an analysis of the style of the grammar, punctuation, errors, vocabulary, and other idiosyncrasies. This method requires a source record for comparison, such as documents or emails that have already been attributed to the suspect. This method has "obtained 95% accuracy and has been successfully used in investigating and adjudicating several crimes involving digital evidence" (Chaski, 2005).

Since the type of document created (email, word processing, etc.) is usually created for different purposes, the style may also be different. An example would be text in an email written by the suspect which may be short, terse, and to the point, whereas a letter written via a word processor may be more fully developed. A comparison between the short email and more fully developed letter most likely will not give accurate results.

Current research in identifying authorship is being conducted and software developed that is able to pinpoint differences between persons through analyzing sentence structure and syntax. Two such software tools in development by graduate students at Drexel University help identify authors of disputed documents or help keep authors anonymous (Perlroth, 2012). Other approaches of authorship attribution are based on comparing writing patterns in emails, in which "the frequent patterns themselves serve as strong evidence for supporting the conclusion of authorship" (Iqbal, Hadjidj, Fung, & Debbabi, 2008).

Through biometrics, the dynamics of keystrokes can identify a person through typing patterns, speed, and timing of each keystroke. However, this method is generally used as a credential verifier for login access rather than identification of a person on past historical computer use. With keystroke dynamics, each person has a unique pattern of typing on a keyboard. By use of keystroke dynamic software, the dynamics of a person's manner of typing can be analyzed and attributed to a person. Subsequent login attempts are compared to the previously analyzed typing to allow or deny access. This allows for an authorized computer user to access a system based on password credentials and their keystroke dynamics.

With this security, any other person attempting to use a valid password will not be able to access the system due to having a different keystroke dynamic. Computer systems that have this security have a much greater potential of placing specific persons behind the keyboard, solely because of the heightened measures to gain access by authorized users.

PROFILING

Entire texts have been written and careers devoted to criminal profiling. With certain types of crimes, criminal profiling may be effective. Perhaps 20 years ago, criminals using computers may have been easier to profile because of fewer persons having the skill level to use computers or write malicious software programs. Today, many people use computers daily and the programs available for specific work spans a wide spectrum including the ability to simply purchase malicious or hacking software without knowing how it works.

Narrowing a list of suspects using the traditional "motive and opportunity" theory also needs reconsideration. At this stage of technology, any person using a computer with Internet access has the opportunity to commit nearly any computer related crime from any global location. As to motives, human nature has not changed nor has motives to commit crimes. Even hackers have varied motives which may be difficult to determine. According to Steven Branigan, a founding member of the New York Electronic Crimes Task Force, "Hackers are motivated to do what they do for different reasons, such as money, revenge and curiosity."

It is the unfettered access allowed by an Internet connected computer that allows the opportunity to exist anywhere, by anyone, for any reason. This ease of global opportunity and widely available malicious software access does not make the profiling of cybercriminals any easier.

Profiling a known suspect against an incident will have to be based upon that suspect's past behavior and history. Is the incident under investigation like others committed by the suspect? Is this behavior consistent with the suspect's past behavior? Questions such as these determine present and future behavior based on past behavior.

BIOLOGICAL FORENSIC EVIDENCE

Blood. Hair. Fingerprints. Biological evidence is not just for non-computer crime scenes. Computers can also contain each and every one of these types of evidence. Keyboards and the entire systems can be fingerprinted, hair strands recovered for forensic examination and comparison. Even blood or other bodily fluids can exist on computer systems.

Perhaps the most certain evidence that the suspect was in proximity of a system would be the recovery of the suspect's fingerprints or DNA from the system. This alone cannot show the suspect accessed the system, but it will show the suspect at one point in time, was in close physical proximity to the computer system, or even touched it in some manner.

In cases where it is imperative to show the suspect had access to any device, fingerprinting will be the best evidence. Photos of the suspect and electronic evidence are powerful, but only if the photographed systems can be positively identified as the evidence in question.

TRIAGE AND PREVIEWS

In addition to the forensic analysis attempts to place suspects behind the keyboard, an effective approach to this goal is a triage, or preview, of electronic media, on location with the suspect. There are varying opinions and definitions of "triage" and "preview" of electronic media, but in the context of this section, both triage and preview refer to the examination of electronic media to find evidence of immediate and actionable value. Immediate and actionable value evidence is also known as "low hanging fruit".

This method of looking for evidence is typically conducted onsite, with the computer owner present. The situations can range from being given consent to search by the suspect, a search based on court authority such as a parole check, or even a search warrant or civil data collection. As the suspect or computer custodian is present, in close proximity to the computer systems, and having the authority to give consent (thereby, admit to being in control), the suspect has been placed at the computer. The suspect's access to the computer will be undisputed. The suspect is there with the computer. It will be the results of the triage that will place the suspect at the computer during the dates and times in question.

By using any number of methods to triage a computer, evidence in plain view can be addressed by the investigator immediately, potentially resulting in admissions or confessions from the suspect. Two methods of triaging/previewing a suspect computer are when the computer is on and when the computer is off. Most procedures of data collection and triage with computers that are on recommend that the computer remain on during the procedure and if off, remain off. This is primarily due to potential encryption issues that can render data recover practically inaccessible if the computer is turned off.

For computers that are running, a wide variety of programs dedicated to the task of previewing a live system are available. Two such programs are Field Search (Figure 4.25) and osTriage (Figure 4.26).

Either of these triage/preview applications can effectively and quickly find relevant evidence. This includes Internet history, searched keywords, documents, photos and videos, and computer system information.

FIGURE 4.25 Field Search, http://www.kbsolutions.com/html/field_search.html.

FIGURE 4.26 osTriage, http://feeble-industries.com/forums.

The live triage of a running system coupled with collection of physical memory serves an important purpose. The possibility of a defendant claiming the Trojan Defense, in that someone installed malicious software onto the evidence system that committed alleged acts, may arise. Defending against this claim can be difficult as it is impossible to prove that malicious software did not exist while the computer was on and subsequently was erased from physical memory when the computer was shut down.

Through the collection of physical memory, to include the running processes, open ports, and open connections, this defense can be challenged, or proven to be correct, through a forensic analysis.

Computers that are not running when approached can still be triaged if not encrypted without turning on the operating system. This can be done by removing the hard drives and connecting the drives to a forensic workstation or by booting the computer to a forensically modified compact disk or USB drive that can run operating systems which have been modified to be forensically sound. One commonly used operating system for a forensic bootable environment is one of many variations of forensically modified Linux distributions. Another option is a forensically modified Windows operating system, such as the Windows Forensic Environment developed by Troy Larson of Microsoft.

Although conducting a triage/preview with the suspect near the computer does not automatically place the suspect behind the keyboard at the time of an incident, it just may be the closest you can get and sometimes, that may all that you need.

SUMMARY

Attributing computer use to a specific person or persons is just as important as a forensic analysis of the computer device to uncover the criminal activity, civil violations, or internal policy violations. The ongoing process of creating a timeline does not have a beginning or end, as it is constantly changing with new information added as it is discovered.

Although there are few, if any, evidentiary items which can place a suspect behind a keyboard with absolute certainty, the culmination of a forensic analysis of activity combined with traditional investigative methods can result in substantial circumstantial evidence. Circumstantial evidence that eliminates persons of interest integrated with corroborating sources of evidence contributes to conclusions that no other person but the suspect could have been behind the keyboard.

Bibliography

Allen, E. (2010). *Speech by Ernie Allen.* <http://www.missingkids.com/missingkids/servlet/NewsEve ntServlet?LanguageCountry=en_US&PageId=4279> Retrieved June 11, 2012.

Bisbing, R. (2006). *The forensic laboratory handbook.* Totowa, New Jersey: Humana Press.

Carvey, H. (2011). *Windows registry forensics: advanced digital forensic analysis of the windows registry.* Burlington, Massachusetts: Elsevier.

Chaski, C. (2005). *Who's at the keyboard? authorship attribution in digital evidence investigations,* <http://www.utica.edu/academic/institutes/ecii/publications/articles/B49F9C4A-0362-765C-6A235CB8ABDFACFE.pdf> Retrieved June 11, 2012.

Hofmann, M. (2011) *Why IP addresses alone don't identify criminals.* <https://www.eff.org/deep-links/2011/08/why-ip-addresses-alone-dont-identify-criminals> Retrieved June 11, 2012.

Iqbal, F., Hadjidj, R., Fung, B., & Debbabi, M. (2008). *A novel approach of mining write-prints for authorship attribution in e-mail forensics.* <http://www.dfrws.org/2008/proceedings/p42-iqbal.pdf> Retrieved June 11, 2012.

Perlroth, N. (2012) *Software helps identify anonymous writers or helps them stay that way.* <http://bits.blogs.nytimes.com/2012/01/03/software-helps-identify-anonymous-writers-or-helps-them-stay-that-way/> Retrieved June 11, 2012.

Further reading

Field Search, <http://www.kbsolutions.com/html/field_search.html>.

Internet Examiner, <http://www.siquest.com>.

osTriage, <http://feeble-industries.com/forums>.

Oxygen Forensics Suite 2012, <http://www.oxygen-forensic.com/en/>.

PhotoME, <http://.www.photome.de>.

Playstation, <http://us.playstation.com/>.

Registry Decoder, <http://www.digitalforensicssolutions.com/registrydecoder/>.

RegRipper, <http://regripper.wordpress.com>.

Tor Project, <http://www.torproject.org>.

Windows Forensic Environment, <http://winfe.wordpress.com>.

Windows Registry File Viewer, <http://www.mitec.cz/>.

X-Box, <http://www.xbox.com>.

CHAPTER 5

Putting It All Together

INFORMATION IN THIS CHAPTER:

- "2 + 2 = Putting it all together"
- Timelines
- Follow the evidence
- Rabbit holes

CONTENTS

"2 + 2 = PUTTING IT ALL TOGETHER"

This chapter gives tips for identifying the suspect as well as eliminating possible suspects by helping develop your investigative mindset. Investigators and forensic examiners can easily become extremely focused on a specific person or incident. So much so, this extreme focus may prevent understanding the totality of the investigation. Incorrect assumptions, false investigative leads, or erroneous conclusions can turn an investigation into a train wreck where the guilty goes free and in worst case scenarios, innocent persons are wrongly accused. These incidents can happen when investigative goals and objectives are not clear.

The tips in this chapter show methods of compiling information to weed irrelevant data to develop a suspect list. Many of the methods used to develop a list of suspects can be used in presenting these facts of the case in legal hearings or internal review boards. Particularly in larger investigations, it will benefit the investigator in maintaining a structure of data organization throughout the case.

In those cases where a suspect will admit guilt, many of these concepts to identify the suspect may not even need to be employed. But sometimes, to obtain an admission of guilt, analyzing all information is needed to ask the right questions to obtain the truth.

Reconstructing the crime scene is a scientific process. Evidence needs to be identified, collected, and analyzed. Persons involved in the incident, including witnesses, need to be interviewed. Beyond the scientific method, investigators need to consider that creativity plays a large part of solving any crime and sometimes, that is the most difficult trait to teach. The following methods are intended to spark creativity.

The evidence as a whole

The seriousness of the incident coupled with the time and resources available directly impact the amount of evidence collected. That just means important cases usually have more evidence and less important cases have less effort used. This is simply a matter of prioritizing the case load for effective time management.

An example to a case with minimal evidence would be the deletion of one document from a single laptop in a civil litigation case. This case may require only one analyst to recover the deleted document from the laptop. Conversely, a criminal organization that creates and globally distributes child pornography across the Internet will require substantially more resources resulting in a massive set of evidence, both physical and electronic. Each investigation determines resources needed and the evidence to be collected.

Whether the evidence consists of a few items or an entire storage locker of physical evidence plus external drives containing terabytes of electronic evidence, looking at the items individually is just as important as looking at all the items as a whole. Items collected that initially appear to be irrelevant may be able to corroborate relevant evidence or give additional leads. One example would be employee timecards, where a suspect appears to have been at work at the same time user activity occurred on his home computer.

On the face value of the timesheets, this would suggest that another person was at the computer, or perhaps, it could have been remotely accessed by the suspect at work. Either way, further investigation is required rather than jumping to conclusions that the user account name is also the suspect's name.

Every criminal act or corporate internal violation of policy involving electronic storage devices involves at least two evidence processing scenes; the devices used (the electronic crime) and the location (the physical crime scene). From that point, there may be additional electronic crime scenes on just one or maybe thousands of victim computers. Looking at all crime scenes overall as one incident helps put a puzzle together of how each scene interacted with another.

Avoiding assumptions

Sometimes, guesses are correct without corroborating evidence. Assumptions made without corroborating evidence can be correct. Then again, assumptions are akin to guessing and the odds of being wrong are too high to risk making substantial decisions on guesswork. Even when all scientific evidence points to a specific person, there is always the chance of an innocent person being framed for a crime. An example can be seen in United States v. Barry Vincent Ardolf (2011), involving an incident between two neighbors in which an innocent person was framed for crimes by a neighbor. The neighbor, Barry Ardolf, bypassed the wireless security settings of the victim's Internet router.

After gaining access to the wireless router of his neighbor, Ardolf accessed the victim's computer systems and conducted criminal activity that appeared to have been originated by the victim. Child pornography was not only downloaded to the victim computers, but Ardolf created and used emails in the victim's name to send child pornography to others and sent death threats to the Vice President of the United States. The victims cooperated with the Secret Service by allowing the use of sniffer software applications on the victim's wireless network. The analysis of captured Internet packets led to identifying Ardolf as the real suspect, leading to his conviction and 18-year prison sentence.

The importance of this example cannot be overstated as the victim did use encryption on the wireless network, which was bypassed within 2 weeks by the suspect. All evidence prior to capturing Ardolf's access to the victim network pointed directly at the victim. This case of wrongfully targeted citizens based solely on an IP address is a too common occurrence and can be avoided through additional investigative work.

Who did it?

Skilled forensic analysts and investigators are great when they not only determine the computer user activity of a suspect, but also answer the basic investigative questions of *who, what, when, where, why,* and *how.* The answer to one question may only be derived by answering another. The answer to *who* committed the act may be derived by answering the question of *why* someone would commit the act. As important with every forensic analysis to determine *what* happened and *how* it happened, it is just as important to find other answers to determine *who* did it.

Unfortunately, it may be practically impossible to determine the person that was behind any keyboard based solely on forensic analysis. With exceptions such as biometric logging devices, the electronic data recovered from any computer simply shows that certain keys were pressed on the keyboard at certain times causing specific activity to occur with or on the computer. Unless the computer system is creating a video capture of the computer user and saving that video locally to the machine, any person can be at the keyboard without additional circumstantial evidence. As this is rarely the case, traditional investigative methods and creative thinking need to be engaged.

Motive and opportunity

There are certain crimes and incidents in which determining the motive and opportunity may quickly solve the investigation. A defendant receiving a legal preservation notice to preserve an electronic document which is later discovered to have been deleted has motive. If the electronic document existed on the defendant's computer hard drive, the opportunity also existed. As long as there are no other factors such as multiple persons having had access to the previously deleted electronic file, a primary suspect may have been identified quickly and easily.

This becomes more complicated as opportunity has become almost effortless due to the interconnectivity of computer systems. Opportunity does not necessarily require physical access to an evidence computer system, which greatly increases the possible list of suspects through remote access.

Multiple persons may have different motives in the same incident, whether the motive is to hide evidence through the destruction of electronic data in a business or perhaps a conspiracy of persons to profit through online fraud. Investigations many times will show that more than one person had both different motives and multiple opportunities. Because of that factor, without additional information, a suspect can be overlooked or innocent persons being accused with suspects.

Hidden motives may be more difficult to determine in some cases. Such would be the motive to profit from a crime. Profiting financially is obviously a motive, but a hidden motive may not be so obvious. A hidden motive to profit could be for a drug addiction problem, late bills, revenge, or to pay for a luxury vacation. A motive to profit without specifics may not be enough to show motive for a specific person and sometimes, the only motive needed by a suspect is "just because."

Process of elimination

One of the most effective means of identifying a suspect and placing the suspect at a scene is through the process of elimination. Of course, a list of possible suspects needs to be identified first and that is not possible in every case. A civil litigation investigation in which all activity occurred within a corporate network will be easier to develop a list of suspects based on known employee access to electronic devices. An intrusion conducted using anonymous proxies may be close to impossible to develop any identifiable persons without further investigation and even with additional investigation, may still be impossible.

A combination of physical investigative methods, such as surveillance and interviews, plus the analysis of electronic devices and call data records can be used to create and narrow a list of suspects. Given any number of suspects, call data records can place their cell phones at specific locations by date and time.

Analysis of their workstations and personal computers can show user activity that may be attributed to their use.

Having a long list of suspects requires effort to eliminate names; however, this is a better scenario than not having any possible suspects identified at all. Charts and spreadsheets are effective in keeping track of possible suspect names and helpful in visually identifying relationships. A simplistic example of creating a list of suspects is seen in Figure 5.1. In this example, where there are 3 days of activity in question, each possible suspect has been noted for each day of having physical access to a shared business computer system. This type of technique is also known as a matrix chart.

Complex investigations involving multiple storage devices and systems do not automatically make such a list as Figure 5.1 complex. It is quite the opposite in that the more incidents in question, fewer persons will be able to have accessed a shared machine over a long period of time for all of the incidents.

Plotting geolocation data obtained from investigative sources onto a map creates a visual representation that is helpful in eliminating or identifying persons as suspects. An example seen in Figure 5.2 shows three identified persons with their locations and one location where the investigated incident occurred at 9:25 am on Turner's workstation. Assuming the persons were located as noted, either an unknown person used Turner's workstation at 9:25 pm locally or it was accessed remotely by an identified person.

Geolocations of all suspect controlled devices can be plotted by date and time, showing travel and use. The traveling laptop of a suspect that matches the geolocation of the suspect's cell phone records strongly implies the suspect had control of both items at the time unless reported stolen or loaned to another person.

	A	B	C	D
	G7		f_x	
1	Person	Day 1	Day 2	Day 3
2	Joe Turner	x	x	x
3	Karen Smart	x		x
4	Jeff Turnbow		x	x
5	Eddie May	x	x	x
6	Scott Mayberry		x	
7				

FIGURE 5.1 Example of a matrix chart used to identify suspects and their activity.

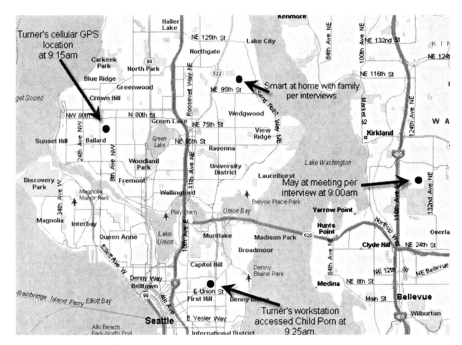

FIGURE 5.2 Plotting locations of suspects in relation to an alleged incident helps to place suspects at the scene while eliminating possible suspects if they are placed elsewhere.

Shared computer systems used in an incident, whether criminal or civil, pose problems in tying a single person to the acts, especially if there may have been several persons using the system as conspirators. In a corporate setting, individual workstations might be physically accessed by any person in the building if security measures are not employed. In those types of cases, a detailed investigation into the whereabouts of all employees may be required including interviews and potentially, examination of their individual workstations in order to determine user activity that can place them at a specific spot.

A diagram of an office is shown in Figure 5.3 depicting multiple persons potentially being suspects in illegal computer use. There are six persons with physical access to every workstation in this sample office. In this example, employee Turnbow's workstation accessed child pornography at 10:18 am, however, a fax was also sent listing Turnbow as the sender at 10:15 am. There are two other persons, Pearson and Turner, whose workstations were not in use during the time of the incident, inferring that either could have accessed Turnbow's workstation. Turnbow may have a plausible denial of not committing this act due to the fax being sent in close relation of time and that there are at least two other persons with access to his workstation at that time.

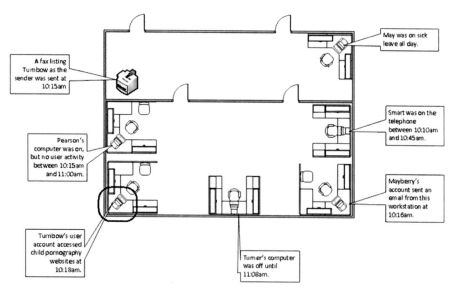

May was on sick leave all day.

A fax listing Turnbow as the sender was sent at 10:15am.

Smart was on the telephone between 10:10am and 10:45am.

Pearson's computer was on, but no user activity between 10:15am and 11:00am.

Mayberry's account sent an email from this workstation at 10:16am.

Turnbow's user account accessed child pornography websites at 10:18am.

Turner's computer was off until 11:08am.

FIGURE 5.3 An example of plotting possible suspects in an office setting to aid in the identification and elimination of suspects.

This example applies not only to a single criminal incident, but applies also to large corporations involving many persons that committed violations in conjunction with others or individually. This concept of eliminating suspects applies across a broad spectrum of cases where multiple persons have access to the evidence devices. In the most basic form, each person must be plotted with electronic devices based on the times of alleged incidents.

TIMELINES

As the information increases, visual representations become more helpful in seeing how events are tied to each other, dependent upon another, and give investigative leads to more evidence. Timelines have most likely been used in legal cases since the beginning of legal cases. In the simplest description, a timeline is a chronological listing of events. The method of displaying timelines changes, whether a timeline is document listing events in order or an electronic display of colors, symbols, charts, graphs, and videos.

The use of timelines to present information in legal or corporate settings will be discussed as a presentation method in the next chapter. Investigators can use timelines to sort massive amounts of information resulting in filtering out irrelevant data, tagging important data, and gathering inferences that help reconstruct the incident. The reconstruction of the electronic crime scene is a major factor in the identification and elimination of possible suspects just as it is with a physical crime scene.

Timeline creations containing large datasets can be accomplished using specific software applications, such as log2timeline from http://log2timeline. net/ or even as an exported file listing from most any forensic application. The type of information used in a timeline is specific to the investigation at hand. Exporting every logged event, file access, Internet history, and all the myriad items of user activity to a single spreadsheet can result in millions of rows, from a single workstation. Although this massive export of data may be necessary during the investigation, most likely, the millions of rows would not be presented in legal hearings without being culled specifically to data relevant to the case.

Spreadsheets efficiently sort data in a meaningful manner based on selected criteria. Whether by date and time, type of event, or by file name, spreadsheets can display relevant information quickly. Figure 5.4 shows an example of a timeline spreadsheet, sorted by date, with a sample evidence file selected. As can be seen, this is a raw data dump of information without much meaning. Although this is a simple example of one evidence file in question, a timeline spreadsheet can contain extremely detailed information gathered from a forensic analysis such as event logs, registry files, and external devices.

	A	B	C	D
	Name	Created	Modified	Accessed
44767	empty[1].gif	7/15/2012 9:26	7/15/2012 9:26	7/15/2012 9:26
44768	423c086f-0099-4a05-9dd9-886624391144[1].jpg	7/15/2012 9:26	7/15/2012 9:26	7/15/2012 9:26
44769	24_months_40x40px-icon[1].png	7/15/2012 9:26	7/15/2012 9:26	7/15/2012 9:26
44770	939461eb-9472-43b3-a2d2-8ac3a6e3ee17[1].jpg	7/15/2012 9:26	7/15/2012 9:26	7/15/2012 9:26
44771	b83f01d3-1565-e011-971f-0030487d8897[1].jpg	7/15/2012 9:26	7/15/2012 9:26	7/15/2012 9:26
44772	f985cbec-887e-4be1-a829-12582e1257a0[1].jpg	7/15/2012 9:26	7/15/2012 9:26	7/15/2012 9:26
44773	a921dc69-a5cd-485f-82c7-06dd5e181440[1].jpg	7/15/2012 9:26	7/15/2012 9:26	7/15/2012 9:26
44774	5002ef24	7/15/2012 9:26	7/15/2012 9:26	7/15/2012 9:26
44775	client list.docx	7/15/2012 9:26	7/15/2012 9:26	7/15/2012 9:26
44776	WGPLU.LNK	7/15/2012 9:26	7/15/2012 9:26	7/15/2012 9:26
44777	2b1be1.msi	7/15/2012 9:26	7/15/2012 9:26	7/15/2012 9:28
44778	SDM_EN.msi	7/15/2012 9:26	7/15/2012 9:26	7/15/2012 9:26
44779	{cf6ddca3-4208-4417-9efd-16fed88d70de}_OnDiskSna	7/15/2012 9:28	7/15/2012 9:28	7/15/2012 9:28
44780	{cba8e548-ce92-11e1-8b08-001eecdb43cc}{3808876b-	7/15/2012 9:28	7/15/2012 11:12	7/15/2012 9:28
44781	_853F67D554F05449430E7E.exe	7/15/2012 9:28	7/15/2012 9:28	7/15/2012 9:28
44782	_112D608FD02CD87FDC7735.exe	7/15/2012 9:28	7/15/2012 9:28	7/15/2012 9:28
44783	_D741DE45EC951A9C783889.exe	7/15/2012 9:28	7/15/2012 9:28	7/15/2012 9:28

FIGURE 5.4 A basic file listing sorted by the created date and time.

Using a timeline spreadsheet to identify and eliminate possible suspects based solely on a forensic examination may not result in enough information to be useful. As any computer only shows the activity of any person that used the computer, additional circumstantial evidence needs to be added to the timeline spreadsheet.

Building upon the timeline spreadsheet from Figure 5.4, other information relating to all possible suspects can be added. In this manner, a person who has been physically placed at the same location of the evidence computer at the time of use can be easily shown on the timeline spreadsheet. The additional suspect information is derived from any or all of the previously mentioned methods such as geolocation of cell phones, physical surveillance, or interviews.

Figure 5.5 shows an example of additional information derived from sources other than a forensic analysis of the evidence system. These two rows of additional information both add a possible suspect related to the evidence file and eliminate a suspect by virtue of their previously determined geolocations. Employee Turnbow is seen to be at the office (row 244776) during the time the evidence file was created while employee Sanchez is seen to be outside the office (row 2144777) at that time.

Part of the task of collecting information is organizing it for a meaningful interpretation. Continually adding and deleting rows to any spreadsheet quickly adds confusion if there is not a system to keeping track of the information. Reconstruction of an incident involving more than one device in which the data is merged into a single timeline spreadsheet can make the timeline too difficult to process or completely confusing.

	A	Created	Modified	Accessed
1	Name			
244773	a921dc69-a5cd-485f-82c7-06dd5e181440[1].jpg	7/15/2012 9:26	7/15/2012 9:26	7/15/2012 9:26
244774	5002ef24	7/15/2012 9:26	7/15/2012 9:26	7/15/2012 9:26
244775	Turnbow checked into office per Proxy card	7/15/2012 9:00	NA	NA
244776	client list.docx	7/15/2012 9:26	7/15/2012 9:26	7/15/2012 9:26
244777	Sanchez in Kirkland per cell phone geolocation	7/15/2012 9:26		
244778	WGPLU.LNK	7/15/2012 9:26	7/15/2012 9:26	7/15/2012 9:26
244779	2b1be1.msi	7/15/2012 9:26	7/15/2012 9:26	7/15/2012 9:28
244780	SDM_EN.msi	7/15/2012 9:26	7/15/2012 9:26	7/15/2012 9:26
244781	{cf6ddca3-4208-4417-9efd-16fed88d70de}_OnDiskSna	7/15/2012 9:28	7/15/2012 9:28	7/15/2012 9:28
244782	{cba8e548-ce92-11e1-8b08-001eecdb43cc}{3808876b-‹	7/15/2012 9:28	7/15/2012 11:12	7/15/2012 9:28
244783	853EE7D554E05449430E7E exe	7/15/2012 9:28	7/15/2012 9:28	7/15/2012 9:28

FIGURE 5.5 Simply adding suspect geolocation information quickly shows patterns and relationships.

	A	B	C	D	E	
1	Item	Relevant	Source	Name	Created	
244773	54 B		Turnbow PC	a921dc69-a5cd-485f-82c7-06dd5e181440[1].jpg	7/15/2012 9:26	
244774	55 B		Turnbow PC	5002ef24	7/15/2012 9:26	
244775	56 B	Y	Company logs	Turnbow checked into office per Proxy card	7/15/2012 9:00	
244776	57 B	Y	Turnbow PC	client list.docx	7/15/2012 9:26	
244777	58 B	Y	Sanchez Cell	Sanchez in Kirkland per cell phone geolocation	7/15/2012 9:26	
244778	59 B		Turnbow PC	WGPLU.LNK	7/15/2012 9:26	
244779	60 B		Turnbow PC	2b1be1.msi	7/15/2012 9:26	
244780	61 B		Turnbow PC	SDM_EN.msi	7/15/2012 9:26	
244781	62 B		Turnbow PC	{cf6ddca3-4208-4417-9efd-16fed88d70de}_OnDiskSna	7/15/2012 9:28	
244782	63 B		Turnbow PC	{cba8e548-ce92-11e1-8b08-001eecdb43cc}{3808876b-i	7/15/2012 9:28	

FIGURE 5.6 Additional identifying columns help to keep order in the timeline as well as sort for specific information quickly.

Some tips on maintaining order in a timeline spreadsheet include numbering rows, identifying the source of information, and marking pertinent data for ease of viewing or sorting by relevance. Figure 5.6 shows examples of each of these tips. Color coding rows are also effective in ease of viewing per relevance; however, printed spreadsheets lose some of their value if not printed in color.

Information on the timeline spreadsheet can also be rated for its veracity of authenticity. An email can be verified through several means, such as an analysis of the email if collected at various locations, such as a source computer, recipient computer, and perhaps an email server. On a reliability scale, a verified email would rate as *reliable*. Information obtained through an anonymous source could be rated as *unknown reliability* or maybe even *unreliable* if other information discredits the source. A scale of reliability between these ends of a reliability spectrum attached to pertinent items of information in the timeline spreadsheet allows for an analysis of the veracity of all information as it relates to each other.

Creating attractive visual displays of timelines is discussed in the next chapter, which contain only the relevant information needed for the purpose of the investigation. The timeline spreadsheets used in this manner of investigation for suspect identification will contain much more than is needed in a trial and will not convey a reconstructed incident as well as a culled dataset will.

FOLLOW THE EVIDENCE

A gut feeling or intuition may work in the movies but not in a legal case. You need to be able to articulate your feelings and belief to be credible and your articulation must be based on factual evidence and inferences. Even your investigative actions are based on evidence, no matter how insignificant one piece of information may be; evidence must be followed to wherever it takes the investigator. So as long as you follow the evidence, you'll find the answers to your investigation if it is at all possible.

This is especially important when there is a long list of possible suspects. I've never met any investigator that wanted an innocent person arrested; yet, this can inadvertently happen if an investigator forces the evidence to point to a specific person. For that reason alone, investigators should consider themselves on an evidence bus and go along for the ride to where the bus goes. That includes forensic analysis of any electronic device. Evidence doesn't lie and doesn't need to be shoehorned to fit a belief. Data is what it is unless proven otherwise.

Doing the best job you can, in which all possible suspects have been identified and eliminated, where the evidence shows the facts without further explanation prevents preconceived beliefs from interfering with the evidence. At worst, the investigation can show that no person except the identified suspect could have committed the alleged act. At best, you show that it was the identified suspect.

Computer user activity

Although this chapter does not go into detail on specific forensic analysis to determine user activity, it is not implied that forensic analysis of storage devices cannot be used to identify suspects. On the contrary, information recovered from evidence devices must be used to determine the *how* of the alleged acts and hopefully, specific information can be found that identifies suspects. Such instances include the computer user logging into email accounts or creating personal documents specific and unique to the computer user for identification.

Analyzing and looking at the activity as a whole also allows a holistic view of the investigation where patterns of activity may be seen. Comparable to a physical crime scene, an electronic crime scene may be able to show the mindset and preparation of the suspect. A haphazard use of the computer in deleting files may be that of a spontaneous act, such as after receipt of a legal hold or court order. Indications of wiped files, anonymous logins, and encryption could show a thorough manner of execution and planning by the suspect.

As the intention and theme of this book is placing the suspect behind the keyboard, all aspects of the investigation are to be used. A complete picture must be painted to ensure the suspect, and not an innocent person, is correctly identified.

RABBIT HOLES

I am a believer that not every case can be solved, or at least be solved when you want it to be solved. Sometimes it may take months or years to get a break in a case. These breaks are sometimes due to a mistake made by the suspect, new evidence being discovered, or advances in technology. As a point of frustration, I've always preferred to solve puzzles and keep moving forward but practically, I know there is a line to be drawn on closing a case, at least temporarily.

There are also situations in which a case and investigator need to take a break. At least it is needed to have a fresh set of eyes to look over the information. As mentioned earlier, it is common to become solely focused on the details of a case and not reflect on the totality of all the information. Having persons new to your case look at your work may be effective for them to see something you overlooked or just didn't put together. This is not a sign of weakness to ask, but instead it is a sign of being a good investigator.

Other cases may have no leads at all. Anonymous logins, proxy servers, unsecured wireless access points, no witnesses, and a one-time act with no identifying information can lead to a case that is unsolvable with the current information. This type of investigation is easy to work because there isn't much to work with at all.

All investigations have a finite supply of resources to expend in an attempt to reach a resolution. Every forensic analysis on a hard drive also has its finite supply of resources. These resources are most always controlled by someone other than the analyst or investigator. Corporations or government entities determine the amount of resources and time to be spent on each case. These decisions come down to the financial cost to eventually solve the investigation based on the need to solve the incident balanced with the cost.

If there are no identifiable suspects and none that can be foreseen identifiable in the future, the rabbit hole needs to be closed unless circumstances change. By being creative and attempting to identify suspects using more than one method, the chances of having a successful resolution to your case will be higher than not. Some cases may have no virtual limit to expend because of the importance of the case, but practically, money, time, and personnel are not in infinite supply.

SUMMARY

I tend to believe that the investigators and forensic analysts who want to solve puzzles involving acts committed by people must have creative minds in order to be successful. There are organizations that employ both specialized investigators and forensic analysts. Other organizations may assign an investigation to the same person that conducts the forensic analysis. Neither method may better than the other but in each case, the investigator and forensic analyst need to be aware of the totality of the investigation in order to see the events as a whole. Compartmentalization of information, where few people know the entirety of an investigation, may be good for national security incidents, but for putting a case together, everyone needs to know as much as everyone else.

Lastly, after a suspect has been identified through circumstantial evidence, as the investigator or analyst, you still should have an open mind to new evidence. A case where a suspect has been identified can be turned upside down with exculpatory evidence. Follow the evidence and make sure you identify the right suspect.

Bibliography

Log2timeline. <http://log2timeline.net/>.

United States of America v. Barry Vincent Ardolf (United States District Court, District of Maryland, 2011).

Investigative Case Management

CONTENTS

INTRODUCTION

This chapter introduces several methods which may allow you to see inferences as you manage the information in your case. These inferences help connect the dots between evidence and suspects. Instead of simply taking notes during your investigation, create a system that can lead to discoveries otherwise missed. Gone are the days of writing reports and placing reports in binders such as seen in Figure 6.1. A case with any amount electronic evidence from a single storage device will quickly overwhelm a system of binders.

Investigative case management enables you to find information quickly and help you understand your investigation as a whole. Comprehending your reconstruction of the incident in your investigation will allow you to see the totality of the reconstructed incident as if you were there when it occurred. You will have more "Eureka!" moments when data can be seen as a whole and inferences between suspects and acts stand out clearly among all information.

FIGURE 6.1 Finding a single document in a shelf of binders can take more time than necessary compared to searching an electronic folder.

There may be a few investigators and analysts who can keep a neat desk during complex cases where the rest of us struggle to keep ahead of growing mounds of paper. Hundreds of pages are printed to be sorted throughout the case, duplicates of forms, photos, mail, court orders, and evidence requests are constantly generated to be filed in some manner, and this can quickly engulf anyone. With multiple cases and exams of multiple storage devices in each case generating even more case records, a common scene of the work area can appear to look like the results of a small office hurricane. Work areas that are cluttered and disorganized will also coincidently consist of cases that are not solved quickly, or even solved at all. This chapter intends to give methods of controlling information and analyzing it at the same time.

Basic case tracking

If there is one rule to remember, it is to handle evidence and information as it is collected. As long as each item is bagged and tagged in your system, the odds of losing or overlooking information are minimized. Bagging and tagging can easily be accomplished using logs where evidence or information that arrives is logged on paper, as it arrives, and filed away.

All other methods of dealing with evidence make your case management that much easier. If you have a good system already, perhaps it can be made better with one of

---

TIP

A stitch in time saves nine

I have never seen success with any method of evidence that does not involve handling it immediately when collected. Evidence that is placed aside to deal with at a later time usually results in lost or missing evidence or forgetting where items of evidence originated. Handle it as soon as you touch it or you may never see it again.

the methods described. And if one suggestion saves you minutes or hours over a period of time, then that would have been one worthwhile change to have made.

Although electronic data can be reproduced and fingerprint cards photocopied and scanned, the reproductions of the actual physical items cannot be cloned. The storage of these types of items requires safe storage within a secured facility. Physical evidence storage is vitally important, but this will not be the focus of this chapter. The focus is to manage your investigation information so that suspects can be clearly identified and evidence supporting suppositions are evident.

The case name

Before you can analyze your own information, you need to be able to find it. As seemingly unimportant it sounds, naming your cases deserves some attention. Depending upon your agency or organization, there may be an automated system for case names and you have no choice other than what the system gives you. There is nothing wrong with that as an internal system is already in place.

But what if you are responsible for creating the name for all your cases? In that instance, especially if there is more than one person that works cases in your organization, having any system is better than having more than one system or no system at all. Figure 6.2 shows a simple case numbering system that is based on the date the case was created with an additional sequential number if more than one case is drawn on that particular day.

It might seem easier to name a case with its legal name, such as Doe v Smith, or maybe even use the name of the client, suspect, or victim. Realistically, this is not the best method as clients may change during a civil case, identified suspects may be cleared, or additional victims identified. Even a court case number can change if the court venue is changed, perhaps from a state case to a federal case. There are too many variables that can change with any such designated name. A date-based format is unaffected by any variables as it is based on the date created and not the content of an investigation.

The electronic file names within an investigation may be organized by using your case name. Simply, each file's name can be preceded by its respective case number

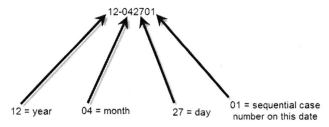

FIGURE 6.2 Case numbering system based on the case creation date.

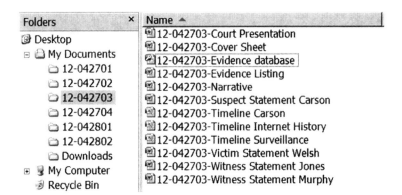

FIGURE 6.3 Simplicity in electronic document management will help you keep track of case information.

for ease of searching and cataloging. An example is seen in Figure 6.3, where case folders contain files named by the case and type of file. Cases where more than one person creates documents require a central repository for all documents, which could be stored on a shared network drive or internal database. Electronic records propagate quickly and can just as quickly be lost or overlooked.

If you currently have cases where your electronic case files have no order in naming conventions, what can you do? Spend hours renaming dozens or more individual files to some order? To save time and get your files in order, you could use a file renaming software utility, such as the Bulk Rename Utility seen in Figure 6.4. In one fell swoop, an entire folder can have the pre-fix of your case inserted into each file name.

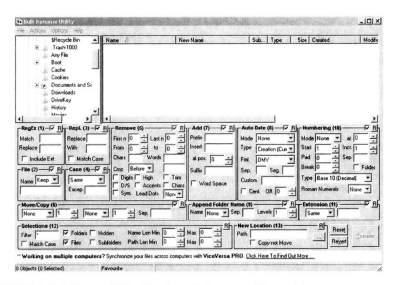

FIGURE 6.4 Bulk Rename Utility, http://www.bulkrenameutility.co.uk/

Note taking

Sometimes, during the investigative or analysis steps of an investigation, facts jump out and directly point to a suspect. Other times, it can take much longer to review and follow up on information just to be able to develop a list of potential suspects. Unless an investigation clearly points to a single suspect, the effort to develop leads begins with taking notes and reviewing those notes as the case develops.

Taking notes should be seen more than documenting your investigative steps. Note taking is one of your investigative steps. Whether your notes are scribbled in a notepad or entered into a database, when reviewed at later dates, you most likely will be able to put one piece of information together with another that you didn't see before, forming an inference and potentially leading to case resolution. It's getting a "Eureka!" moment when you least expect it by analyzing your own notes and reports.

One method of keeping all investigative notes and related information in one place can be accomplished through multifaceted programs, such as the One-Note from Microsoft (http://office.microsoft.com/en-us/onenote/) and Ever-Note (https://evernote.com/). There are similarities between both programs, such as being able to save all your notes in one location with search capabilities. Your notes can include pictures, audio and video recordings, faxes, emails, and almost any electronic file format you may be using as you conduct your analysis and investigation.

A benefit of programs like OneNote (Figure 6.5) and EverNote (Figure 6.6) is that the information can be sent and accessed in the field through mobile devices. Investigators can take a photo of evidence with a mobile device in the

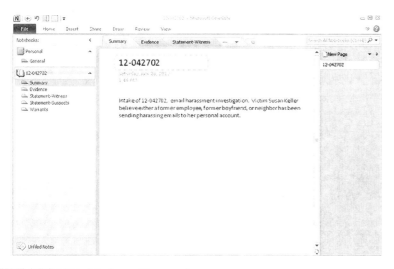

FIGURE 6.5 OneNote interface with a sample case.

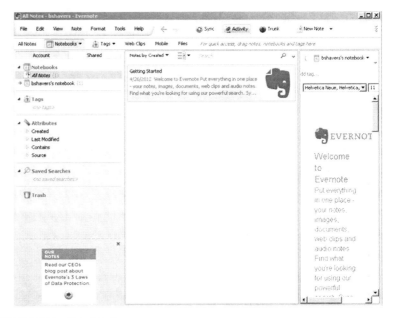

FIGURE 6.6 EverNote interface.

field and send it directly into the case file. Web screenshots can also be saved directly into the program. As an information management option, these types of programs may be useful to your investigation to organize case data.

Analyzing your notes

Gone are the days of typewriters. Reports are now typed using any one of many word processing software applications or typed directly into an internal system. Report narratives, summaries, and briefs are created and stored electronically. The ability to search these electronic files for information that may have been entered months or years earlier eliminates the need for physically searching for paper documents. Spending hours sifting through a dozen boxes of case files looking for one document can be done electronically in seconds.

TIP

Screen captures and graphics

There is truth to the adage "a picture is worth a thousand words." Visual representations of your data show the totality of case aspects much faster and clearer than reading pages of information which describe it.

But is typing your notes using a word processing application good enough? For a final report, most any word processing application will work, however, reviewing a word processed report may not be the easiest to analyze. As notes are written and typed chronologically, reviewing all instances of a specific event is a difficult process with a chronological report. As an example would be finding all instances that a USB device was connected in multiple systems. A typed, chronological report requires reading through every page to find every instance this information was typed. Sometimes, being able to review notes out of chronological order helps find the information needed to understand a case. Perhaps an application that is not a simple word processing program would be better.

One example of such an application is KeepNote (http://www.keepnote.org), a cross platform, note taking utility. As seen in Figure 6.7, data is stored in a hierarchy format and customizable to a specific case or need. The information is able to be searched electronically, files of various formats can be attached, and reports generated in html or xml format. KeepNote can also be run from a portable storage device. Although KeepNote has a simple interface, it provides the analysis of investigator notes with supporting evidence without completely relying upon chronological information.

There are other similar applications, available freely through open source or freeware applications. Some of these are primarily report writing utilities or light case management utilities, which leaves scalability as a drawback.

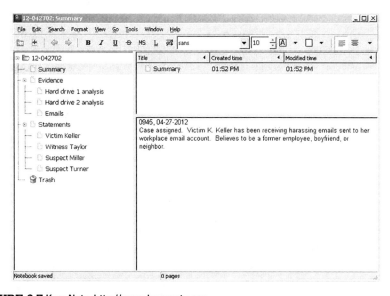

FIGURE 6.7 KeepNote, http://www.keepnote.org.

A program like KeepNote is NoteKeeper (http://www.tolon.co.uk/software/notekeeper/). NoteKeeper is also freeware and useful for organizing investigative notes. Another note taking utility with capabilities of encryption and tamperproof notes is CaseNotes (http://qccis.com/resources/forensic-tools/casenotes-lite/). CaseNotes, like NoteKeeper and KeepNotes, is freely available.

The point to be made in analyzing your notes is that although the information in the notes consists of investigative steps taken, including analysis of electronic evidence, being able to analyze your actual notes can be productive. Sometimes, a short sentence created weeks earlier can take on a whole new meaning when reviewed with other notes created later.

Analysis with spreadsheets

The spreadsheet is perhaps one of the most commonly used, versatile, and powerful software applications used in digital forensics investigations. The spreadsheet could be used for entering text as if it were a word processing application, but it shines when used to analyze massive amounts of information such as displaying events in a chronological timeline. Timeline analysis allows viewing and interpreting of data through sorting of the data by various criteria, such as chronological dates or specific event types.

Timelines can be used to display Internet history, event logs, registry files, or a combination of system and file data. Important events in a timeline can be given focus through the use of color and bold text to draw attention during review of the data. As spreadsheets can be sorted by columns, any header of interest can be chosen to view in ascending or descending order, or other selection of criteria available. The header columns are the titles for the metadata for each data item. The metadata consists of timestamps, filenames, file paths, or any user selected metadata descriptor that may be available.

Manipulating a spreadsheet in this manner allows finding specific information quickly, even if there are hundreds of thousands of data rows. This manipulation of how data is viewed also helps to change your perspective on the data to perhaps see information leading to investigative leads or conclusions.

Creating a timeline usually involves importing a raw or filtered amount of information in .csv format into a spreadsheet that can range from thousands to millions of rows of data. This data can be collected using timeline applications, including such applications as Log2timeline (http://log2timeline.net/), Aftertime (http://www.holmes.nl/NFIlabs/Aftertime), or through scripts and applications such as RegRipper (http://code.google.com/p/regripper/) developed for collecting timeline data.

Even the export of file lists from forensic analysis applications such as X-Ways Forensics (http://www.x-ways.net) can be used to create a timeline. However, exporting massive amounts of data most likely will contain an amount of information not needed for your investigation. At that point, time will be needed to substantially cull the data in order to understand specifics and context of a certain incident.

As information can be imported into a timeline that is specific to a file type, separate timelines are able to show focus on specific events. For instance, graphic files, documents, or system related data such as registry files can be either combined into one timeline or separated into individual timelines depending on your objective. Figure 6.8 shows filtered data of USB device use only, sorted by date created, as an example of a narrowly focused timeline, or mini-timeline, displayed in a spreadsheet.

Since a spreadsheet timeline can contain millions of rows of data, analysts may simply underutilize this method of analysis simply for being overwhelmed. Even if a massive spreadsheet was sorted and filtered for review, the time spent can be intensive. However, I know of no better method of showing the chronology of events than a timeline.

Charts and graphs created in spreadsheet applications are an effective means to visualize massive amounts of data. Using data in a particular spreadsheet, charts and graphs can be updated as information is updated. Visual representations

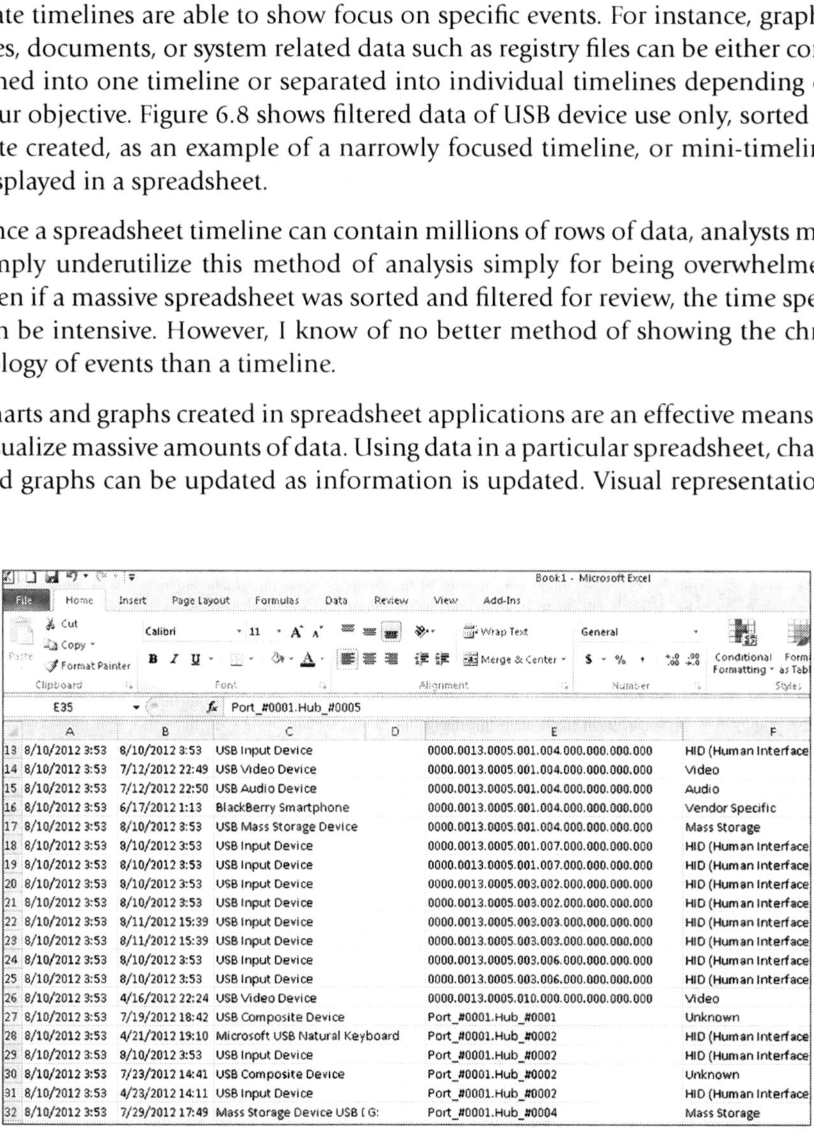

	A	B	C	D	E	F
13	8/10/2012 3:53	8/10/2012 3:53	USB Input Device		0000.0013.0005.001.004.000.000.000.000	HID (Human Interface
14	8/10/2012 3:53	7/12/2012 22:49	USB Video Device		0000.0013.0005.001.004.000.000.000.000	Video
15	8/10/2012 3:53	7/12/2012 22:50	USB Audio Device		0000.0013.0005.001.004.000.000.000.000	Audio
16	8/10/2012 3:53	6/17/2012 1:13	BlackBerry Smartphone		0000.0013.0005.001.004.000.000.000.000	Vendor Specific
17	8/10/2012 3:53	8/10/2012 3:53	USB Mass Storage Device		0000.0013.0005.001.004.000.000.000.000	Mass Storage
18	8/10/2012 3:53	8/10/2012 3:53	USB Input Device		0000.0013.0005.001.007.000.000.000.000	HID (Human Interface
19	8/10/2012 3:53	8/10/2012 3:53	USB Input Device		0000.0013.0005.001.007.000.000.000.000	HID (Human Interface
20	8/10/2012 3:53	8/10/2012 3:53	USB Input Device		0000.0013.0005.003.002.000.000.000.000	HID (Human Interface
21	8/10/2012 3:53	8/10/2012 3:53	USB Input Device		0000.0013.0005.003.002.000.000.000.000	HID (Human Interface
22	8/10/2012 3:53	8/11/2012 15:39	USB Input Device		0000.0013.0005.003.003.000.000.000.000	HID (Human Interface
23	8/10/2012 3:53	8/11/2012 15:39	USB Input Device		0000.0013.0005.003.003.000.000.000.000	HID (Human Interface
24	8/10/2012 3:53	8/10/2012 3:53	USB Input Device		0000.0013.0005.003.006.000.000.000.000	HID (Human Interface
25	8/10/2012 3:53	8/10/2012 3:53	USB Input Device		0000.0013.0005.003.006.000.000.000.000	HID (Human Interface
26	8/10/2012 3:53	4/16/2012 22:24	USB Video Device		0000.0013.0005.010.000.000.000.000.000	Video
27	8/10/2012 3:53	7/19/2012 18:42	USB Composite Device		Port_#0001.Hub_#0001	Unknown
28	8/10/2012 3:53	4/21/2012 19:10	Microsoft USB Natural Keyboard		Port_#0001.Hub_#0002	HID (Human Interface
29	8/10/2012 3:53	8/10/2012 3:53	USB Input Device		Port_#0001.Hub_#0002	HID (Human Interface
30	8/10/2012 3:53	7/23/2012 14:41	USB Composite Device		Port_#0001.Hub_#0002	Unknown
31	8/10/2012 3:53	4/23/2012 14:11	USB Input Device		Port_#0001.Hub_#0002	HID (Human Interface
32	8/10/2012 3:53	7/29/2012 17:49	Mass Storage Device USB (G:		Port_#0001.Hub_#0004	Mass Storage

FIGURE 6.8 Spreadsheet timeline example with USB device data.

of data may be easier to comprehend the nuances of relationships between events. The visual impact of a chart as compared to a listing of information is shown in Figures 6.9 and 6.10. Figure 6.9 is an example of Internet history shown in a spreadsheet which includes the number of visits per website. Creating a chart of this data gives a clearer picture of the differences of website visits as seen in Figure 6.10.

The chart seen in Figure 6.10 shows that the "Ccleaner" website was visited much more than the other listed websites. As a case presentation method, this is impactful to explain data. As an analysis method, it can be insightful into your data. Given massive datasets of Internet history, outliers of pertinent facts are glaringly obvious.

The spreadsheet timeline is an effect method of analyzing data, finding patterns or anomalies, and differentiating which data is evidence from data which is not. Although using charts and graphs in spreadsheets assists in the analysis of data, these same methods can be used in the presentation of data, which will be discussed in a following chapter.

	A	B	C	D
1	Evidence Item	URL	Title	Visit Count
2	02-042701-001	http://www.ccleaner.com	Ccleaner	55
3	02-042701-001	http://eraser.heidi.ie	Eraser	46
4	02-042701-001	http://www.foxnews.com	Fox News Breaking News	4
5	02-042701-001	http://www.google.com	Google	23
6	02-042701-001	http://www.accessdata.com	e-Discovery, Computer Forensics	17

FIGURE 6.9 Example of a spreadsheet displaying Internet history.

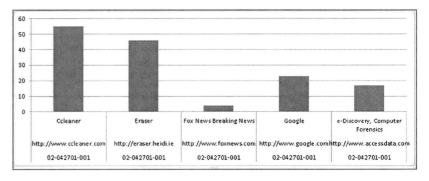

FIGURE 6.10 Example of a graph visually displaying the number of website visits.

Analysis with databases

As storage device capacity grows, the amount of data grows with it. Spreadsheets can become overwhelmed with data and at that point, become useless. A database is an option to consider helping with data analysis when the amount has outpaced a spreadsheet. Relational databases, such as Microsoft Access seen in Figure 6.11, can be linked to spreadsheets, searched, shared, and used to determine relationships between data.

Depending upon the chosen database application, scalability can extend from small teams of investigators to an entire organization. A spreadsheet timeline can be imported into a database or converted into a database for analysis. Since databases have a powerful ability to store, organize, and manage large datasets, the ability to import multiple spreadsheet timelines allow management of many separate datasets as one.

Especially when multiple timelines have been created for multiple computer systems, databases are an effective means of analyzing the timelines through importing into a single database. Creating queries to generate tables and reports based on a single or multiple filters can be run against millions of rows of imported spreadsheet timelines. One example of a query could be a search for a USB device serial number or particular file. When queried, a database will output a table or report of all instances of that file, across all imported

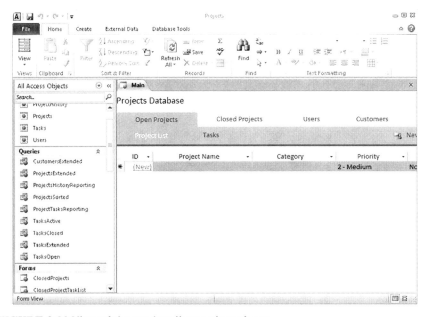

FIGURE 6.11 Microsoft Access, http://www.microsoft.com.

spreadsheet timelines. Mini-timelines consisting of hundreds or fewer rows can be created from a query in a short period of time rather than searching millions of rows in multiple spreadsheets for the same information.

Since timelines are based on timestamps from the filesystem, combining different timelines into a single database requires converting all timestamps into a common time zone, such as Coordinated Universal Time (UTC) also known as Greenwich Mean Time (GMT). UTC/GMT is the time standard used worldwide and is a good option of standardization multiple time zones in your investigation. Otherwise, the timeline will be confusing at best.

An example of the searching capability of a database is seen in Figure 6.12. Using FileMaker Pro (http://www.filemaker.com), multiple spreadsheet timelines have been imported into one database. Through the search feature, any number of metadata fields can be specified for searching, either through one selected evidence item or all evidence items.

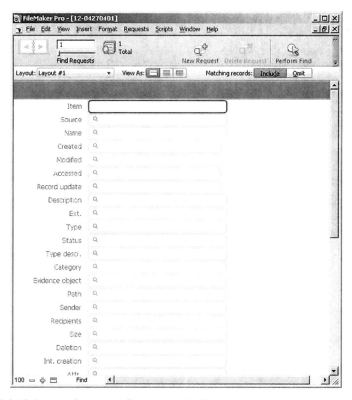

FIGURE 6.12 Sample of metadata fields created in FileMaker Pro.

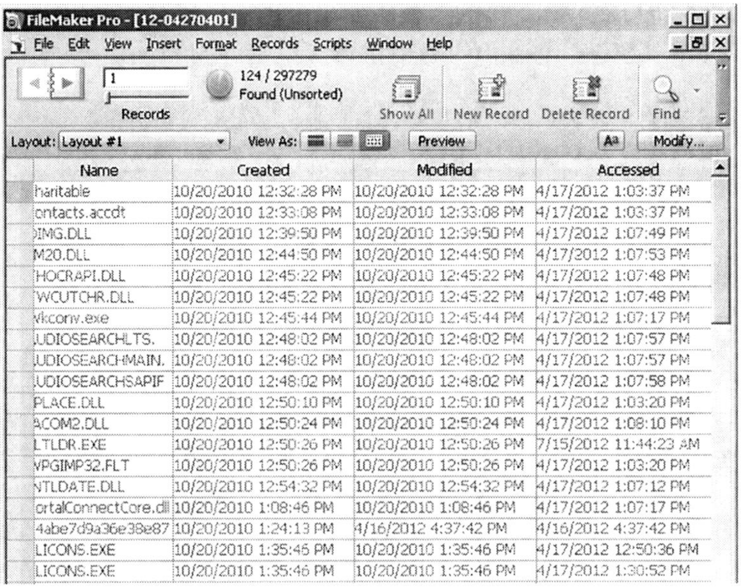

FIGURE 6.13 Results of a date search using FileMaker Pro database.

The result of a search can be viewed within the database program or exported into a mini-timeline spreadsheet or document. One search example for a date of 10/20/2010 is seen in Figure 6.13. Through the use of a database, individual or multiple timelines, especially those with millions of rows, can more easily be searched, managed, and exported into smaller and narrowly focused timelines.

Nearly all forensic analysis applications can sort and search like the described database programs. The forensic analysis applications can even export the results to a spreadsheet format too. However, the more powerful capability of a database program is the manipulation of data to create a uniquely desired product suited for a specific purpose. Through this manipulation of displaying data, inferences can be gained toward reaching that Eureka! moment where you recognize the evidence placing your suspect at the computer.

Analysis using charts

Charting information allows for visual representations that can help interpret data, and turn a complex investigation into an easy to understand concept. The type of chart depends upon the type of information to be displayed. Link charts and matrix charts show relationships, flow charts and event charts show a sequence of events or processes, and organization charts show hierarchy.

The matrix chart has been discussed in a previous chapter as a means of identifying and eliminating potential suspects. Although simple, the matrix chart is extremely effective given almost any number of potential suspects and can quickly be understood. See Figure 5.1 as an example of a matrix chart.

Link charting is another method to quickly visualize relationships between persons or events. As a data analysis method, suspected or confirmed relationships are immediately made obvious through symbols. A basic foundation of symbols used in a link chart can be seen in Figure 6.14. Through the use of basic and simple symbols, clarity in relationships becomes obvious.

Using the basic design symbols from Figure 6.14, an example has been created in Figure 6.15. In this example, it is clearly seen that only Suspect B has access to both evidence computers, PC 1 and PC 2. Suspect C has access only to one evidence computer and Suspect A might have access to PC 1.

Suggestions for link charts include avoiding crossing lines to avoid confusion, and keep the charts simple and to as few points as possible. Solid connecting lines are confirmed relationships whereas dotted lines are not confirmed.

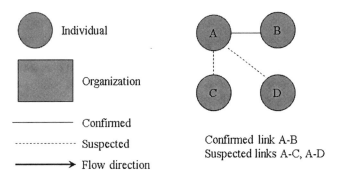

FIGURE 6.14 Basic foundation of link chart symbols.

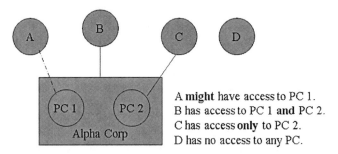

FIGURE 6.15 An example of a link chart showing relationships between persons and personal computers.

If there is not a relationship between a person and/or evidence item, then no connecting line is made, showing no relationship. Although Figure 6.15 is a simple example, it only takes seconds to see relationships without requiring explanation even if the data was more intensive.

The creation of link charts can be made using paper and pens or using any number of software applications. Microsoft Visio (http://www.microsoft.com) is one example of a program developed for this type of diagram. As seen in Figure 6.16, Visio allows for easy creation of link charts and analysis with pre-defined shapes and symbols. Programs developed specifically for data analysis, such as the IBM i2 Analyst's Notebook (http://www.i2group.com), allow for automated creation of links, charts, and graphs. These more powerful programs have advanced features of data analysis beyond creating link analysis diagrams which may be necessary in large investigations.

Event and flow charts can be used to display a chronological chain of events of an investigation or a computer application process. Figure 6.17 shows the requirements to physically access a computer which was used to send an email under investigation. The chart implies only one employee had physical and login access rights to the suspect computer out of over 100 persons at the location. Actual cases will most likely require more complex charting but the concept remains the same; visually show facts to more easily see the less obvious.

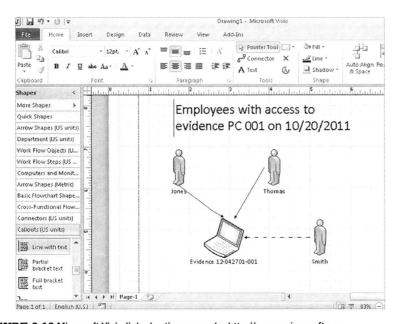

FIGURE 6.16 Microsoft Visio link charting example; http://www.microsoft.com.

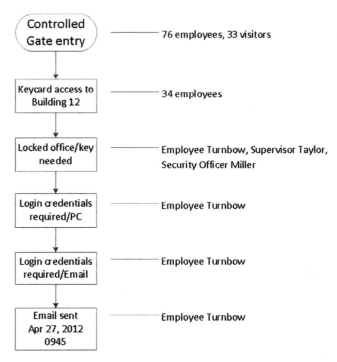

FIGURE 6.17 Event flow chart depicting physical access to an evidence computer, where 109 persons are initially suspected, but only 1 person had access.

Used in combination to the information displayed in Figure 6.16, a visual timeline created from both a forensic analysis of the suspect computer and investigative information can be seen in Figure 6.18. By employing several analytical methods to analyze information, a narrowing list of suspects is created or may show that only one suspect could have committed the alleged acts.

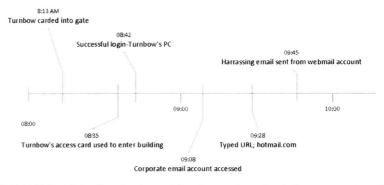

FIGURE 6.18 Visual timeline showing activity of an employee in relation to computer activity.

Analysis using maps

Previously discussed geolocation data showed that suspects can be tracked by several means, such as call data records, IP addresses, and physical surveillance. Plotting this data on a map shows a suspect's movements and location in relation to an investigated event, such as downloading contraband or unauthorized access to networks. Of course, a mobile device must be attributed to a suspect before assuming the geolocation in a particular device belongs to the suspect. This can be done in varied ways, such as reviewing the call records and verifying calls made were the suspect's. These calls can be to the suspect's home, workplace, or to witnesses corroborating the calls.

Plotting geolocation can be accomplished manually, either by plotting each separate location onto a map or by creating mapping data files which can be read and imported by geolocation plotting applications. One such application is GPS Visualizer (http://www.gpsvisualizer.com). GPS Visualizer is a free online utility that creates maps from GPS data. The GPS data can be a combination of way points, EXIF geolocation data, or manually imported locations.

Given a mobile device, the amount of data to analyze may be more than simply creating a map and need specialized software. An example of an application well suited for cell phone analysis is GeoTime (http://www.geotime.com). As seen in Figure 6.19, GeoTime can show the time and location of a mobile device. GeoTime can also show the frequency of calls made.

Perhaps the biggest benefit to using specialized analysis applications is the ability to easily manipulate the viewing of the data. As opposed to manually

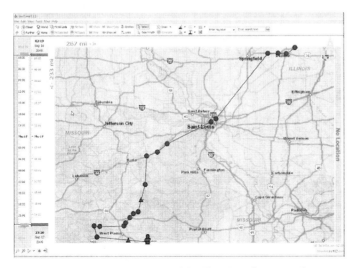

FIGURE 6.19 GeoTime screenshot, courtesy of GeoTime, http://www.geotime.com.

FIGURE 6.20 PerpHound, courtesy of NW3C, http://www.nw3c.org.

updating and revising visual appearances, programs such as GeoTime allow for instantaneous changing of views and data through an intuitive interface.

PerpHound, a law enforcement only program provided by NW3C, provides a similar function to GeoTime. PerpHound also exports call data records into a Google Map, showing a suspect's movements. Figure 6.20 is a screenshot showing a call data records of a suspect in relation to his home.

As with any analytical method, mapping coordinates without a purpose may lead to being overwhelmed with information but also is a powerful method that visually places a suspect at locations of activity under investigation.

Fresh set of eyes

Sometimes, by staring at data for long periods of time, the only result is eye strain. Even working a long-term investigation can result in a lack of results by not being able to truly understand the context of events. When that happens, it's time for a new set of eyes. This requires the analyst to take a step back and regroup.

Or even better, someone else should take a look at the data and case. Having a different perspective makes a huge difference in how information is seen and understood. Having several sets of eyes looking at the same information usually results in new ideas, better comprehension, and finding the evidence that was sitting there the entire time. That makes all the difference in a case.

SUMMARY

The forensic analysis of electronic storage devices uncovers details of activity under an investigation, whether it is criminal violations of law or internal corporate violations. Yet, without supporting evidence, the forensic analysis does not unequivocally place a suspect to that activity. This chapter gives insight into the analysis of information, both recovered through digital forensics and that of traditional investigation methods.

Another aspect to consider when analyzing datasets is that all types of information can be analyzed to develop investigative leads and additional evidence. As deleted emails can be recovered from a hard drive for analysis, the actual words of the email can be analyzed for comparison against sample writings of the suspect. The analysis of text can show how specific words are used, the frequency of words, grammar, and level of writing, all of which may be attributed to a person.

Internet history in and of itself will show use of browsers and the websites visited. An analysis of the actual types of websites, typed URLs, bookmarked pages, and number of visits to each page can show the intention and knowledge of the computer user related to alleged acts.

The secret ingredient in this chapter has been to look into the data, look into each specific data, and look at the data holistically to find the meaning of the evidence, not just hard facts. Even as the suspect's data can be analyzed, your own notes may hold the key that is missing to place the suspect at the keyboard.

Bibliography

Bulk Rename Utility. <http://www.bulkrenameutility.co.uk>.

Carvey H. (2012, June 11). Timeline analysis. <http://windowsir.blogspot.com/2012/06/timeline-analysis.html>.CaseNotes. <http://qccis.com/resources/forensic-tools/casenotes-lite1>.

EverNote. <http://www.evernote.com>.

FileMaker. <http://www.filemaker.com>.

GeoTime. <http://www.geotime.com>.

GPS Visualizer. <http://www.gpsvisualizer.com>.

IBM i2 Analyst's Notebook. <http://www.i2group.com>.

KeepNote. <http://www.keepnote.org>.

Log2timeline. <http://log2timeline.net/>.

Microsoft Office. <http://www.microsoft.com>.

NoteKeeper. <http://www.tolon.co.uk/software/notekeeper>.

Case Presentation

INFORMATION IN THIS CHAPTER:

- It's not whether you win or lose
- Investigative mindset
- Your audience
- Preparation
- Organizing case information
- Value of visuals
- Presentation media
- Slideshows and animations
- Charts and diagrams
- The suspect machine
- Analogies
- Avoid TMI (Too Much Information)
- Your presentation

INTRODUCTION

This chapter will discuss methods of presenting electronic evidence for a variety of audiences. The admissibility, authentication, chain of custody, and other aspects of *what is evidence* are extremely important to every case; however, this chapter will only minimally discuss the actual evidence and focus more on methods of presenting your case. After all, the objective of any investigation is to convey to an audience the facts of the case in a manner that they understand it.

Keep in mind that your goal of placing the suspect behind the keyboard rests upon your presentation clearly describing your case. Articulating your case in a manner in which your audience will have a picture in their mind, will also have your audience place the suspect behind the keyboard. This can be accomplished without you having to say it directly as the audience will say it for you.

IT'S NOT WHETHER YOU WIN OR LOSE

As a witness, your primary function in presenting case information is simply explaining the facts. Experts will give opinions, keeping that these experts' opinions are just as truthful as any fact and include their interpretations of computer user activity.

Investigations are conducted to uncover the truth, where both inculpatory and exculpatory evidence is authenticated, corroborated, analyzed, and interpreted for relevance and veracity. To have any preconceived beliefs or opinions discredits a fair investigation. You must be open to all possibilities and eliminate possible suspects through a fair investigation until you are left with only a list of reasonable suspects.

With an open and inquisitive mind, the facts will lead you to the truth of the investigation and analysis. Proving and disproving theories, corroborating and discrediting alibis, and verifying information will allow the case to speak for itself. But how do you convey this information to your audience and how can you have an inquisitive or investigative mindset to accomplish this?

INVESTIGATIVE MINDSET

Having an investigative mindset helps you to prepare your presentation as you need to know the *why* and the *how* of presenting information to convey the facts just as you did investigating your case. One of your goals in presenting your case is showcasing how you arrived at your beliefs without actually saying it. As you answer the fundamental investigative questions of *who, what, why, where, when, and how*, your audience can put the case together in their own minds, as if they were the investigator. When that happens, your audience places the suspect behind the keyboard, not you.

Good investigators get asked the same questions time and time again. How do you do it? Why are you so lucky? What is your secret? Another set of similar types of questions are asked at trials and hearings. Why did you suspect this person and not that person? Did you focus your entire investigation on one person? These types of questions are intended to discover your mindset and to find out what you were thinking. The investigative mindset not only helps you be a great examiner or investigator, but it also helps you prepare your case for presentation by being able to articulate your thought processes.

Whether you are an investigator conducting surveillance on a suspect or examining the registry for computer system settings, being curious most always leads to uncovering evidence or leads to evidence. Perhaps there is one clue that happens after days or weeks of intense focus, but sometimes that one clue is what makes a case. Whether you wait for a clue to appear or relentlessly dig for it, the clue is there. You just have to find it and know it when you see it. You want your audience to see it just as you did.

An example I have given in workshops on investigative mindsets is a personal experience where I've seen two police officers, standing side by side, and both looking at the same street corner. One officer saw several criminal acts occur where the other did not, even though they were looking at the same activity. This occurred many times. Simply, one officer observed and asked *why* is that person there and *what* is he doing, whereas the other officer accepted two people standing on a street corner as just being there. Just as important is the ability to effectively communicate these observations, feelings, and beliefs to your audience.

Digital forensics is not so different when looking at computer activity. Being able to ask questions such as, "*why* does this file have a modification data stamp that precedes the creation data stamp" does not require a law enforcement commission to possess the superpower of curiosity. If any detail of an investigation doesn't seem right, maybe it is not right and should be examined more closely. This even applies to your gut feeling or intuition where you should ask yourself, "*why* do I get the feeling something is missing."

Asking these questions during your investigation and analysis allows you to miss less evidence. This mindset will help you to develop an effective means to convey your investigation to others for your case presentation so your audience will also have a clear understanding.

YOUR AUDIENCE

You need to know your audience and the venue for your case presentation to be effective. This chapter gives several methods of presenting your information, but not every method will be appropriate for every type of audience. Your presentation could be informally presented to a supervisor or formally before a Congressional hearing. Even different courtrooms and judges will have varied rules on how digital evidence is presented.

Not knowing your intended audience or their needs most likely will result in at least embarrassment of a presentation or the complete failure of presenting your case effectively. There are instances where an audience, such as an attorney, just wants to know if the evidence points to guilt or innocence of a client, without having to read dozens of pages of forensic analysis. Other audiences require minute details of analysis, but both audiences require the presenter to be aware of the objectives for presentations.

The one thing to avoid is to think that you are the audience. As much as you may want to toot your horn, show off your great work, and speak in complicated technical jargon, the only person that will be impressed is you. Everyone else will be dazed, confused, and not at all impressed. Some in your audience may be plainly irritated. Case presentation is for your audience and you succeed when your information is clearly understood and this requires preparation.

PREPARATION

The work of preparing your presentation may be the only part of case presentation where you have total control. The information is in your hands, arranged in the manner you prefer, and any technical problems can be tested and corrected. Since you have this luxury during the preparation phase, take advantage of it because during the presentation, the control of the information may be completely out of your hands.

The amount of time to prepare depends on the complexity of the investigation and your audience. One case presentation may require an hour to prepare while another requires weeks to prepare. The objective in both of these scenarios is the same, only the time needed will vary.

ORGANIZING CASE INFORMATION

Maybe you are the sole investigator tasked with an entire case, conduct all forensic analysis and interviews personally, and maintain all information centrally. If that is the situation, gathering and organizing case information will be fairly easy. However, many investigations have more than one person involved to include a variety of third parties such as Internet Service Providers, witnesses, co-case agents, and multiple examiners. For these situations, collecting and organizing case information takes a life of its own just trying to track down all reports that may have been written. But it has to be done, especially finding all written reports.

Read all the reports. Read them all again. Find any inconsistencies and loose ends and make sure each written statement is corroborated with supporting evidence. During this process of reviewing reports, should anything negative to the case be found, take corrective measures and inform your client or legal counsel immediately. No one likes surprises during a presentation of evidence.

If supplemental reports are needed to clarify information, make sure they are written and submitted to the case file.

Organize your information. Printed information can be organized in folders, but what about a gigabyte or more of data collected throughout the case? Emails, electronic documents, scanned letters, and other electronic evidence files contained on an external drive may need immediate and unplanned production at any time during case presentation. One answer is to use forensic applications that can double in organizing your case data. An example seen in Figure 7.1 is dtSearch, an indexing application typically used as a forensic tool but also excels at indexing your case information to be searched on the fly.

Complex cases that contain hundreds of thousands of electronic files are better served being indexed, that is, a database of words and numbers of the files created for ease of searching. dtSearch not only indexes large datasets, but it can create reports of the searches, export the files found, and even highlight the keywords found. A utility such as dtSearch enables you to find information quickly that might have been easily be overlooked when manually searching files on a hard drive. Being asked a question on the spot by your boss, client, or judge for whom you don't have answer is stressful enough, but not being able to find the answer makes it that much worse.

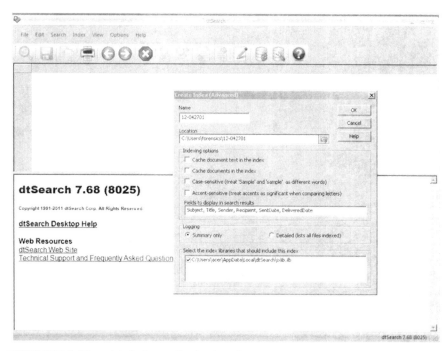

FIGURE 7.1 dtSearch indexing application, http://www.dtsearch.com.

VALUE OF VISUALS

The cliché that a picture is worth a thousand words does not accurately describe a visual used in your presentation. In a case presentation, one visual can be worth the entire case. As most people grow up learning visually, whether in math class using charts and graphs to see numbers or through art, understanding by seeing is an effective method of learning.

In the tale of three blind men attempting to describe an elephant with words, each basing their description on the part of the elephant each person touched, such as the tusk or the tail, they could not agree on the totality of the elephant's description. Presentations require the spoken word for descriptions, but visuals can make sure that each person in your audience understands and sees the same thing.

Compare the following examples. Figure 7.2 shows a paragraph describing an average evidence scene with multiple evidence items.

The accompanying figure to the written description is seen in Figure 7.3. Although this is a simple photo of the items described in Figure 7.2, the photo clarifies the scene in the mind of your audience without misunderstanding.

Although the report accurately reflected the physical evidence scene, the ease at which a visual aid clarifies the words is dramatic. Taking this one step further to clarify the physical connections described in the report, review Figure 7.4 as an example of a visual created to visually show the connections.

The value of visuals cannot be understated but can be overused. As long as your audience has the sense of sight, visuals will enable all to see that which you verbally describe. The key ingredient, however, is to choose the right type of visual to use for each situation and only use visuals when needed, not just for the sake of creating visual aids.

Presentation media

Not all media presentation methods, visuals, or equipment used may be suitable for every type of presentation. Your audience may be a technically

```
I observed five computer processing units (CPU) and one computer
monitor situated on a desk in the suspect's bedroom. Two CPU units
(evidence items 1 and 2) were stacked on top of each other while the
remaining three units (evidence items 3, 4, 5) were standing side to
side.  A computer monitor (evidence item 6) and keyboard (evidence
item 7) were on top of CPU evidence item 4. The monitor and keyboard
were connected to CPU evidence 5.
```

FIGURE 7.2 Written description of an evidence scene with multiple items.

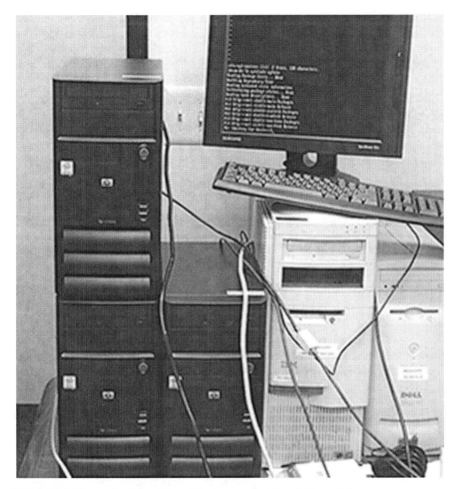

FIGURE 7.3 A sample photo of the evidence seen described in Figure 7.2.

proficient supervisor who will not need visual aids to understand a verbal presentation. Another audience could be a jury where your audience's technical knowledge is unknown and can range from someone never operating computers to computer experts.

Within this range are presentation limitations based on limited technical resources or even restrictions on using specific types of technical resources by a specific judge. Therefore, having access to a wide range of presentation media and the ability to use each effectively will allow you to tailor your presentations accordingly.

As much as any forensic examiner uses technology, reliance on any technology cannot be taken for granted nor expected to work all the time.

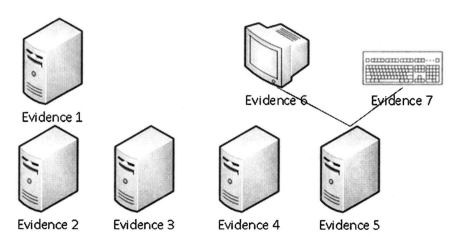

FIGURE 7.4 Visual created to show connections between devices.

Computers and software programs crash, a surprise shortage of outlets prevents use of a projector, bulbs burn out, and sometimes, nothing seems to work as expected when needed. These electronic devices, such as projectors, computers, video players, and televisions, will eventually fail, all of them, at some point in their normal lifecycle. Expecting that this day of equipment failure will occur when you are presenting your case will make a big difference in the outcome if you are prepared with backup plans.

Backup plans include the use of non-technical media devices such as white boards, flip charts, posters, and even chalk boards. These will work as long as you have writing utensils. When technology fails and you are not allowed the time to correct the issues, having a backup plan may save your presentation. However, there are substantial drawbacks to using these items.

As an example, using a flip chart or standing dry erase board, as seen in Figure 7.5, requires that you write on it, and therefore, be in front of it, blocking the view of the flip chart. Your writing legibility is critical, as is your artistic ability, in order for your audience to read your writing and interpret your drawing.

There are no "do-overs" either, as that what you write and draw, unprepared, has been memorialized. But most importantly, is that at least having non-technical devices as a backup, you will still be able to deliver your information in a credible manner should you need to visually illustrate your information when technology fails.

Beyond the physical devices and articulation needed to convey your investigation, there is the dilemma of choosing the manner that electronic data is visualized. Since electronic data is not a physical object that can be held with hands, choosing the right format to display the data is crucial for understanding by your audience. Luckily, there are many ways to visually display any amount of data.

FIGURE 7.5 Flip chart/standing dry erase board, when technology fails, may be a good backup visual aid.

Slideshows and animations

A slideshow presentation can be one of the best methods to display your case. It can also be the worst if incorrectly used. When used appropriately, a slideshow presentation allows conveying of information in an organized manner. Depending upon technical arrangements, a slideshow can be projected onto large screen or onto individual monitors for each member of your audience. The individual slides most likely will also need to be printed, which allows for note taking and review. Examples of website screen captures are seen in Figure 7.6 with note taking area for each slide. Diagrams, charts, graphs, and other depictions of case information can just as easily be displayed.

The phrase "death by Powerpoint" is a truism when a slideshow consists of excessive, unnecessary, irrelevant, or confusing information. Case presentation can be supported by use of a slideshow if it is put together coherently.

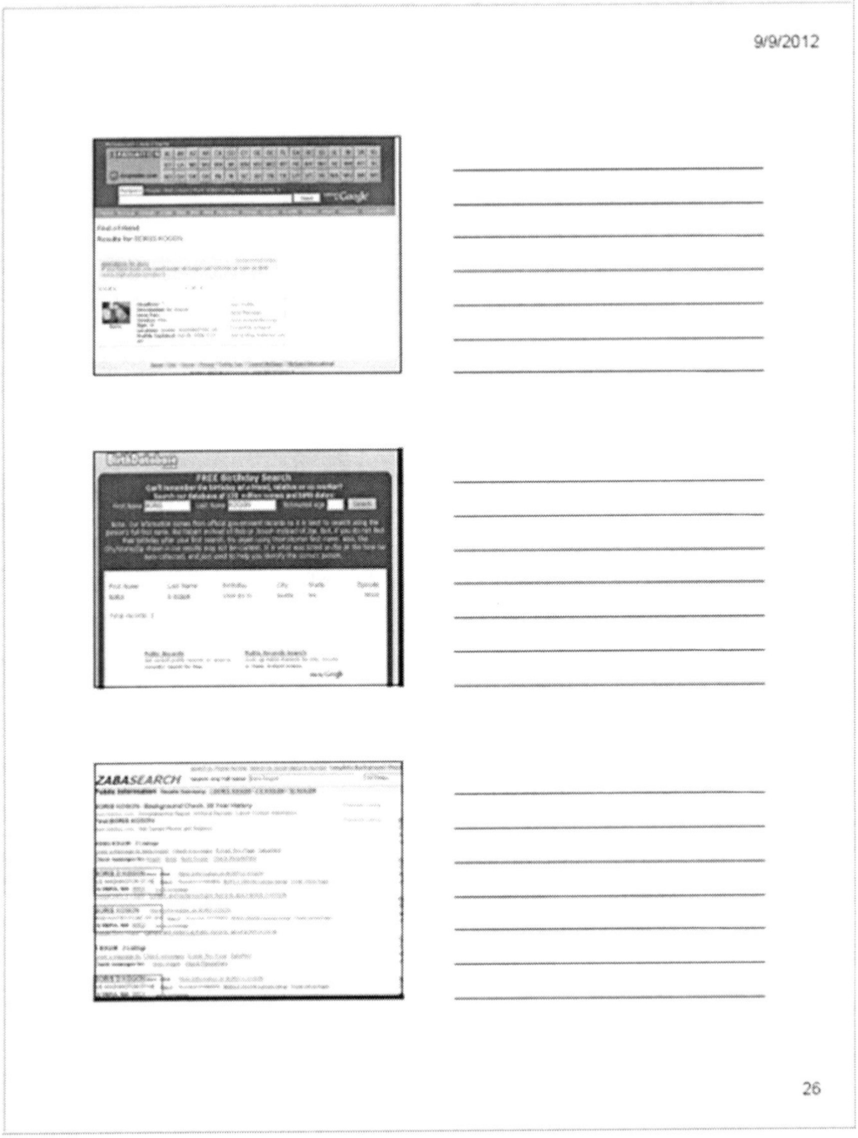

FIGURE 7.6 Example of a printed slideshow presentation showing three website pages.

A slideshow is not your case presentation. Each slide should have specific relevance and give context to the data you are explaining, with as few words on the slide as possible. The goal is not having a pretty presentation, but creating a method that the data can speak for itself by way of visual representations.

Fancy fonts, transition effects, and sounds may not only detract from the meaning of each slide, but can also have a negative impact on a particular person.

These unwanted impacts could be the result of the use of colors used in a graph that have negative connotations based on culture. Even a certain combination of colors can have a negative meaning that detracts from your data presentation. Additionally, any person who is color blind may not be able to see the point of the colors chosen. Some colors may even be likened to causing a prejudicial emphasis. To lessen the risk of offending your audience, avoid the use of colors in your charts and graphs and use shades of black.

Charts and diagrams

The objective of visualizing a dataset depends upon the type of data and the point you want to convey to your audience. These visual aids can be created using commercial software, such as Microsoft Visio or even drawn on poster boards. The visual can be a direct representation of data, such as seen in Figure 7.7. This type of chart easily shows a listing of different types of data by the amount of each kind of data.

This type of chart can be broken down even further within each type of file format to emphasize a fact. Figure 7.8 extrapolates a file type from Figure 7.7 into a separate chart to emphasize the context of graphics. This method can easily be used to show the number of any file type of relevance. Another example could be to show the number of stolen intellectual property spreadsheets as compared to the number of other spreadsheets on a system.

As easy it may be for you to visualize the data that you have come to know in the investigation, as the presenter, your objective is to make your audience quickly and accurately interpret your work as you know it. Charts are an easy and effective means to visualize some types of data in a way that fewer words are needed to explain the data.

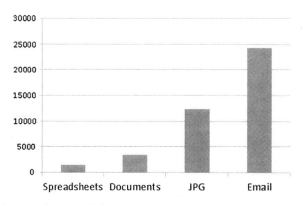

FIGURE 7.7 A graph of number of files on a hard drive as a comparison to each other.

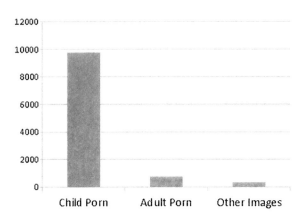

FIGURE 7.8 Extrapolation of graphics taken from figure 7.6 comparing the content of graphics on a computer system.

Complex computer systems, such as corporate networks, are difficult to describe in words. The biggest hurdle is describing computer networks or even describing how a computer works. Many computer users have not seen how computers are physically connected in a network or how data moves between systems. Diagrams may be the best solution, if not the only solution other than building a network, to show the inner workings of complex computer networks. Figure 7.9 shows an example of a shared network printer, where four client computers have access.

As large networks contain many servers of various types with hundreds of client machines, complex diagrams can quickly overwhelm an audience. If the objective is to show the connection between client computers and a shared printer, the diagram should be made simple enough to only show that facet. Unnecessary information only clouds understanding.

Diagrams can also be used to show movement, or flow of processes. The booting of a computer system can be shown through a flow chart diagram, visually depicting each step in the booting process. Flow charts can be used to show how a virus infected a system and spread. Even the historical movement of a file across computer systems can be shown through a flow chart or visual timeline.

An example seen in Figure 7.10 shows one identical evidence file created on different computers depicting a timeline of the file traveling to different computers. This could be through emails, external media, or through a network, but regardless of the method, gives a visual of when this particular file came into existence on different computer systems.

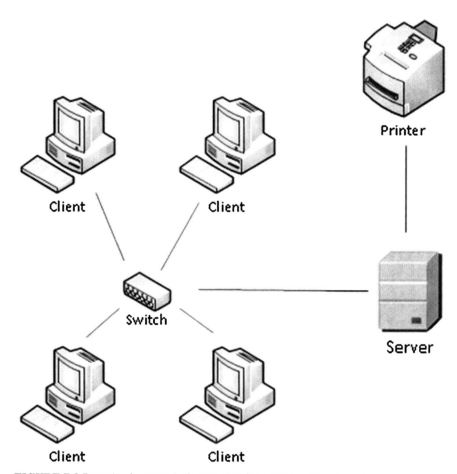

FIGURE 7.9 Example of a network diagram showing a shared network printer.

This same concept of historical file movement and changes on a single system can be shown on the same type of timeline as seen in Figure 7.11. Tables, or spreadsheets, that contain data organized by date and time are effective in showing extreme detail of activity of a computer system. Specific types of activity of importance can be pulled out of the spreadsheet and visually shown to an audience to emphasize the importance of that specific data. Such would be the case seen in Figure 7.11, where one file is shown from creation to deletion, including the possibility of being copied onto a USB device.

Most events taken from detailed spreadsheet timelines can be visually shown in graphic timelines such as these. However, the time required to create each timeline compared with the number of important events must be taken

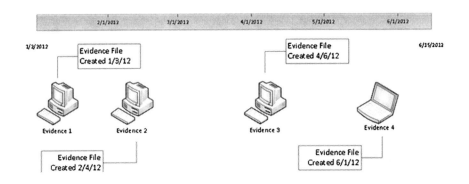

FIGURE 7.10 Example of one identical evidence file as it was created on four different computers over a period of time.

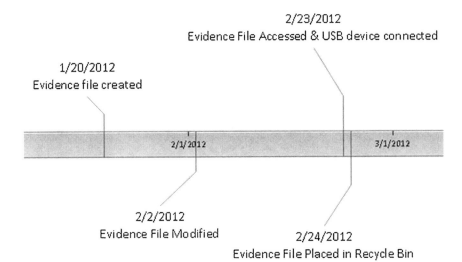

FIGURE 7.11 Historical file movement on a single computer system.

into consideration. Simplicity is also important as not to cause your audience to shut down their senses due to being overwhelmed with information.

Data from timelines can be shown as it relates to each other, outside of relation to dates and times. For example, a listing of phone call records with hundreds of calls is difficult to visualize. Figure 7.12 shows a call detail record from the Casey Anthony trial. As you can see, this is only a portion of the entire record and even though the calls are listed in chronological order, the numbers dialed are not in order, nor could they be. It is difficult, if not impossible, to visualize which numbers most often.

CASEY ANTHONY TELEPHONE TOLLS
JUNE 15-20, 2008

CASEY ANTHONY TOLLS JUNE 15-20, 2008

TARGET NAME	TARGET NUMBER	DATE	TIME	DURATION	RECORD TYPE	DIRECTION	NUMBER DIALED	SUBSCRIBER
CASEY ANTHONY	(407) 619-9286	6/15/2008	0:13:00	0:12:00	Unknown	INCOMING	(631) 902-5443	ANTHONY LAZZARO
CASEY ANTHONY	(407) 619-9286	6/15/2008	6:33:00	0:01:00	Unknown	OUTGOING	(407) 619-9286	CASEY ANTHONY
CASEY ANTHONY	(407) 619-9286	6/15/2008	8:56:00	0:01:00	Unknown	OUTGOING	(954) 328-9214	AMY HUIZENGA
CASEY ANTHONY	(407) 619-9286	6/15/2008	9:15:00	0:01:00	Unknown	OUTGOING	(631) 902-5443	ANTHONY LAZZARO
CASEY ANTHONY	(407) 619-9286	6/15/2008	12:51:00	0:10:00	Unknown	OUTGOING	(954) 328-9214	AMY HUIZENGA
CASEY ANTHONY	(407) 619-9286	6/15/2008	13:01:00	0:01:00	Unknown	OUTGOING	(407) 619-9286	CASEY ANTHONY
CASEY ANTHONY	(407) 619-9286	6/15/2008	14:44:00	0:01:00	Unknown	OUTGOING	(407) 619-9286	CASEY ANTHONY
CASEY ANTHONY	(407) 619-9286	6/15/2008	17:05:00	0:04:00	Unknown	OUTGOING	(407) 275-4909	CYNTHIA ANTHONY
CASEY ANTHONY	(407) 619-9286	6/15/2008	19:10:00	0:01:00	Unknown	OUTGOING	(407) 275-4909	CYNTHIA ANTHONY
CASEY ANTHONY	(407) 619-9286	6/15/2008	20:38:00	0:00:00	Text Message	OUTGOING	(631) 902-5443	ANTHONY LAZZARO
CASEY ANTHONY	(407) 619-9286	6/15/2008	20:48:00	0:01:00	Unknown	OUTGOING	(407) 619-9286	CASEY ANTHONY
CASEY ANTHONY	(407) 619-9286	6/15/2008	21:08:00	0:00:00	Text Message	OUTGOING	(631) 902-5443	ANTHONY LAZZARO
CASEY ANTHONY	(407) 619-9286	6/15/2008	22:06:00	0:11:00	Unknown	OUTGOING	(631) 902-5443	ANTHONY LAZZARO
CASEY ANTHONY	(407) 619-9286	6/15/2008	22:08:00	0:00:00	Text Message	OUTGOING	(631) 902-5443	ANTHONY LAZZARO
CASEY ANTHONY	(407) 619-9286	6/15/2008	22:38:00	0:05:00	Unknown	OUTGOING	(631) 902-5443	ANTHONY LAZZARO
CASEY ANTHONY	(407) 619-9286	6/15/2008	22:45:00	0:04:00	Unknown	INCOMING	(631) 902-5443	ANTHONY LAZZARO
CASEY ANTHONY	(407) 619-9286	6/15/2008	23:44:00	1:21:00	Unknown	OUTGOING	(631) 902-5443	ANTHONY LAZZARO
CASEY ANTHONY	(407) 619-9286	6/15/2008	23:50:00	0:00:00	Text Message	OUTGOING	(631) 902-5443	ANTHONY LAZZARO
CASEY ANTHONY	(407) 619-9286	6/16/2008	2:18:00	0:00:00	Text Message	OUTGOING	(631) 902-5443	ANTHONY LAZZARO
CASEY ANTHONY	(407) 619-9286	6/16/2008	3:07:00	0:15:00	Unknown	INCOMING	(631) 902-5443	ANTHONY LAZZARO
CASEY ANTHONY	(407) 619-9286	6/16/2008	11:47:00	0:19:00	Unknown	INCOMING	(631) 902-5443	ANTHONY LAZZARO
CASEY ANTHONY	(407) 619-9286	6/16/2008	13:00:00	0:14:00	Unknown	INCOMING	(631) 902-5443	ANTHONY LAZZARO

FIGURE 7.12 Portion of a call detail record (State of Florida v. Casey Marie Anthony (2011)).

This information can be displayed in a graph, as the previous Figures 7.7 and 7.8, to show the number of calls to each number compared to each number. Another method of displaying the call detail records other than a list of the information can be seen in Figure 7.13 where outgoing calls made to individual phones are easily understood. Diagrams such as this can be created using software applications that automatically cull data from spreadsheets or even created with markers on a flip chart.

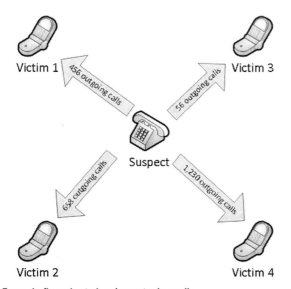

Victim 1   456 outgoing calls   Victim 3   56 outgoing calls

Suspect

658 outgoing calls   1,230 outgoing calls

Victim 2   Victim 4

FIGURE 7.13 Example flow chart showing outgoing calls.

There are many different types of graphs and charts to display any type of data, from pie charts, bar charts, area charts, scatter charts, and bubble charts. Depending upon the data you need to display, the type of chart used will either make it easy to understand or be completely confusing. Examples of poorly chosen charts include pie charts with more than five pieces. Seen in Figure 7.14, there are too many unrelated data items on the same chart resulting in a fairly useless and probably confusing visual aid.

Even bar charts, which are simple to view and understand, can be made complicated if the bars are random and not ordered. Never randomize data as your audience will have to figure out a pattern out of random data. It should be visualized either by location, chronology, category, hierarchy, numerical, alphabetical, size, or amount. Figure 7.15 shows how random bars do not effectively represent the data as compared to ascending or descending bars. In this example, Chart A is the clearer method, whereas Chart B does not have a pattern.

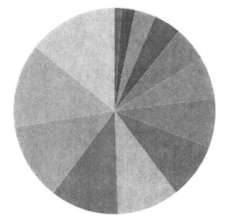

FIGURE 7.14 Ineffective use of a pie chart, where there are more slices of the pie that can be effectively understood.

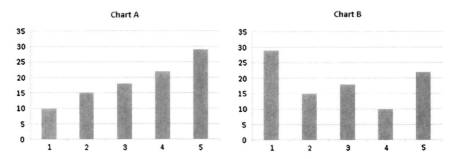

FIGURE 7.15 Examples of an effect bar chart (Chart A) and ineffective bar chart (Chart B).

As the data presented in many forensic exams consist of numbers and that charts and graphs may be used to visualize this data, it is prudent to be aware of basic math as it applies to your data. By not knowing the difference between the Mean (simple average), Median (middle value of a data set), or Mode (most often occurring data) could affect your credibility since you are displaying numerical data.

Even percentages can be misstated with a great negative effect. Stating that 10% of all internet sites visited were related to "murder" is not the same as saying the top ten internet sites visited were related to "murder."

There is high value in using charts and diagrams as long as reasonableness is constantly considered. Overuse or misuse will not only cause confusion, but may counter the point you wanted to get across in the first place. Charts and graphs with incorrect data can discredit your presentation altogether.

THE SUSPECT'S MACHINE

There are instances where a file listing or chart won't do justice as much as seeing the actual file as it exists on the suspect computer. Describing how a suspect computer has been configured is one thing but showing it on a projection screen is much more effective. The best method to show the suspect's computer system is through creating a virtual machine from the suspect's computer system. A virtual machine is a software implementation of a guest virtual operating system that runs within a host physical computer system.

There are several methods in which a forensic image of a suspect's operating system can be converted into a virtual machine which can be run on almost any computer as a program. One of these methods involves using software utilities, such as Virtual Forensic Computer (http://www.virtualforensiccomputing.com/), to create virtual machine configuration files that will allow the forensic image to run as a normal operating system.

The power of a visual to describe a virtual machine can be seen in Figure 7.16, where a guest operating system can be seen running within a host operating system. The virtual machine is a complete operating system, running within a program window and separate from the host machine. The virtual machine can be paused and reset to its original state at any time, making it a great tool of representing the suspect's operating system as part of a case presentation.

There are several benefits to using a virtual machine to visually display a suspect's computer system. The most important benefit is that it avoids having to boot an evidence computer which would irreparably alter electronic data contained on it. A virtual machine can be booted and restored to its original

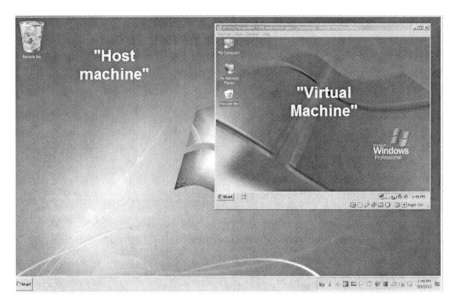

FIGURE 7.16 A "virtual machine" running on a "host machine."

state as many times as needed to test theories and show the file settings chosen by the computer user as the computer user saw it.

The effect this has compared to the written or verbal description is dramatic. Consider describing an evidence file discovered on the suspect's computer. An example of a file residing on the desktop can be described in a report as seen in Figure 7.17. A person unfamiliar with file paths on computer systems could have a difficult time visualizing this description, even if the description is concise and accurate.

Using a virtual machine to show this description of a file's location takes on an entirely different and more accurate meaning as seen in Figure 7.18. Any person who has ever used a computer has also seen the desktop and icons on the desktop. This type of visual demonstration quickly and accurately conveys

> Using X-Ways Forensics, I observed an evidence file named, "Nude boy.jpg" residing on the suspect's hard drive, evidence item 12-4267-002 at filepath C:\Documents and Settings\Smith\Desktop.

FIGURE 7.17 Description of an evidence file by filepath.

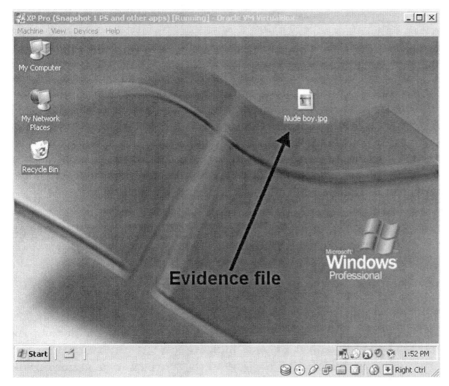

FIGURE 7.18 A suspect's computer system, booted virtually, showing the location of an evidence file on the desktop.

your thoughts to the audience without misunderstandings. Using a virtual machine can be used to show Internet settings, such as bookmarks chosen by the suspect, files residing in the Recycle Bin, and other aspects of user activity as it exists on the suspect's computer.

ANALOGIES

Over the past decade, a new language has been developed in the digital forensics community. A mixture of legalese and technical terms, spoken only by those in the community, tends to confuse those outside this community. Terms such as "prefetch files" and "jump lists" are meaningless to the layperson if not understood. Forensic examiners know the importance of these files as artifacts of user activity, but should not expect the audience to have the same knowledge without some explanation.

Generally, when a presenter knows a subject matter very well, the information can be presented verbally in a manner that can be easily understood in clear language. Sometimes this is not possible and analogies may be needed to describe intangible electronic data by comparing it to tangible objects. Comparisons between items are commonly used, such as comparing the tastes of foods, appearances of objects, and even comparisons between persons.

However, an important aspect to remember is to choose an analogy that can be compared reasonably. As an example, a library is a common object to use as an analogy, such as a hard drive stores electronic files like a library stores books. Libraries are well known and do not need much more description to be understood. Choosing a relative unknown item for comparison, such as a "Mars Rover" to compare with a hard drive not only confuses the audience about a hard drive, but adds a new confusing concept of a vehicle on Mars.

The use of analogies can also create other problems. The opposing counsel or your audience may disagree with your analogy, or twist the intention of the analogy to the point of being meaningless or opposite to your original goal. Other analogies may be too simplified for the subject you are attempting to describe. The risk of using an analogy which your audience may not understand can result in confusion of the analogy, how it relates to the data you are explaining, and a decrease in your credibility of knowing the subject matter. When analogies are to be used, test them with a non-computer literate audience by quizzing your audience to explain it back to you. Better to find your analogy doesn't work in the office rather than during your presentation.

Luckily, due to a multitude of court cases and police television dramas, the public is more aware of electronic evidence than ever before, even if they have some misperceptions. The ability to recover deleted files is nearly a commonly known fact among any computer user. As digital forensics becomes even more widely known and each new generation of computer users are more knowledgeable about technology, the need to use analogies will decrease.

Sometimes, the use of analogies to help place a suspect behind a keyboard can be an effective tactic. Consider having to explain to your audience that the suspect was the only person that could have sent an email from a specific computer and email account, from a specific location such as the suspect's home. A common defense is "some other dude did it."

Through visual aids, such as slideshow showing a computer screen captures, you can show the effort and knowledge needed to send this email. The following section shows a visual timeline of the actions a suspect had to take to send an email.

First, since the computer in this example was seized from the suspect's home, *physical access to the computer* was needed. Physical access usually means having

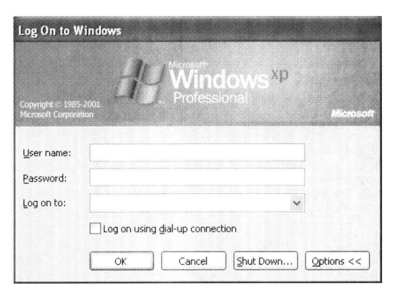

FIGURE 7.19 Windows operating system login screen, requiring user name, password, and domain for access.

a legal right to be in the residence along with the means to enter such as having a *key to unlock the door of the residence*.

Next as seen in Figure 7.19, in order to operate the computer system, the suspect needs to enter the *username, password, and select a domain to log onto* the computer.

After logging into the computer system with this information, in this same example, the suspect would log into webmail as seen in the screen capture in Figure 7.20. Again, the *suspect would need to know the username and password*. This may be the same user name and password used for the computer login or it may be completely different.

So far in this part of your presentation, you have shown the suspect needed to have physical access to the residence, which requires a physical key, plus also have five items of personal information consisting of 2 user names, 2 passwords, and 1 domain name.

One analogy that could be used in this example is that of a password to an email account or computer can be compared to having a key to open the front door of a home. Typically, the resident of the home controls any and all keys and does not lend them out to strangers or make the keys easily accessible. If a password is commonly known and shared with others, then that would be like giving copies of the key to your home to anyone.

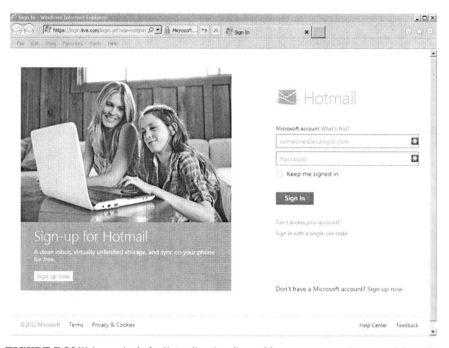

FIGURE 7.20 Webpage login for Hotmail webmail, requiring username and password (http://www.hotmail.com).

An analogy to guessing the password or cracking the password can be compared to trying to open a combination safe. The person attempting to open a locked combination safe would have to guess every combination of turns and numbers to find the right combination. The more complex the combination is for the safe, the more difficult to guess. Passwords are similar in order to correctly guess the password, every combination of letters, numbers, and special characters would have to be attempted until the right password is found. This could take days, years, or centuries.

The use of this type of analogy would ring true for any person that has a key to their home or ever used a combination lock. It also lends credibility to the likelihood that only the suspect would know the personal information needed to log into the computer and email. Granted, given more than one person having access to the home, the investigation needs information identifying this one suspect, but the analogy remains accurate.

Until then, there are many analogies that have been tried and tested which you can use when needed. Comparing hard drives to libraries, books, or buildings to describe partitions and file storage are effective methods of conveying technology to your audience. The goal should also include the analogies to show the suspect's relation to the evidence being explained.

Another example of an analogy tying a suspect to having access to certain files is that of file access rights. If a specific folder seized from a computer network is evidence in your case and that folder had restricted rights, then the list of suspects can be narrowed.

Perhaps only a few users had access to the folders, including the network administrator. The analogy to be used could be that of an apartment building. In an apartment building, tenants have physical access only to their apartment and any common area such as a laundry room. The tenants in the apartment building are like computer users on a network, each having their own access to certain folders, some shared and others not. The landlord would have physical access to all areas of the building for maintenance and can be compared to the network administrator. This analogy not only helps explain user rights on a network, but also helps your audience see for themselves a list of possible suspects.

Remember that any analogy can be broken and use them with care. Even the previous example of a building tenant having physical access to their apartment can be broken. A burglary can occur in an apartment, just as a computer can be hacked.

AVOID TMI (TOO MUCH INFORMATION)

When you spend weeks, months, or years on a case, it is tempting to talk about every detail to your audience. In legal proceedings, your presentation may be controlled by an attorney and this won't be an issue. In other venues, such as within your organization or for a client, you could have unfettered ability to discuss the entire investigation with a potpourri of charts, diagrams, and spreadsheets, describing your great work. This may not be a good idea.

You just want understanding of your investigation that places the suspect behind the keyboard. The selective use of analogies to easily describe complex information, specific charts to visually display massive amounts of information, and perhaps timelines of specific events showing and eliminating all known possible suspects. Most certainly, you probably should not detail every single minutiae of information as at some point, your audience may stop taking in your presentation due to being overloaded with too much unnecessary information.

YOUR PRESENTATION

Any of the methods and examples in this chapter may be of use in your presentation, but probably not all the examples will be used in one presentation. Beyond accurate technical explanations of computer activity, audiences want a roadmap of what they are about to endure. They want to know where they are going and how they are going to get there. You've already done it, now you are going to present the highlights to your audience.

Within this presentation, where you use visual aids and analogies, you are painting a picture in the mind of your audience. Without having to explicitly accuse any suspect of an act, your presentation does it for you. As you have had Eureka! moments during the analysis, so will your audience where they place the suspect behind the keyboard. This can only happen if you know your material well, explain it in layman's terms, treat your audience as if they are more important than you, and remember the objective; place the suspect behind the keyboard.

The skill in presenting goes beyond this book, but is definitely worth talking about. All basic foundations of public speaking apply in every venue of case presentation. Confidence, speaking clearly, professionalism, and being extremely careful with humor all play a part in presenting your information. The use of any visual aids also requires skill and practice. Not blocking the screen or talking to the screen instead of your audience not only detracts from the presentation, but also does not effectively convey your talking points. One of the first rules to become proficient in both public speaking and use of visual aids is practice. The second and third rule is practice more.

SUMMARY

The importance of case presentation is on equal standing of case investigation. A failed investigation cannot be saved by a good presentation and a good investigation can be ruined by a poor presentation. Both require attention to detail and the objective to not only find the alleged activity under investigation, but also identify the suspect or suspects behind that activity and convey that information to your audience.

Your case presentation, using analogies and visual aids, will help your audience determine the suspect and place that suspect behind the keyboard. Building the presentation with direct and indirect evidence, shown for what it is, can show the audience that of course the suspect you identified was responsible for the alleged acts, because no one else could have done it.

Bibliography

dtSearch <http://www.dtsearch.com>.

State of Florida v. Casey Marie Anthony (Ninth Judicial Circuit of Florida,. 2001).

Virtual Forensic Computing <http://www.virtualforensiccomputing.com/>.

Cheat Sheets and Quickstart Guides

INTRODUCTION

The field of digital forensics grows continually as interconnectivity of businesses and people continue to increase. The ability to determine the *who, what, when, where, why,* and *how* becomes more important holistically as an investigation rather than solely conducting a forensic analysis of a computer system. As this encompasses a wide range of forensic artifacts, processes, methods, techniques, and knowledge, it is easy to become lost and overwhelmed to the case objective; placing the suspect behind the keyboard.

This chapter intends to demonstrate the use of reference materials as constant reminders of staying the course in a case in placing the suspect behind the keyboard. There are instances where a small reminder will spark an Eureka! moment and all of us can use those moments on any case. The tips in this chapter are in hopes that you will have more of those moments, even if you are only walking through your office hallways and subconsciously using the tips presented in this chapter.

CHEAT SHEETS AND QUICKSTART GUIDES

The use of "cheat sheets" for test taking is wrong, but for the use of the forensic examiner, the use of cheat sheets is a helpful source of references for specific topics. Scaled down guides of full manuals, such as quickstart guides, are also helpful to save time during an investigation or as a refresher of information when specific information is quickly needed. As an example, researching information on Windows shortcut files, also known as "link" or .lnk files, could result in an hour or more looking through different digital forensics books and websites, only to look for one tidbit of sought-after information.

By having a cheat sheet showing link file information in an easy-to-read format not only saves research time, but it also helps to be an easy study guide. Although a link file is just one electronic file that points to another file, it contains a wealth of metadata, more than what can be probably memorized. A cheat sheet on link files helps to show examiners the context of the metadata as it relates to any forensic analysis without having to memorize every detail. One nice example of a link file cheat sheet can be seen below in Figure 8.1.

There are many online sources of cheat sheets directly related to digital forensics and others indirectly related with Information Technology topics that can be freely downloaded and used as your references. Although I personally do not prefer the word "cheat" in reference material, in the manner these references are used do not imply any cheating on the part of the examiner. Flow charts, check lists, and other means of ordering information are also not "cheating," but merely aid in helping examiners do their job as basic guides.

Other examples of cheat sheets are shown in Figures 8.2 and 8.3. Figure 8.2 is a report writing cheat sheet, in which one of the most important notations is

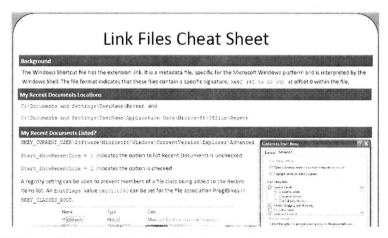

FIGURE 8.1 Portion of a Link Files Cheat Sheet from http://www.lowmanio.co.us/blog/entries/link-files-forensic-cheat-sheet/.

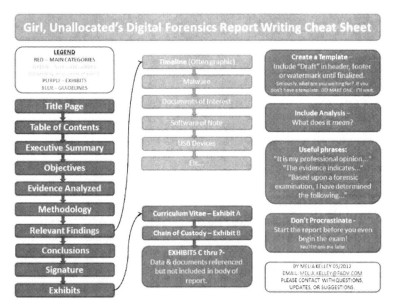

FIGURE 8.2 Report Writing Cheat Sheet, http://girlunallocated.blogspot.com/.

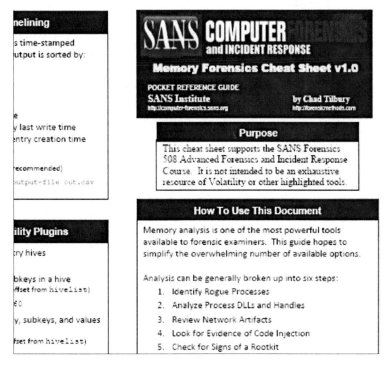

FIGURE 8.3 Memory Forensics Cheat Sheet, SANS Institute, http://www.sans.org.

"Include Analysis—What does it mean?" Sometimes, a simple question such as this can give the examiner an important reminder or hint that can make a big difference in their case.

Another example, seen in Figure 8.3, shows the first page of a two-page Memory Forensics Cheat Sheet, from the SANS Institute. Generally, if there is a complex subject, there just may be a simplified cheat sheet to help understand, remember, and reference the most important information.

Other examples worth mentioning include the SANS cheat sheet for USB Device analysis, as well as several references guides from https://lockandcode.com/.

Turnover folders

One of the many good ideas I've taken from my days in the Marine Corps is that of the "Turnover Folder." As Marines generally move around duty stations and jobs on a regular basis, Turnover Folders exist to make the move into a new job that much easier. Turnover Folders contain just about everything you need to know to be effective in your new job after a few days, rather than trying to figure out how everything works in the new office.

Specific to the job, a Turnover Folder contains templates of forms, examples of orders, flow charts, contact lists, and anything of pertinence that is required for that position. A Turnover Folder for a forensic analyst can contain anything you feel is necessary to help you in your job and help with your cases. Besides the basic information, such as contact lists, cheat sheets and quickstart guides can be stored in the folder. Organized by topic, a Turnover Folder can be created that is specific to how you prefer to work containing the information you need to reference the most. Figure 8.4 shows one example of a folder containing printed copies of cheat sheets. This type of work aid can be put together as easy as it looks, yet can be one of the most used reference binders in your office.

Although digital forensics analysts primarily use computers for almost all aspects of their work, the printed page still has relevance when placed in a folder for easy reference. Indexed, tabbed, or color-coded, the Turnover Folder can lend a hand in finding material that may help save research time. And of course, for the "new" examiner in the office, handing over a Turnover Folder will help the new examiner get right to work with a handy reference of cheat sheets and guides.

As far as investigative help, when an analyst runs out of ideas during an exam, or just hits a mental block in moving forward, the Turnover Folder can help spark an idea or remind of an overlooked aspect of an analysis. Much like reading a book on digital forensics, but without any excess information not needed at the moment, just visual guides and reminders to re-start the brain.

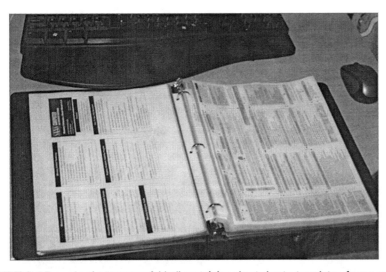

FIGURE 8.4 Example of a "turnover folder" containing cheat sheets, templates, forms, and information relevant to the job of a forensic analyst.

Visual aids

Cheat sheets may also be used as visual aids in presentations if they are relevant to your presentation and audience. Process flow charts, such as visually showing how a computer virus spreads across a computer network, help the examiner in visualizing their case to create a report just as much as it helps an audience understand a written report.

Other references and guides, such as the chart seen in Figure 8.5, can show an overview of specific and related information sources that pertain to a certain aspect of a presentation. In Figure 8.5, a poster created by Rob Lee and the SANS Institute shows a listing of forensic artifacts with details of their relevance to user activity. The use of a chart such as this for a visual aid can show your audience the locations you searched for evidence, which has already been tested by an entire community of forensic analysis professionals.

This same chart, or any such chart like it, can also be used for training purposes and as a constant reminder of forensic artifacts to be aware. Figure 8.6 shows this same poster, plastered across a hallway in a forensic lab. By merely walking between offices, references such as these in the forensic lab can help examiners learn material, refresh what has been learned, and give something to talk about when around the water cooler, other than office talk. Locations to hang cheat sheets, posters, and references are limited only by your imagination. Generally, any place where examiners may be standing around would be a good place to hang a reference guide.

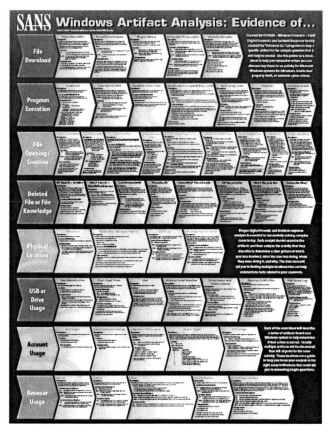

FIGURE 8.5 SANS Windows Artifact Analysis chart, courtesy of Rob Lee, SANS, http://computer-forensics.sans.org.

Investigative aids

Every investigation is different, just as every investigator is different. Therefore, the manner in which someone conducts their analysis will be different from someone else. However, many aspects of an analysis are constant with guidelines for evidence control and commands used in software applications. Cheat sheets can be used to save research time and spark reminders of artifacts to examine.

Cheat sheets are also helpful for those times an examiner may not have someone to bounce ideas or ask questions. There are forensic exams where evidence to place the suspect at the scene of a digital crime isn't being found. Hours can be spent digging and digging without success. Having someone at your side to ask is the quickest and easiest method to have a question answered. When there is no partner, sometimes flipping through cheat sheets may be your best bet to come up with a solution to a problem.

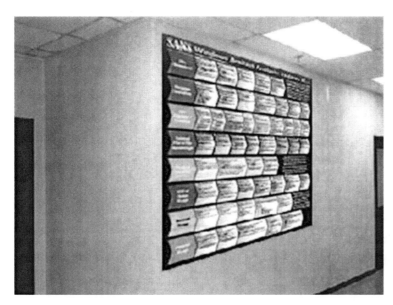

FIGURE 8.6 An enlarged SANS Windows Artifact Analysis poster in a hallway of a forensic lab.

Other benefits of cheat sheets include lists of software commands and software tips. Forensic software applications that are command line driven, or have a command line option, may have more than what can be remembered by an examiner. Without referencing a list, commands can be forgotten, and data that would have been collected, now will be missed. Process flow charts can help visualize simple aspects of computing, such as the boot process, to more complex aspects, such as the effects of malware on a system. Any of these types of cheat sheets and guides may hold that one tidbit of information that helps seal the case with a simple reminder or showing context of what a certain datum means.

Study guides

Yes, cheat sheets can be used for studying, whether it is studying for an exam, a certification, a deposition, or trial. These can be used as reading material during lunch, a long bus ride, or anytime you are free. However, the purpose of mentioning cheat sheets as study guides in this venue is not to pass a test. As a forensic examiner, studying cheat sheets and looking at process charts should be done with a different goal.

The goal is asking yourself, *"How does this information help me place the suspect behind the keyboard?"* Link files are great forensic artifacts, but without asking yourself how this helps fulfill your objective, it is of little value. The same can be said of collecting thousands upon thousands of individual artifacts, displayed in a spreadsheet. Without having a reason for data carving and creating lists of files, the time is wasted if each piece of information doesn't serve a purpose to assist in the investigative goals.

As electronic evidence recovered from an analysis is simply electronic data, the analyst needs to be able to place the information into context in relation to other evidence. A link file may be meaningless by itself, but a separate artifact or piece of information, such as a link file created by use of a flash drive that was owned by the suspect becomes pertinent. Now, the time you see a cheat sheet or chart, ask yourself, *"how can I use this to help me place the suspect behind the keyboard?"*

Make your own

As much as you may expect someone to have made a cheat sheet for every forensic topic you need, that's not the case. Although there are plenty available, sometimes, there is a topic that you want, but just doesn't exist. No problem. I would encourage every examiner to create their own cheat sheets and right afterward, share them. That which you make will probably save other examiner hours of time. As you download and print pre-made cheat sheets, you can almost as easily create and upload yours for the community.

SHARE AND SHARE ALIKE

Increase your effectiveness by sharing

By sharing your discoveries in forensic analysis with other examiners, your findings can be vetted and validated by the community at large. This can benefit you professionally as other experts may be able to expand upon or correct your work. More important is that your discoveries in new methods or forensic artifacts can be a contributing factor in the development of digital forensics.

Besides using basic software applications, you can also use online sources for creating a cheat sheet. One great online resource for creating cheat sheets is Cheatography at http://www.cheatography.com. This free resource helps you create a cheat sheet that is stored online, shared publicly, searchable, and can be downloaded in a pdf.

One of the great benefits of having digital forensics books as references is that you can use the books as references in your daily work. Pages can be dog eared, passages highlighted, and your notes written on pages for reminders of some point that was important to you. Another benefit of digital forensic books as references is that you can create your cheat sheet of your reference book, for that material which directly suits your needs. One example of this would be creating a cheat sheet of this book, Placing the Suspect Behind the Keyboard, with annotations to pages or chapters on the cheat sheet.

CHECKLISTS

The thought of using checklists brings fear to many forensic examiners. Part of this fear comes from past experiences in testimony where an examiner may not have been able to give a clear answer as to why "step 3" was skipped in their standard checklist. Rather than explain why steps are skipped, many choose to avoid checklists altogether.

Another problem seen by having a checklist is that since every examination is different, one checklist isn't going to cover all types of situations. There are too many variables in operating systems, computer systems, and types of data to cover in a single checklist. Again, the common answer is to avoid having a checklist.

I'd like to look at checklists a little more differently as a positive aid rather than potential hindrance. To eliminate the fear that a checklist is a negative, consider that your pilot in the plane you may fly uses a checklist to make sure the plane is airworthy. Your doctor that may be operating on you also uses a checklist to make sure you survive your operation. Police reports can also be seen as a checklist, as the form flows through a report by descriptions of persons, incidents, and narrative. Even attorneys use checklists in their cases so as not to miss important deadlines.

The point is that checklists help ensure you don't forget an important detail and keeps your mind focused on the task at hand. Digital forensics should be included as a field needing a checklist.

As to the granularity of the checklist, that is up to you. Perhaps a general checklist of case workflow will suffice, or maybe a detailed checklist for a specific investigation will be better on a case-by-case basis. A checklist for evidence can be used to keep consistency in how your office handles electronic evidence. Any situation that is repetitive is a situation that a checklist could be helpful to prevent failure.

The answer to the question that all anti-checklist examiners have in regard to how does the examiner explain skipping steps in one case but not another, the answer is simply, *"that step didn't apply in this case."* You can simply give the reason why it didn't apply. An example to this would be skipping the step of a checklist that advises to pull the plug from the back of a computer to seize it. If the examiner decided to not pull the plug, perhaps it was because physical memory had to be captured first, or perhaps the operating system was encrypted. In these cases, that step gets a N/A marked on the list.

I would say it is better to have to answer the question as to why you skipped a step rather than answer the question as to why you wing it every time. All of us are prone to forgetting something at some point and if we don't write it down or go through a list, it may be an embarrassing moment when we are reminded by someone else of our omissions.

SUMMARY

There are some cases where hours are poured into forensic analysis with no result of finding relevant evidence. Frustration and impatience are two of the worst enemies in a task requiring patience and a steady attention to detail such as digital forensics. To lessen the risks of mental blocks, overlooking important electronic evidence, and as reminders of evidence to recover, the use of cheat sheets help stay on track.

Cheat sheets can serve more than as a reference, but also as a training guide, study guide, refresher, and visual aid. When referenced regularly, they could be the one thing that creates a spark and connects the dots in a case as you flip through a binder of cheat sheets you printed months earlier.

Checklists help in not forgetting small details that can result in major problems later in a case. Deadlines, evidence handling, and reporting deadlines are items that can be covered in a checklist. The use of checklists can also help in reviewing a case as a supervisor to ensure work is being performed correctly and completely.

Bibliography

Cheatography. <http://www.cheatography.com>.
Link Files Cheatsheet. <http://www.lowmanio.co.us/>.
Report Writing Cheatsheet. <http://girlunallocated.blogspot.com/>.
SANS Institute. <http://www.sans.org>.

CHAPTER 9

Some Things Will Become Easier, Others Not So Much

INFORMATION IN THIS CHAPTER:

- It will become easier to place a suspect behind the keyboard
- It will become more difficult to place a suspect behind the keyboard

INTRODUCTION

The digital forensics field evolves faster than most other fields simply because technology changes rapidly. With each new operating system or new version of an operating system, digital forensics must keep up with the advances. Not only must digital forensic examiners try to keep up with each technological advance in computing, but also keep up with ever changing laws.

Sometimes, these changes make it easier for digital forensics and the investigator's ability to place a suspect behind a keyboard. Other times, these changes can make it difficult or impossible. Expecting which changes will occur in the future is anyone's guess, but no matter the changes, the digital forensics field must be flexible to stay abreast.

IT WILL BECOME EASIER TO PLACE A SUSPECT BEHIND THE KEYBOARD

With each new version of operating systems, many in the community of digital forensics examiners discover innovative methods that more easily help place the suspect behind the keyboard. This is made possible due to advancements in operating systems and forensic software capable of exploiting forensic artifacts created by computer users.

Investigations where computer systems are involved also create changes in laws that can benefit digital forensics examiners. Combined with a number of these advances and legal changes, placing a suspect behind a keyboard becomes easier as time passes. Knowing which aspects make it easier to accomplish this goal should be a priority for every examiner.

Operating systems will make it easier

With each new version of an operating system, more electronic evidence artifacts are created by the operating system and subsequently discovered by forensic examiners. It is highly unlikely that for any new feature of an operating system, no new forensic artifact will be related to it. More features simply mean more artifacts, each of which may by itself or in relation to other artifacts, help place the suspect behind the keyboard with more circumstantial electronic evidence.

One example is that of the Volume Shadow Copy Service (VSS) found in Microsoft Windows. The Volume Shadow Copy Service was introduced in Windows Server 2003 through the current version of Windows 8. The VSS creates a series of incremental backup of modified files, known as shadow copies. The VSS process operates in the background, without the need for user intervention to create the shadow copies. In many cases, computer users are completely unaware that their files are being backed up and will not be deleted if they delete only the current version of any file.

Computer users can restore multiple revisions of one single word processing file from multiple shadow copies, even if the current file has been deleted or wiped from the system. Although earlier versions of Windows, such as Windows XP, have a similar function, it is much more limited in scope and persistence. Figure 9.1 shows the ease to access a previous version of a file through a simple GUI interface. A list of previous versions of the file is given, which the user can select and restore.

Each version of a file recovered from a shadow copy gives the examiner additional metadata, such as file creation or modification dates and times, that contributes to user activity evidence. As this is a background service in the operating system, the average computer user is unaware of the evidence that is continually created with computer use.

For evidence collection, shadow copies contain a wealth of information, much more so than previous operating systems. As the average computer user may be unaware of these incremental backups, more evidence can be recovered. Suspects unaware of shadow copies are mistaken in their beliefs of security when deleting or wiping their evidence when they ignore shadow copy files.

The Volume Shadow Copy Service is only one example from one operating system, in which improvements by an operating system for an enhancement to the

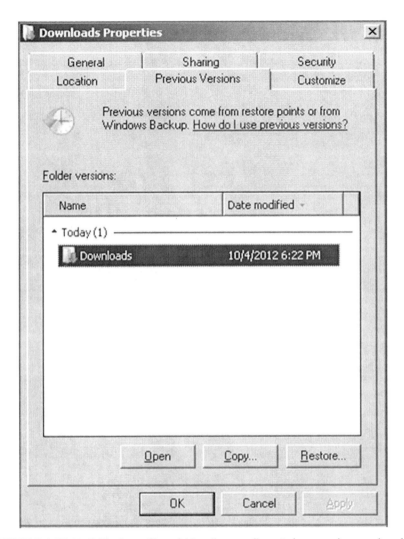

FIGURE 9.1 "Right clicking" on a file or folder allows easily restoring a previous version of a file or folder from one or more shadow copies.

computer user experience, result in additional troves of electronic evidence. More features in operating systems equates to more user-related forensic artifacts.

Computer hardware and software applications will make it easier

The manufacturers and developers of digital forensic tools, both software and hardware, continue to make great strides in making forensic examinations easier and quicker. Forensic software maximizes computing power to recover

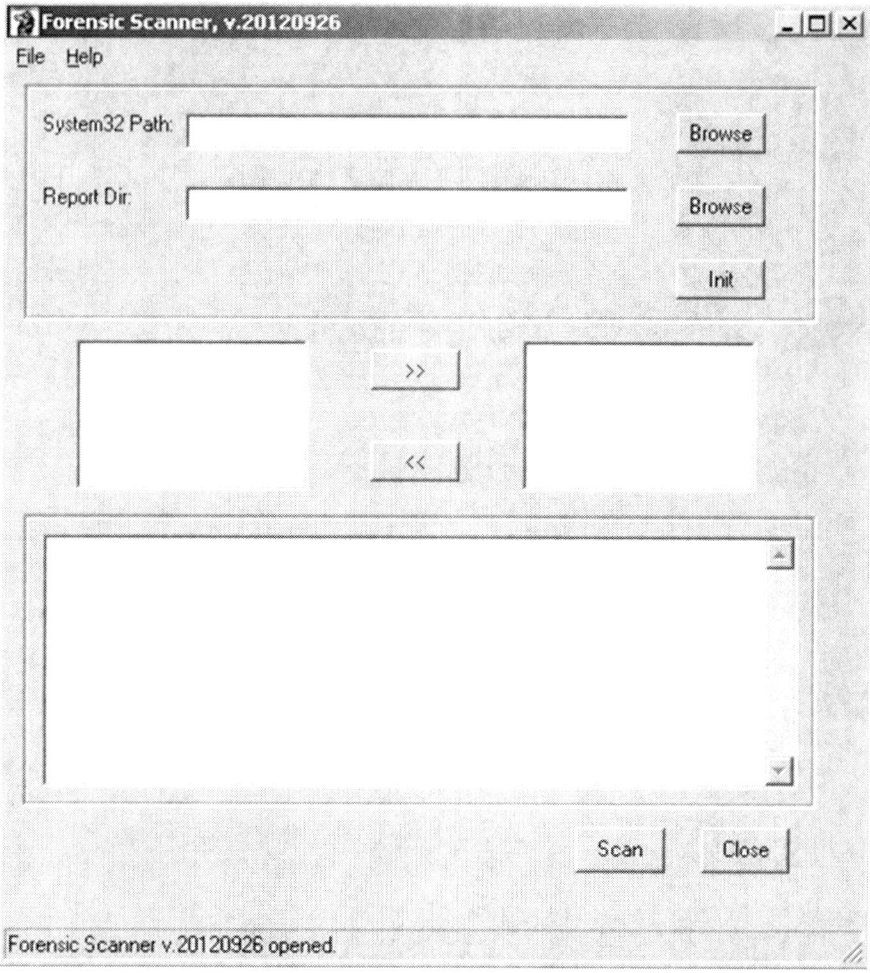

FIGURE 9.2 Forensic Scanner, developed by Harlan Carvey http://code.google.com/p/forensic-scanner/.

deleted files, create indexes of data, and search for keywords and files across enormous amounts of data. Password bypassing applications can access protected files in seconds whereas only a few years ago, these same files could be considered inaccessible.

Even the selection of software applications specific to a certain need has given forensic examiners the ability to provide intensity on an aspect with greater depth than ever before. Early forensic software was neither intuitive nor easy to operate, whereas today, current forensic software can be almost described as point and click applications.

The speed of electronic evidence collection, which can have an effect on an investigation that is time sensitive, is simply incredible as compared to any previous year. An example is the collection of specific information from a computer system in order to help determine initial investigative steps to take. Although a fully featured forensic suite can be used to collect massive amounts of data, smaller and more focused applications may be more efficient.

Figure 9.2 shows the interface of Forensic Scanner, an open source forensic software application developed to collect targeted information from a computer system in less than one minute. By browsing to a mounted target folder and selecting a directory for the output report, user account information is pulled from the system and placed into a text file in seconds. Not more than a half a decade ago, this type of ability was unheard of and impossible without spending an hour or more to collect the same information.

The continued development of forensic software designed to accomplish specific tasks quickly, such as the Forensic Scanner, will only increase the ease of use, speed of data collection, and simplicity of the analysis. As computing power increases, the increased processing speeds allow for even faster case processing of data. These factors effectively make the interpretation of computer user data clearer through massive amounts of circumstantial evidence to make your case.

New and innovative computing devices will make it easier

Human ingenuity continues to create some of the most creative and useful computing devices. The cellular phone, once the size of a small gym bag carried by an elite few, has now been shrunk to fit in the palm of a hand, and carried everywhere by adults and teenagers alike.

Figure 9.3 shows an iPhone by Apple (http://www.apple.com), which continues to store more information with more features, with a compact design. As these devices continue to be developed and used as everyday activities, the data trail of evidence will also continue to grow. Smartphones can be considered one of the best sources of evidence to place a suspect not only behind a keyboard, but at any location the device has traveled.

Data storage and access will make it easier

Just as computing power increases, data storage capacity also increases. As the price for data storage decreases, there is almost a direct relation in an increase of data storage capacity. With the ease and capacity to store massive amounts of data created by computer users, there is simply more electronic evidence to be collected and analyzed. Since any one case can consist of thousands upon

FIGURE 9.3 An iPhone with gigabytes of storage capacity, GPS tracking, text messaging, Internet, and email. All of this data is useful in the investigation of cybercriminals.

thousands of individual evidence files and artifacts, circumstantial evidence of computer use and the amount of electronic contraband becomes extensive with just one hard drive.

Today's storage devices are not only measured in terabytes, but also measured by their small size. Portable external hard drives that can fit in the pocket of trousers can hold terabytes of data. These inexpensive and commonly used storage devices encourage the collection of data by any computer user. Smaller storage devices allow for extreme amount of data storage and a risk of misplacing these small items. A misplaced storage device by a suspect may be a goldmine of evidence if found by an investigator. Figure 9.4 shows an example of a 16 Gbyte USB flash drive compared to the size of a penny.

Data is created, copied, stored, backed up, modified, and backed up numerous more times across multiple hard drives by computer users, including cybercriminals. All of this massive data duplication and storage aids investigators by increasing the chances of finding electronic evidence that a suspect may have destroyed on any other hard drive. Rather than focusing on a single hard drive from a suspect's computer, there is usually a potpourri of associated storage devices containing pertinent electronic evidence.

Online storage, a convenient method to store and back up user data, contributes to potential evidence sources. Whether the services are provided by commercial sources or freely available, each file stored online offers an investigator the opportunity to find and attribute evidence to a suspect.

FIGURE 9.4 Data storage devices increase in capacity, decrease in size, and decrease in cost, such as this 16 Gbyte USB flash drive.

Public awareness and education will make it easier

Cybercrime has become a common term with regular media attention. The public has been inundated with high profile media cases of hacking, intrusions, and identity theft broadcast across printed and televised media. This results in victims self-identifying themselves as victims faster. This faster identification of victims gives investigators more time to identify electronic evidence before it is destroyed.

Education of forensic examiners continues to increase in quality, depth, and opportunities. Just within the last half decade, many universities have created certificate and degree programs either specific to digital forensics or Information Technology Programs with an emphasis on digital forensics. US Government agencies faced with exploding cybercrime issue further support educational institutions by providing partially and fully funded cybercrime scholarships.

Digital forensics has entered the forefront of desirable careers and impact on the security of infrastructure across a broad spectrum of businesses and government entities. This education, public knowledge, and even entertainment references of digital forensics in popular television programs have contributed to a frontline of examiners ready to identify cybercriminals.

The suspect will make it easier

For basic computer use, cybercriminals use computers just like everyone else. Passwords are still written down and taped to the bottom of the keyboard, by

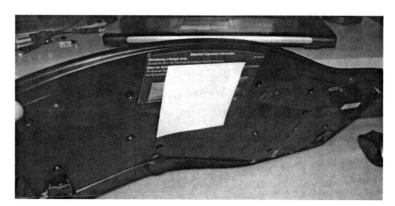

FIGURE 9.5 Commonly used methods by all computer users are used by cybercriminals, such as writing passwords for reminders.

everyday computer users and cybercriminals, such as seen in Figure 9.5. Weak passwords are used for logins, and communicating online is conducted in a manner as if no one will ever read the chats or comments made in social networking websites. Cybercriminals will still continue to brag about their crimes in online public forums and chats as if immune to detection.

Cybercriminals also backup their systems, using the same programs that everyone else uses. Some cybercriminals are unaware of evidence they create as they commit crimes, such as illegally accessing a network when using their home computer and IP address. Harassing emails and text messages are sent and deleted without thought of investigators tracing each email and message.

Basic human nature has always helped investigators in all criminal investigations, not just cybercrime investigations. In many cases, breaks in an investigation are solely due to a mistake or laziness on the part of the cybercriminal, which most likely will never change. These mistakes by cybercriminals turn a seemingly impossible case into an easy, open, and shut case.

Pre-placed surveillance systems will make it easier

As it stands in major cities now, it is virtually impossible for any person to conduct daily business or travels without being under video surveillance at some point. The majority of these video surveillance systems are in place by private businesses for the prevention and detection of crime on their premises. Any of these can be sources of information to place the suspect at a location, given legal authority to demand the information from private businesses.

Additionally, surveillance systems are being placed in public by government agencies at a faster rate than ever before. High crime areas in some cities already have surveillance systems in place; however, many cities are now installing more video cameras in high pedestrian traffic areas in addition to traffic cameras. As with private business security systems, any of these can place a person at a location, to either prove or disprove alibis. If lucky enough, an investigator may even place a suspect at a publicly available computer such as at a computer store, while the suspect committed any number of online crimes through store surveillance cameras.

New laws and employer rights will make it easier

As terrorism breeds risk to national security, laws are continually created or updated to include increased surveillance on citizens. Since terrorism also includes cyber-terrorism, this will result in more data collected which is beneficial to investigations.

In the private sector, laws and employer rights generally include the right to monitor employees in the workplace. This can be through video surveillance or computer monitoring software. Already, employee use of business equipment is under the explicit approval of and monitoring by the employer. The monitoring of computer use, including emails and Internet history is considered to be part of employee monitoring in the workplace.

This reduction of privacy in public and private businesses generates a massive amount of information of all persons being monitored, which hopefully includes those engaged in cybercrimes.

IT WILL BECOME MORE DIFFICULT TO PLACE A SUSPECT BEHIND THE KEYBOARD

Just as the future holds more ease in placing suspects at a keyboard, it is also a fair statement that as it becomes easy in some aspects, it becomes difficult in others. At times, investigations may be impossible to complete successfully depending upon the effort undertaken by a suspect and technology hinderances.

The following topics give a broad overview of increased difficulty that is currently faced by investigators. Many of these obstacles will continue in complexity, but at any point, a breakthrough in technology can make the impossible, possible.

Encryption will make it more difficult

Encryption, in the most basic definition, makes electronic data unreadable without supplying a key, or password. Encryption can be bypassed with sophisticated software and hardware which can try thousands of potential passwords per second in the attempt to guess the password. However, the stronger the encryption algorithm and the more complex of a password used, the less likely an encrypted file or computer system will be accessed.

By any standards, the use of encryption does not automatically imply that criminal evidence is being hidden. It is quite the opposite in that encryption is commonly used to protect sensitive personal, corporate, or government data. In a forensic examination of encrypted data, the only method to know if the encrypted data is evidence is to bypass the encryption protection.

As more operating systems are being sold with encryption built into the operating system, the odds of encountering encryption are increasing. As seen in Figure 9.6, several Microsoft Windows Operating Systems offer the option of encrypting the entire hard drive and other attached hard drives with Bitlocker Drive Encryption by simply clicking "Turn On BitLocker."

Operating systems that do not include encryption features can still be encrypted with third party software applications. Many of these encryption applications

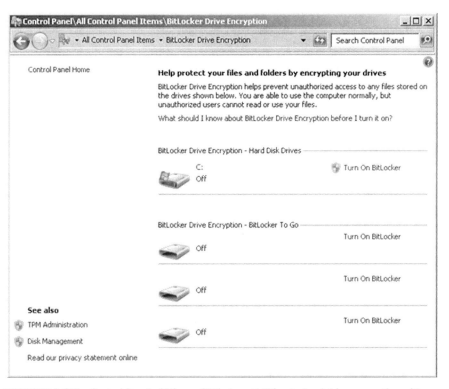

FIGURE 9.6 The Control Panel of Microsoft Windows 7 Ultimate, hard drive encryption with BitLocker Drive Encryption. (http://www.microsoft.com).

are open source and freeware, such as TrueCrypt and by being freely available, increase the chances that more users will install these types of programs. Figure 9.7 shows the dialog box of TrueCrypt, giving the user options of encrypting the entire partition or drive and creating hidden volumes.

Full disk encryption, such as BitLocker Drive Encryption, requires possession of the key, which may be an alphanumeric phrase or any number of additional protections such as a physical USB device containing a startup key. Without the key, access to the hard drive and any information on the hard drive is virtually inaccessible.

Other uses of encryption also render data useless, such as encrypting files, folders, and electronic communication. Emails can be encrypted prior to and during transit. Internet use can also be encrypted or obscured through Internet proxies. Cellular calls are also capable of encryption. Any of these uses of encryption can render electronic storage devices uses as a source of evidence, unless the key is available or the encryption can be broken.

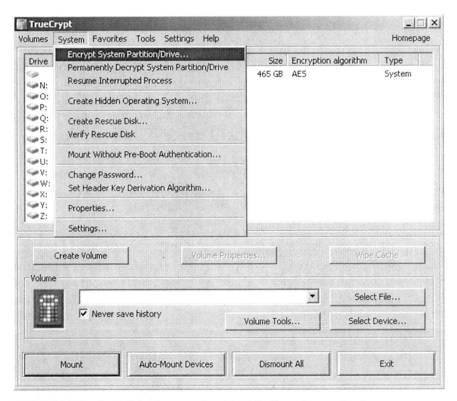

FIGURE 9.7 TrueCrypt dialog for encrypting data. (http://www.truecrypt.org).

Public awareness will make it more difficult

Just as public awareness may prevent and detect cybercrime, this same awareness may also contribute to creating difficulties in forensic examinations. The average computer user has become aware of encryption to protect personal data, creating complex passwords to prevent someone guessing their password, and generally being aware of the potential hazards of computer use. And just as the average user has become more aware, so has the cybercriminals.

Although television crime dramas are not completely accurate with investigative methods, these dramas and crime novels do create to a broader perception of what examiners may be able to find on computers. This perception includes both accurate and false beliefs as to the abilities of investigative methods. Also known as the "CSI Effect," where television dramas solve crimes within an hour, public perception may falsely believe the impossible is possible. This belief negatively affects law enforcement examiners in the courtroom just as much as it effects private sector examiners in the boardroom. The paranoia created through the entertainment world inspires cybercriminals to be even more cautious than they would have been otherwise, making investigative efforts that much more difficult.

Additionally, the education available for potential and future cybercriminals not only consists of the same colleges and universities offering cybersecurity degrees, but there also exists an entire network of online hackers which share information among each other. The information on how to commit cybercrimes is as readily available as information on how to combat cybercrime.

Remote control of systems will make it more difficult

Almost every computer on the planet is practically connected to every other computer, as long as the computer is connected to the Internet. Networks are protected with firewalls and computers are generally configured to not accept remote connections without approval of the computer user.

But as with any security system, methods to gain entry exist through electronic means, such as hacking into a system, or being allowed into a system through social engineering. Social engineering, which consists of a suspect gaining trust of a person through false pretenses, is just as dangerous for security as any malware. If a victim willingly gives remote access or information leading to remote access to a social engineer, the victim's computer could be used to facilitate a crime.

The difficulty in placing a suspect behind a keyboard arises when the keyboard at the evidence computer is actually a different location than the computer. A suspect who can access a victim computer system or even his own computer system from another location might not be able to be traced to the suspect's physical location. The act of remotely accessing multiple systems further complicates an investigation, particularly if the actual physical location of the suspect has been obscured through proxies and the use of public wireless access points.

The examination of a suspect's computer system, which was suspected used in a cybercrime, will most likely show the exact dates and times the criminal activity occurred. But your investigation could show that the most likely suspects were at work, on vacation, or on the other side of the world. With remote access potential, this does not eliminate the likely suspects if the analysis shows remote connections on the system.

Open Wi-Fi hotspots will make it more difficult

Wireless Internet is perhaps the most convenient technology creation for anyone who travels with mobile devices. The ability to instantly connect to the Internet and access email, surf the web, and conduct business cannot be overstated. Private businesses draw patrons to their business by offering free wireless. Coffee shops, grocery stores, and hotels each offer free wireless services.

Besides private business, many government entities offer free wireless for their citizens. Also, private households inadvertently or intentionally offer free wireless access through their home networks. A single apartment building can literally have dozens of open wireless access points where any computer in range will be able to access without restriction.

The difficulty arises as a traveling cybercriminal may access a number of open wireless networks and commits any number of online crimes. The owners of the wireless networks are then at risk of being accused of these crimes. This not only causes investigators to wrongly assume the identity of a suspect, but also causes unnecessary resources to be spent on chasing the wrong leads.

Massive and duplicate data will make it more difficult

I stated that the massive amounts of data, stored across multiple storage devices, can be helpful to an investigation, as evidence can exist on any of the devices. By the same token, because of the massive amount of data, much of which may be duplicative, the time necessary to cull and analyze the data contributes to the difficulty of an investigation. As an example, hundreds of compact disks, or several external hard drives containing hundreds of gigabytes of data, not only take time to analyze, but the analysis may end with a negative result for evidence.

It is the time involved to adequately search and analyze mountains of electronic data that add to the complexity of investigations. Particularly where time is of the essence, not knowing which hard drive contains the most pertinent and important evidence means that every hard drive may have to be examined. That which would have taken days may now take weeks or months, during which time, victims are being further victimized and suspects continuing to roam free. This includes the data stored online through any means of online storage providers needing to be sought after, found, collected, and examined.

Virtual machines will make it more difficult

Any way you look at it, a virtual machine is just as much a complete operating system and contains just as much system and user created files as any "real" operating system. On a suspect's computer, where a virtual machine exists, two forensic examinations are needed: one of the actual physical machine and another on the virtual machine.

Technically, the issues of examining a virtual machine are not unlike those of the physical system. The virtual machine can be imaged, data carved, indexed, and analyzed. But technically, the same issues of complications can arise, such as encryption, along with a other roadblocks to any forensic analysis.

Making matters worse, a single physical computer can host multiple virtual machines. An example seen in Figure 9.8, five separate virtual machines are

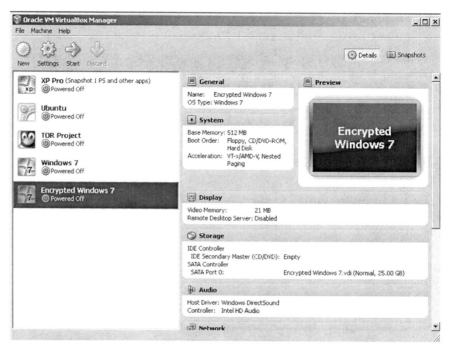

FIGURE 9.8 VirtualBox interface showing five virtual machines. (http://www.virtualbox.org).

seen existing on one physical machine. This figure does not show the virtual machines that may have been deleted, nor does it show any virtual machine that was run from a portable USB device. But at a minimum, Figure 9.8 shows that for a complete forensic examination, there are six operating systems to exam (five virtual systems and one physical system).

The difficulty caused by virtual machines goes beyond the time involved for an analysis of each virtual machine. As a virtual machine can be run from a USB flashdrive, the evidence stored in the virtual machine may not even exist on the physical computer hard drive. The evidence would exist on the USB flashdrive, which, in a difficult scenario, could also be encrypted or thrown away by the suspect.

Another aspect of difficulty with virtual machines is the feature of virtual Snapshots. Figure 9.9 shows an example of a virtual machine with Snapshots. A Snapshot stores the current state of a virtual machine which at any time may be used to revert back in time. By referring to a Snapshot, electronic evidence created on the virtual after the chosen Snapshot is effectively destroyed. In this manner, a virtual machine can be reused often for any cybercrime, yet the evidence destroyed after reverting back to a Snapshot.

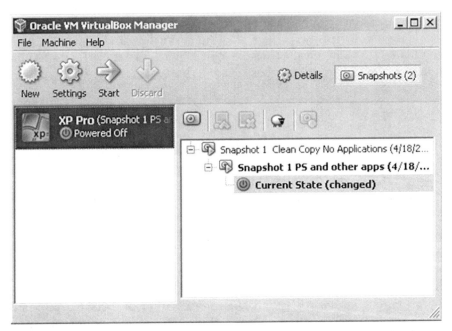

FIGURE 9.9 VirtualBox allows for Snapshots to be stored of the current state of a virtual machine. These can be used to revert previous states, eliminating electronic evidence.

The use of a virtual machine to facilitate cybercrimes strongly benefits the suspect and is a detriment to the investigator. Internet access through the virtual machine can still be conducted through open wireless access points or through the use of proxies to obscure the suspect's actual IP address. Crime committed within a virtual machine stays within that virtual machine, which is really just a file on a computer or USB drive. This single file or storage device can be wiped beyond recovery or simply tossed on a freeway to prevent discovery.

Even more techniques will make it difficult

Counter-forensics, or anti-forensics techniques, is any method to make forensics difficult or impossible. Some of these discussed already include encryption and the use of virtual machines. Other methods that are just as easy and effect are data wiping and data hiding, where evidence is either overwritten with random data or hidden behind other data. Employing a combination of these techniques can effectively render forensic analysis on a storage medium useless.

Perhaps the most effective means of disrupting a forensic examination is that of the complete destruction and disposal of the suspect's computer system. Because storage devices drop continue to decrease in price as they increase in storage capacity, the disposal of these containers of evidence by suspects is of small consequence compared to prosecution. Desktop computers and laptops also have become so inexpensive, that the destruction and disposal may be commonplace. Computer systems can even be purchased solely for the facilitation of a crime and quickly disposed after its use.

SUMMARY

Without a confession from a suspect, placing the suspect behind the keyboard requires effort, ingenuity, patience, and more than one Eureka! moment. Even with a confession, reliance upon one piece of evidence is a risky decision when a confession can be suppressed, recanted, or proven to be inaccurate.

The future holds easier solutions to placing the suspect behind the keyboard, just as it will provide obstacles to that end. It is up to the investigator, the examiner, and the investigator-examiner to be a problem solver and think beyond traditional means of investigations. A forensic analysis can stand on its own regarding only the interpretation of the data recovered. It cannot, however, be the sole piece of evidence to place a suspect at the computer without further investigative methods and other circumstantial evidence.

Bibliography

BitLocker Drive Encryption. <http://windows.microsoft.com/>.

Forensic Scanner. <http://code.google.com/p/forensicscanner/>.

TrueCrypt. <http://www.truecrypt.org>.

VirtualBox. <http://www.virtualbox.org>.

CHAPTER 10

Online Investigations

INFORMATION IN THIS CHAPTER:

- Online investigations
- Capturing webpages as evidence

CONTENTS

INTRODUCTION

Online investigations are one of the most powerful tools you have available in your objective of placing the suspect at a keyboard or location, identifying your suspect, and identifying co-conspirators of your suspect. You can even identify the victims and witnesses in investigations.

This chapter is not about online undercover investigations. Primarily, this chapter will give you advanced techniques to search for information beyond simply using a search engine. Social networking sites, forums, blogs, and the deep web contain much more information that any one search engine. The goal of this chapter is to show how to find your suspect online so you can eventually find him in person.

ONLINE INVESTIGATIONS

As you can see in the Case Studies chapter, several high-profile investigations involved searching the Internet for information to identify suspects. As a corporate investigator, you may have access to public databases on a subscription basis. Law enforcement investigators have access to government databases, such as those containing criminal history information, including non-conviction data.

These databases have an advantage over information found online, in that the information can be considered very credible. An arrest record is not needed to be verified with the arresting agency, but if it were, documents would be found such as fingerprint cards, mug shots, and arrest reports. But generally, a record of an arrest is taken at face value as being credible.

Information found online is not as credible and in fact, may be completely and intentionally falsified. Anything that is posted on a website, blog, or forum has no requirement that it be backed by physical proof. With this type of free-for-all wild west of publishing information on the Internet, why would any investigator consider using it at all? The answer lies in the source of the information.

Unlike a criminal or public records database where the information is entered by a third party, information found online offers something you can't get any-where else. The information is published by the suspect, personally, by the suspect's own hands. Whether the information is factual or false bears little weight as the content is not always the factor needed in your investigation. Any character typed on a keyboard by the suspect that is posted on any webpage is a breadcrumb for you to follow to his doorstep. The best part is that the infor-mation posted online may be as close to *real-time information* on your suspect you can find. In most cases, the data posted online is stored by third parties that have nothing to do with your suspect, nor may even allow your suspect to remove from their systems. That's the power of online investigations.

Why the internet?

The Internet as it relates to investigations is much more than commercials for products. It is a means of communication with email, chatting, social network-ing, forums, and blogs. Internet users can share information and ideas or give their opinions in publicly viewable forums.

With the interconnectivity of mobile devices in which photos and messages can be instantly uploaded to the Internet, more people are online, all of the time. Those that wish to share every detail online can do so uninhibited. This includes those that wish to brag about their exploits, which could be your sus-pect anonymously bragging about his criminal acts.

Again, the content of a posting may not be important to your case compared to the timing of when a comment was posted. Potentially, an IP address may lead to a physical location that has not been obscured through an anonymous means. And most important, the *Internet might be your only chance of identifying your suspect.*

What can be found online?

Just about everything can be found on the Internet and for the most part, online content stays online. If the content is interesting enough it will multiply through mirrored webpages. At a certain point, it is difficult if not impossible to remove information on the Internet.

The difficulty is weeding through millions of webpages to find only the information you need without having to spend days at a computer screen. Without a plan or the knowledge of how to search for information, you will miss important clues a suspect has left for you to find.

Some of the most pertinent areas to look for information on your suspect are comments to articles that your suspect finds interesting. Forums that relate to his need to brag, express anger, or simply communicate with others like him. Your suspect may not have his own webpage or domain, but may have any number of personal social networking pages such as a Facebook page. He may have one or many usernames in different forums. Your goal is to find the first clue and typically you already have it.

If your case involves harassing emails, you have one or more email addresses. If the case involves the posting of threatening comments on a blog, you have the usernames of your suspect. Even if your suspect has given a false name, you have the false name at least to start your online search.

How to build your "super" browser

Before you get started with an intensive manhunt online, there are tools you can configure that will greatly reduce the amount of time spent searching. Your primary tool will be the web browser. With a few tweaks to the browser, online research can be more effectively accomplished.

A web browser allows you to read webpages, watch videos, and interact with others online. Search engines, such as Google, allow you to search the Internet for webpages on the search terms you choose. Tweaking your web browser to accomplish searches automatically, systematically, and thoroughly will make your online time much more efficient.

Using Mozilla's Firefox as an example, there are a few changes to the browser you can accomplish in a few minutes. From the Mozilla website (http://www.mozilla.org), Firefox can be downloaded freely and installed. From the same website, "Add-ons" can be downloaded and installed to the browser.

Add-ons are additional features that add push button efficiency to your online searches. For example, in Figure 10.1, an Add-on that searches multiple social networking sites at one time can be added with the click of a button. As many Add-ons you see fit for use can be added to the Firefox browser. The time saving feature for this one example will allow searching over 40 social networking sites at once rather than searching individually.

FIGURE 10.1 An Add-on for the Firefox web browser from http://www.mozilla.org that allows searching social networking sites.

With each Add-on giving your browser combinations of searches to be conducted at once, the amount of data specific to your searches will be produced faster. Another additional feature for the Firefox browser is from SEARCH. SEARCH is an online resource for investigations. From SEARCH, you can download and install the SEARCH Investigative Community Toolbar, which installs directly to Firefox. The SEARCH toolbar adds bookmarks to the browser specific to areas of an online research, such as IP address information, cell phone information, and social networking websites.

Other web browsers also offer Add-ons type features, such as Google's Chrome browser which allows for extensions for the browser. Some toolbar Add-ons, like the SEARCH Investigative Toolbar are compatible across several browsers. Regardless of the browser you choose, set it up from the start and you will quickly have a systematic method of online searching that will save you more days of research than you would have liked to endure.

Internet search engines and directories

All search engines are not created equal. In the world of search engines, there are catagories of search engines that are specific to a topic, which are helpful to narrow your results. All-purpose category search engines, such as Google or Bing, search across the Internet for any hits on your search term, if the website has been indexed by that search engine. As each search engine has been developed by different organizations, using different indexing methods, their results may differ slightly. That means that many times you may need to try the same search term using different search engines.

FIGURE 10.2 A blog search engine, Icerocket, http://www.icerocket.com.

One example of a category-specific search engine is Icerocket, which is a search engine for blogs. Figure 10.2 shows the search dialog box for Icerocket. Other category search engines are developed for catagories such as searching for books, businesses, email, forums, games, people, and news. If there is a specific search topic you need to accomplish, there may be a search engine designed for your search. One website that maintains a list of search engines separated by category is The Search Engine List at http://www.thesearchenginelist.com.

Another source of online information is directories. A directory, like a phonebook, is a listing of information, which includes online phonebooks. Some of these online directories may not be indexed with a search engine and as such, a general-purpose search engine may completely miss any results in a directory.

Usernames

Usernames may be the only lead you have in a case. Besides attempting to determine the meaning of a username, it is probably more important to find if the username has been used in other online services. There are a few websites that allow searching across many social networking sites by username. Figure 10.3 shows one example, NameChk, which can search for matches across a wide range of websites.

However, if the same username is found on more than one website as a comment or blog post, it does not necessarily mean it is the same person. Usernames are specific to an account on the Internet, not to the Internet as a whole. Finding the same username in more than one location means time is needed to investigate if the owner of the username is the same person.

The benefit to you in searching usernames is that if your suspect chooses a username for criminal activity, it is possible that he may use the same username for legitimate activity, even though the email addresses associated with the username may be different.

FIGURE 10.3 NameChk (http://www.namechk.com) allows searching for a username across many social networking websites.

Social networking websites

Searching for your suspect online obviously includes searching social networking websites. By this time in your searching, you should have installed several Add-ons or extensions to your browser to help. In addition to the added features, there are several search engines developed for searching these websites. One example is seen in Figure 10.4 with SocialMention, which can search a user specified selection of social networking websites or all at once.

FIGURE 10.4 SocialMention is one of many search engines designed for searching social networking websites. http://www.socialmention.com.

Recent privacy concerns have resulted in many people setting their personal social networking websites to private only settings, where only friends and family can view. Without legal authority, you cannot view these pages directly. A workaround may be the friends of your suspect who may keep their pages open for public view. Once a friend or family member has been identified, if they allow open public view, you too can see the page and possibly information posted by your suspect.

I would not get caught up with only the most popular social networking sites. There are literally thousands of social networking sites on the Internet, any of which may hold the key to your suspect's identification. Many of these sites are created by category, unlike a general social networking site. If your suspect is involved in hacking, there is a possibility he may have an account with a hacking networking site along with others like him. Or maybe he enjoys knitting and belongs to both a hacking and knitting social networking site. Either way, it doesn't matter which social networking topic the suspect belongs, as long as you can find it.

Blogs, forums, and wikis

Blogs, forums, and wikis require a separate discussion apart from social networking sites. Generally, a social networking site is administered by a third party, such as Facebook. Users with Facebook accounts do not control their data on the service, nor does a user have control over data retention of the service. For information posted by a user on some of these sites, it will remain and the user may not have the means to alter or delete it.

This does not always hold true for the blogs, forums, and wikis. For the blogs, forums, and wikis, the control of the information may or may not be in a third party's hand and the user can alter or delete their information as desired. Many times, your suspect may be the administrator of the blog or forum, in which case, sending a legal demand for information may not be in the investigation's best interest. Even a blog that resides with a third party, but created by a user, you may not be able to locate a post by the suspect if the suspect deletes it. The deleted post may still be available from the third party, but you won't know that it ever existed if it were deleted.

An example would be a blog service provided by Google, Blogger, seen in Figure 10.5. A suspect can create a blog using Blogger, and post incriminating or identifying information, but at any point, the suspect can simply delete the blog. Without finding the information before deletion, you'll never know it was there. A wiki, which is like an online encyclopedia, also allows for users to access, create, and modify content. These changes are usually logged by the wiki, listing the changes by username. Since a suspect could delete their own information on a wiki, it may be missed. Potentially, if discovered after a

FIGURE 10.5 Blogger, by Google. http://www.google.com.

deletion, the information may still exist and be able for production upon legal request, such as a search warrant.

Forums pose some of the same issues as a blog if the forum administrator is your suspect. Forums also offer more opportunities for information about your suspect. Given any forum on any topic, users can post to a threaded topic, like replying to an email, only that these are usually in public view.

Since most forums require a username and profile, there may be information specific to your suspect in the profile, especially since the profile is self-identifying. One example of a pertinent piece of information can be seen in Figure 10.6. In this example, the user's profile photo is a handgun. Although this is just a photo of a handgun, it gives rise to officer safety concerns when the suspect is eventually contacted or arrested. As the saying goes, a picture is worth a thousand words.

The trust users lend to forums most always leads to a compromise in personal information, which benefits an investigation. One example where forum

FIGURE 10.6 Profile photos in forums give some information of importance about a suspect.

postings were instrumental in a case involved a pursuit by police officers where the suspect eluded officers and the suspect's license plate was not identified.

One of the officers involved in the pursuit searched online and found a forum discussing the same pursuit that occurred a few days earlier. In this forum, the anonymous suspect admitted to getting away from the police and bragged about it, however, the suspect was not using a real name in the forum.

Looking further, the same username was found in another forum topic selling motorcycle parts, giving away the city where he lived, but still, not quite enough information for identification.

Eventually, a different forum was found with the same suspect bragging about beating a speeding ticket. This suspect was so proud of beating the system, that he scanned a copy of a check received from the court as a refund for bail when he won his case. The suspect redacted his name on the check and posted the scanned image to the forum in an attempt to protect his identity.

It took one phone call to the court listed on the check to get the full name, date of birth, and home address of the suspect. Five minutes later, having the suspect's real name, his photo was found online in yet another forum where he was standing next to the same motorcycle he was riding when he eluded the police. This online search took less than an hour.

The Dark Web

There are places on the Internet that few venture into. In this place known as the Dark Web, or The Onion Web, you can find anything. Drugs, sex, child pornography, hackers for hire, hit men for hire. Literally anything that you would ever want to see exists in the Dark Web. Perhaps your suspect visits the Dark Web and you want to check. Let's take a quick look at some of the problems you'll have.

First, to access the Dark Web, you must use Tor, as you can't get in otherwise. When you run Tor, your IP address is hidden through a number of anonymous relays, worldwide. That means your suspect's IP address is also hidden.

Once you have accessed the Dark Web, website addresses take a new meaning. Instead of webpages with understandable characters, like the name of a company, the address appear like this: http://silkroadvb5piz3r.onion/index.php.

This particular example of an address is for the "Silk Road Anonymous Market". The Silk Road offers visitors anything they want, mostly illegal items and substances. A screenshot of the Silk Road website can be seen in Figure 10.7. As you can see, marijuana, heroin, hash, and other drugs are openly sold online, all from sellers hiding behind the same system as the buyers.

FIGURE 10.7 The Silk Road Anonymous Market website, http://silkroadvb5piz3r.onion/index.php.

I can assume that many of the items and services in this Dark Web are scams and cons from anonymous criminals selling to anonymous buyers through electronic payments. None being the wiser of the other or being able to track each other, surely results in problems for the buyers being ripped off in some manner. The black market is the black market, even if it is online.

Your obstacles in identifying your suspect in the Dark Web start with IP addresses. If your suspect is in there, using forums or participating in the black market, chasing the IP address will waste valuable time. Another problem is that websites and forums in the Dark Web are extremely transitory. Probably the biggest problem is that if you could identify the owner of a website or forum, you may not have any luck with cooperation.

Following the bread crumbs

Perhaps the biggest question to this chapter is *"so what does this do to help put a suspect behind a keyboard?"* Besides identifying your suspect, which can be a major break in your case by itself, there is a ton of evidence waiting for you to grab online. For every comment posted to news articles, or comments to blogs, or continued forum posts, exist one or more IP addresses and email addresses.

Behind each email address there are more even IP addresses for when the account was created and each time accessed.

Some of these accesses by the suspect may be obscured by using virtual private networks, if the suspect takes the time to use a VPN all the time. *All you need is to find that one time that the suspect made a mistake.* Once you tie the suspect to a physical address, you have half the obstacles in your investigation solved. Surveillance operations can be planned and executed, a background conducted on the newly identified suspect, and you will no longer be investigating John Doe.

The other benefit to following bread crumbs of evidence and logging each item found online is that of suspect activity, by date and time. Each bit of activity online shows the suspect was at a computer at that date and time. There are exceptions to this, such as configuring a blog post to upload at a later time, but generally, you will have dates and times consist to actually being at a computer.

CAPTURING WEBPAGES AS EVIDENCE

One thing about the draw to the Internet is that it is dynamic and changing. Dynamic websites change constantly with ads, comments, or other content. Information that exists at 1:00 pm may not exist at 1:01 pm. Sometimes this information can be critical to your case. So how do you save it?

One general rule to save a webpage of interest is to immediately print it when you find it. Don't bother reading the entirety of the website first, or grab your partner to brag what you just discovered. Print it. Make sure it printed. Then treat that printed page as if it is the only copy in the world because it just could end up being the only copy if the webpage changes.

At that point, you can take several measures to preserve the webpage or website. You can create a PDF file of the entire website or single pages with Adobe Acrobat or you can download the entire site with a program designed for saving websites. One example is the free software, HTTrack Website Copier, seen in Figure 10.8. This program can download an entire website to a local folder in native files, meaning the html code used. It also downloads the files associated with the website such as videos, graphics, and documents.

Commercial products exist for capturing Internet pages with more features designed for evidence control, but printing the pages, creating a PDF of the website, and downloading the website with a program such as HTTrack Website Copier can accomplish the goal of saving your evidence locally. For court admissibility, documents of website captures only require that they be entered as evidence if they accurately reflect what was seen on your monitor. A printed webpage fills that need if all else fails.

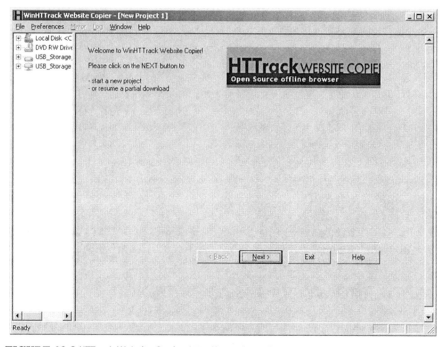

FIGURE 10.8 HTTrack Website Copier, http://www.httrack.com.

Be careful of your visits online

A very important consideration before you go online to find your suspect is to prevent being discovered by the suspect. If your suspect is technology savvy, runs their own websites, writes malicious scripts, or otherwise examines their website logs, be prepared for your IP address to show up in front of him and for the suspect to take advantage of the information.

Also be prepared that a website run by your suspect could be a honeypot of sorts to infect machines through malicious links, in particular, infect those that are intent on finding him. This applies to any website run by any criminal element. It may be an idea to use a method to hide your IP address, such as Tor or a VPN and like you've heard on every police drama, *be careful out there*.

SUMMARY

Prepare for your online investigation before you actually start searching. There are steps you can take now that will save hours of work and narrow your search results to a manageable amount. Online investigations do not mean solely using a general purpose search engine to look for your suspect. An online investigation exploits the Internet using every tool available to find exactly what you need. It would be a rare cybercriminal that is not on the Internet in some form or fashion.

For some, the Internet holds all the answers to life. For you, the Internet may hold the identity of your suspect. It can also hold the eventual physical address of your suspect, his contacts and co-conspirators, admissions and confessions, and maybe even a photo posted of him and his motorcycle.

Bibliography

Adobe Acrobat. <http://www.adobe.com>.

Bing. <http://www.bing.com>.

Facebook. <http://www.facebook.com>.

Google. <http://www.google.com>.

HTTrack Website Copier. <http://www.httrack.com>.

Icerocket. <http://www.icerocket.com>.

Mozilla Firefox. <http://www.mozilla.org>.

NameChk. <http://www.namechk.com>.

SEARCH Investigative Community Toolbar. <http://www.search.org>.

Silk Road Anonymous Market. <http://silkroadvb5piz3r.onion/index.php>.

SocialMention. <http://www.socialmention.com>.

CHAPTER 11

Case Studies

INFORMATION IN THIS CHAPTER:

- A day in the life of a cybercriminal
- The life and casework of a cyber investigator
- Testifying to your work

CONTENTS

INTRODUCTION

In theory, investigations should succeed as planned and expected. However, in practice, theory is only the starting point for real-life situations requiring creative solutions to obstacles. A review of case studies provides a means to show theory and practical applications in real-life case scenarios, with both positive and negative results. A thorough examination of one case for a targeted study goes well beyond this book due to the amount of information any single case possesses, but we can use many examples to reinforce investigative concepts.

In order to give examples showing how successful concepts in this book have been applied in real life, this chapter will show a collection of briefed examples across a wide range of case studies. Keep in mind that there is more than one solution to any single problem you will encounter and certainly more solutions that can be given in this chapter.

And as some examples are clearly criminal investigations where the availability of demanding evidence through search warrants exists, civil cases allow for evidence to be gathered without warrants, such as electronic evidence owned by a business and used by an employee. Whichever type of case you have, use the resources and legal authority available to secure the evidence. Sometimes you can just ask for it; other times, you may need a judge to order it.

The specific examples come with disclaimers. Depending upon the type of operating system and even the version of an operating system, certain artifacts will not exist or be recoverable. Depending upon the actions of the suspect, artifacts that existed at one point may not exist after being overwritten by other data. Even depending upon the forensic application used, some artifacts may be incapable of being recovered. So, a statement that electronic evidence *may* be recovered in a specific situation literally means maybe, because it depends on other factors. Usually, the answer as to if a forensic artifact of evidence can be recovered is simply, it depends.

A DAY IN THE LIFE OF A CYBERCRIMINAL

The scenarios given in each following section are fictional, but much of the content has been taken from cases I've worked. Each scenario has a referenced case ("Case in Point") for a real-life example of a high profile case. Most of these can be found online through open source or court records to read detailed information on investigative methods used.

As an investigation can be comprised of one independent incident or a multitude of crimes over a period of time, utilizing different operating systems and versions of operating systems, your investigation processes and methods will need to flow with your evidence. Some of the investigative tips discussed in this chapter will work with some cases, others won't.

Backdating documents

Scenario: A business purchase agreement document in PDF format is alleged to have been altered to benefit one party in the agreement. Certain verbiage is claimed to have been changed as has the date of the agreement. Both the plaintiff and defendant claim their version of the document is accurate and the other document version being a manipulated copy.

Investigative Tips: Antedating is creating files with intentionally inaccurate time stamps. A common antedating action is backdating of electronic documents. Backdating documents is changing the date of a document, such as a business

---

CASE IN POINT

Paul D. Ceglia v Mark Elliot Zuckerberg, and Facebook Inc., 2012
This case hinged on the authenticity of a contract between Ceglia and Zuckerberg as it related to the development of Facebook. A forensic analysis was conducted resulting in conclusions that electronic documents and emails were manipulated and backdated.

contract creation date changed to an earlier date to gain a benefit. The benefit could be to cover knowledge of a crime or to benefit financially in a business dispute. Another example of backdating could be to create a suicide message after the fact, using a computer in an attempt to cover a murder. The printed date on a document is easy to manipulate and difficult to validate. The electronic time stamp is a different story.

Firstly, examining the metadata of an electronic file gives a baseline of information, whether or not the dates and times are authentic. Each copy or version of the documents under investigation will need the metadata extracted for comparison to create a historical timeline for each document.

In any document backdating investigation, being able to examine the machine on which the document was created may be the most beneficial source of information. Secondary items of evidence that the document may have been copied onto or emailed are also important as comparisons.

Documents which have been emailed as attachments create a credible source of information in the email headers. A document showing a creation date after an email date would be suspect as being modified. This example would be easy of course, but more important is building the timeline of historical relevance for the documents using all available information, including email header time stamps.

One method of manipulating document time stamps is through the use of software intended for altering metadata. Whether used for legitimate file management or nefarious purposes, these applications enable computer users with average skills to manipulate the time stamps on electronic files. One such example is seen in Figure 11.1, showing the dialog box for Stexbar, an open source extension for Windows Explorer. This particular extension can be downloaded from http://code.google.com/p/stexbar/ and easily installed. Once installed, computer users can change the metadata time stamps on any file by right clicking the file, choosing "properties," and selecting the TimeStamps tab to alter the metadata.

If the evidence in question is a file absent its respective computer on which it was created, validating the time stamps is problematic. More information is needed to validate the metadata. By examining the computing system, recovering time stamp information from the Master File Table (MFT), which will contain the time stamp of when the last modification of the file occurred ("Entry Modified"), when the file's attributes have changed, along with information on other actions affecting the evidence file.

Changing the computer time before creating an electronic document is another method of antedating, as the metadata for the newly created electronic file will be based on the incorrect setting of the system. Antedating using more than

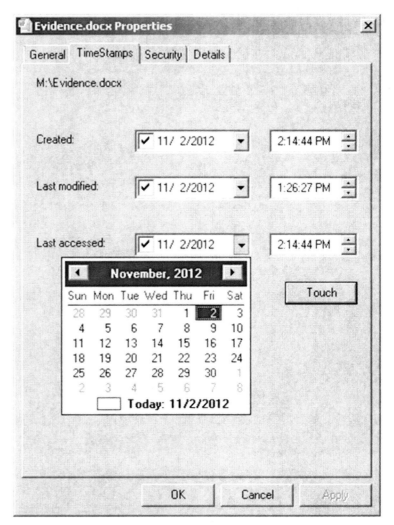

FIGURE 11.1 Stexbar, a Windows Explorer extension allowing an easy method of altering a file's time stamps.

one means only complicates an analysis. Once there is doubt to the validity of any file's time stamp, the computer system must be analyzed to correlate dates and times as well as determine if a suspect manipulated the system.

Internet web browsers are full of time stamped records from reliable sources such as from an Internet Service Provider or website. These can be compared to files on the system in relation to the evidence files. Event logs in Windows are also a great source of information to determine if antedating occurred, such as the system logging a computer clock change. Other log files, like anti-virus program logs, may also have time stamps to help correlate activity on the system.

Generally, antedated documents are made with a substantial gap in the actual date and time compared to the altered date and time. For these situations, the differences are obvious. For situations where the time gap may be small, finding the differences requires attention to minute detail. Also, the time stamps of files do not change consistently. Depending upon how a file was copied or moved, will affect which time stamps are modified. Time stamps can be updated when extracted from a zip file, downloaded from the Internet, or moved to a folder when using the command line. Conversely, simply moving a file from one folder to another will not update the Create time.

The versions of software used to create a document give an indication if a file has been antedated. An example would be an evidence file, such as a Microsoft Word document which has been produced as authentic evidence in the file format of ".docx," yet the claim is the document was created and not modified since the year 2001. The file format of the document is immediately questionable since it did not exist in 2001.

To antedate a file and make it appear credible, the suspect has to take into consideration the relation of the date chosen to backdate the file to the software and hardware used. Obviously, purchasing a new laptop in 2012, with the most current operating system and programs installed, will not be the best choice to create a file made to appear as if it were created in 2004. The file format type, metadata of the file, and system clock changes will each show any number of techniques to backdate the file.

When presented with a goal to validate time, you need to take into consideration the factors specific to the evidence in front of you. The operating system, the method of file creation and movement, log files, and even the printed documents need to be correlated for discrepancies. Without an authentic time-line of events, including accurate file time stamps, placing a suspect at the keyboard is an extremely difficult task. First things first; develop the time line, and then take the steps to identify possible suspects.

False names and disposable email accounts

Scenario: A victim has been receiving harassing and threatening emails from an unknown person. The names used in the emails are false names and the email accounts are commonly used, free webmail accounts.

Investigative Tips: This case includes great examples of suspect elimination. Interviews, polygraphs, and searches of computers and emails eliminated most potential suspects, leaving Bruce Ivins as the prime suspect. From the

---

CASE IN POINT

FBI Anthrax Investigation (Arredondo 2008)

Doctor Bruce Ivins, a biodefense researcher at the US Army Medical Research Institute of Infectious Diseases was suspected of mailing anthrax contaminated letters causing five deaths and injury to dozens of more people. Ivins used disposable email accounts with false names during the time of the anthrax attacks. Although Ivins committed suicide before being charged, he was the primary suspect in these anthrax attacks in 2001.

---

elimination of suspects, focus on Ivins resulted in obtaining the evidence needed to determine he had to be the suspect in the murders.

Techniques used to gather information on Ivins comprised pen registers on email accounts and telephones, search warrants on his residence and cars, covert collection of his trash, and the installation of GPS devices on his vehicles. The pen registers, or trap-and-trace, allow for investigators to have near real-time information on phone numbers called/received and email addresses of correspondence, but without accessing the content of either voice or data.

Doctor Ivins sent anonymous emails days before the anthrax attacks with the warning of "WE HAVE THIS ANTHRAX. DEATH TO AMERICA. DEATH TO ISRAEL." Linking these emails to Doctor Ivins required a pen register which revealed additional email addresses related to the case. Additionally, an email address was linked to an online posting on Wikipedia.

Following the trail of evidence on Wikipedia led to information obtained where Ivins communicated with others with an email having his real name in the name field of the email. Other emails believed to be owned by Irvins were identified, where Irvins was sending emails to himself, between email accounts.

The investigation of a single email address may lead to another email or to the identification of an online account with accurate user name information. The inclusion of IP address verification in your investigations is an important aspect if the IP addresses can be traced to an actual physical location. Otherwise, the investigative means will be to trace and follow emails through online sources such as online bulletin boards and forums to eventually end at the legitimate information of your suspect.

Evidence leads to more evidence

During the collection of storage media at a search warrant related to a gang shooting, a smartphone is seized. There are several computer systems to be examined and only one forensic examiner. Where do you start?

State of Wisconsin v Brian Pierick, 2010
During a search warrant executed at a residence, two iPhones were seized along with other items. An analysis of the iPhones recovered sexually explicit chat messages with juveniles. Coupled with child pornography discovered on seized computers, investigators continued the investigation to obtain even more evidence of these crimes, including postings on Craigslist that were pertinent to the case.

Investigative Tips: The forensic examiner starts the first forensic examination first. Ideally, the first examination is the one that cries for attention as a priority. In one case, this could be the laptop. In another case, it may be the smartphone or a flash drive. All things being equal, the smartphone may be a good piece of evidence to search your examinations.

As in the case in point above, investigators not only examined the iPhones, but requested the call detail records which helped to identify victims. The analysis of mobile devices such as smartphones can yield a wealth of evidence and much of that evidence can place a suspect at any one location that has been either logged by GPS on the phone or through cell tower records. Being able to create a historical location and movement of a suspect helps prove or disprove alibis. It also helps to potentially identify locations where additional evidence may exist.

Although smartphones capable of geolocation through GPS logging or by embedding EXIF data in photos are incredible items of evidence for suspect locations, laptops may contain some of the same location information, as they are almost as portable as a smartphone.

As shown throughout this book, the combination of investigative techniques and forensic processes helps place the suspect at a location and behind a keyboard, but these same processes help find clues and lead to additional evidence and victim identification. Of course, there is always the question of how much effort to place in an investigation when there is enough evidence to prove an allegation in a legal hearing, but when unidentified victims exist, sometimes you should consider going the extra ten yards. The victims will appreciate your effort.

Searching for all the bad things

Scenario: The suspect is alleged to have planned the murder of his ex-wife to end paying alimony. After his arrest and search warrant of his home, a computer is seized for examination. The goal is to determine if evidence of the

CASE IN POINT

The people of the state of illinois v steven zirko, 2009
In this case, Steven Zirko was charged with first degree murders of two persons and the solicitation of murder. A forensic examination of Internet activity on Zirko's computer revealed evidence directly related to his charges. Internet searches for "killer," "nitrous oxide," "unconscious," "hire a hitman," and "hire plus mercenary" were performed by a computer user. Websites visited included www.hireahitman.com and www.gunshows.usa.com. florida.

The investigation showed that this computer belonged to the Zirko and he was not traveling during this activity on the computer. Considering the content of the websites visited, the search words used, and the timing of use, these items were determined to show intent and motive to commit the crimes and that it was Zirko that typed the search terms.

crime exists on the computer and determine if the electronic evidence can be tied to the suspect.

Investigative Tips: Intent, motivation, opportunity, and knowledge. Each of these constitutes factors to help identify a suspect. Typed URLs are clearly indicative of intent to at least view specific websites of interest. Typed search terms to find websites of interest also show intent. Other Internet and browsing activity which can show knowledge and intent includes bookmarking webpages, printing or saving webpages, and numerous revisits to specific webpages. Creating a timeline of Internet history can show determination to research a topic or attempts to find contraband online.

However, Internet history by itself doesn't have much weight as evidence unless it is tied to a suspect. Other than a computer belonging to a suspect, a process of elimination still needs to occur to narrow the list of suspects. A single family residence where a single person lives helps narrow the list of suspects having access to a computer. Multi-family homes and computers accessed by any person in a common area increase the amount of data to examine and decrease the ability to tie specific actions to a single person.

A method to help determine a specific user's activity on a computer is to examine another computer or device that the suspect has access. This can be an Internet enabled smartphone or work computer. Potentially, the Internet history on all devices will be comparable with each other. A suspect can be more easily placed at a job location than somewhere outside the workplace. Within the workplace, access to an assigned computer reduces the chance that only the suspect uses his assigned computer. Given a suspect can be placed at his work, on his computer where the same Internet bookmarks and searches were conducted as on his home computer, his home use of the computer can be inferred.

So even as the intent of Internet searches is very relevant to an investigation, the searches of one computer at a work location, which mirror the searches of another computer at a home location, may effectively place that suspect behind both computers.

Scenario—threatening blog posts

A suspect has been making anonymous threatening posts on an Internet blog against specific persons. The posts are clearly death threats, yet the suspect is obviously using a false name. Depending upon how the suspect posted to the blog will determine the odds of being able to identify the suspect.

Investigative Tips: IP addresses can be gold in your investigation. Although to obtain the actual physical address requires law enforcement authority, being able to securely identify a physical address along with the subscriber of the Internet account is hard evidence to defend against.

Cybercriminals have become to know that their home IP address is not the Internet connection to use when committing a crime. Suspects that are unaware falsely believe that signing up for a free and anonymous webmail account means they are anonymous to the world. This can lead to the suspect creating evidence on a regular basis, such as posting comments on blogs, from their home, blissfully unaware that every log in and post is logged and waiting for an investigator to obtain.

But before you are too confident with IP addresses, there is still work needed to make sure you have the right suspect when based on any IP address. This additional work means you must do as much as reasonably necessary to ensure you are right, because if you are wrong based on erroneous information, nothing goes right.

CASE IN POINT

US District Court v Clifton Dwayane Brooks, 2012

Clifton Dwayane Brooks posted comments on an Internet blog threatening to kill Maricopa County Sheriff Joe Arpaio. Investigators sent emergency requests to the blog hosting company, Google Incorporated. Google responded with the email address blog poster, and afterward in response to a search warrant, provided the IP address used of the blog poster.

The IP address resolved to Comcast as the Internet Service Provider, who provided investigators with the physical address of their customer, Clifton Brooks.

Making the wrong kind of friends online

An unknown suspect attempts to lure children online for sexual exploitation by offering to be their friend. The only information about the suspect available a social networking user name given to you by a victim's mother.

Investigative Tips: Anonymous tips are like birthday presents. You never really know what is inside until you open it. But unlike a birthday present, an anonymous tip, if credible, can yield great cases. Rather than considering an anonymous tip as a nuisance, consider it a potential goldmine of a case, where you may be able to save a victim and prevent others from becoming a victim.

In this instance, the anonymous tip gave enough information to identify a person, but not enough information to constitute a crime. The investigation uncovered the criminal evidence because the investigator took an active, online undercover role. Forensic analysis doesn't usually come into play with an online investigation until physical electronic evidence is identified and seized.

A sexual predator case conducted through online chatting can be completed against a suspect without going beyond the evidence of the single online crime under investigation. However, by examining all of the suspect's electronic devices, past victims may be identified as well as any possible conspirators. Previously convicted sex offenders with Internet enable smartphones may even have created geolocation evidence on these devices by visiting areas ordered off limits by a court, such as playgrounds.

An investigation is not over until the investigator says it is over. Sometimes, investigators may close a case as soon as there is enough to bring charges so as to move on to the next case. Granted, some cases may only need limited evidence to succeed, but other cases, particularly where there are human

CASE IN POINT

US District Court, Eastern District of Wisconsin v Harry J Janikowski, 2009

Investigators received an anonymous letter with information that Harry Janikowski was involved in child molestation. All details in the anonymous letter were confirmed except for the child molestation allegations. To prove or disprove the allegations, investigators searched online for Janikowski on the MySpace website. Janikowski had a MySpace account and his photo on the MySpace user page matched his driver's license photo obtained from the Department of Transportation.

An undercover online conversation with Janikowski was initiated by an investigator that assumed the role of an underage boy. Chats and instant messages culminated in the probable cause in Janikowski's intention to meet the undercover officer to perform a sexual act. He was subsequently arrested.

victims, such as human trafficking investigations. It may be worth the extra effort during a forensic analysis in attempts to uncover more crimes and victims, just to make sure you do a good job for the victims that otherwise would have been ignored.

A break in the case, otherwise known as a suspect's mistake

Scenario: Suspect uses an anonymous email account to send a harassing email to an ex-girlfriend. The suspect attaches a word processing document stating numerous threats. After sending the email, the suspect learns about metadata and regrets his email.

Investigative Tips: There are investigations that cannot be solved. No amount of resources will do it. No amount of investigative skill will do it. No software or hardware will do it. These types of investigations just can't be cracked no matter how much effort is expended. That doesn't mean you stop trying.

There is a solution and that solution resides in your suspect's actions. Eventually, all suspects will make a mistake. Many of these mistakes go unnoticed, sometimes for 31 years. However, the astute investigator will have an ear to the ground in the event that a mistake is caught at some point. These mistakes are the "breaks in the case" that are unexpected and powerful. An example of metadata from a common document file is seen in Figure 11.2. If the information in the metadata in this deleted file is accurate, then you would have the name of the suspect and potentially the name of his workplace, or at least the owning business of the computer used.

One search warrant in which I participated involved the seizure of a huge safe on the top floor of a multi-story home. The safe contained evidence and

CASE IN POINT

State of Kansas v Dennis Rader, 2005

Dennis Rader, also known as the "BTK Strangler" or "Bind, Torture, Kill," eluded law enforcement for 31 years. Rader murdered 10 people between the years of 1974 and 1991 and sent anonymous letters to the media and law enforcement detailing the murders he committed.

In one of his last anonymous letters, Radar mailed a computer floppy disk to the media which contained his usual message to the police. However, he had also created and deleted another document on the floppy using a computer at his church. Radar would later learn that the metadata in the deleted file was recovered by law enforcement and traced directly to him by name. In mere minutes, 31 years of anonymity as a serial murderer unraveled as BTK was identified as the President of Christ Lutheran Church. Mere minutes. Mere metadata. A 31-year-old case broke wide open in minutes because of metadata.

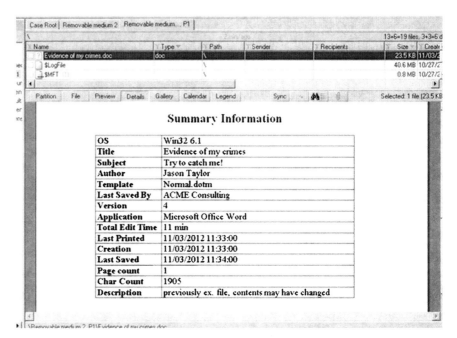

FIGURE 11.2 Metadata recovered from a deleted Microsoft Word document.

proceeds of crimes and was subject to seizure in the search warrant. Of course, the suspect did not cooperate or give us the combination to the safe. The result was a gaggle of cops dragging one of the heaviest items I've ever had to move down more than one flight of stairs and into the back of a truck. Shortly after loading the safe into a truck, the combination to the safe was found on a scrap of paper, lying on the kitchen table. It would have been nice to find that scrap of paper earlier, but at least the safe didn't have to be forced open with even more labor.

Encrypted data that may contain evidence is even more difficult to by pass than a locked safe. If a dictionary attacks doesn't open the files quickly, then the possibility of bypassing the encryption is low. Figure 11.3 shows a spreadsheet from Mandylion Research Labs to obtain time estimates to by pass a password using brute force. In Figure 11.3, the example shows that based on the complexity of this password, it could take over 182,000,000 h to break.

The point in this example is not to discourage trying, but rather to encourage not giving up as you never know when the break (i.e. suspect's mistake) will occur. Perhaps the password chosen by the suspect in an evidence document is the same password you found written on a scrap piece of paper on the kitchen table. You just never know where or when you will find the break in your case.

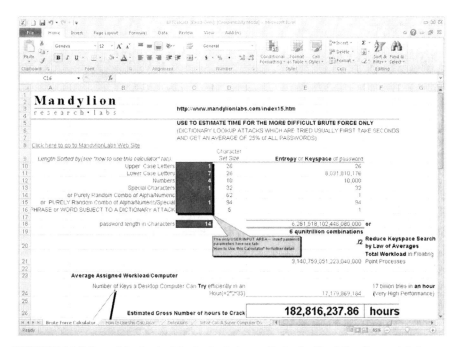

FIGURE 11.3 Spreadsheet calculator for brute force attacks, by Mandylion Research Labs, http://www.mandylionlabs.com/.

Breaks from the suspect may seem to be too good to be true. As in the BTK case, investigators believed that the BTK Killer may have been intentionally leading law enforcement on a wild goose chase, because the name "Dennis Radar" and the name of the church were in the metadata of a deleted document. The document even contained the word "encase," which investigators thought was a reference to the forensic software program. The investigators thought BTK was taunting them through false leads. Surprisingly, "encase" ended up only being a misspelling for "in case." Mistakes by the suspect are the best kind of mistakes to find.

Altered evidence and spoliation

Electronic evidence in the form of word processing documents which were submitted by a party in litigation is alleged to have been altered. Altered electronic evidence has become a common claim with the ability to determine the changes becoming more difficult. How do you know if an email has been altered? What about a text document?

Investigative Tips: All evidence needs to be validated for authenticity. The weight given in legal hearings depends upon the veracity of the evidence.

CASE IN POINT

Odom v Microsoft and Best Buy, 2006

The Odom v Microsoft and Best Buy litigation primarily focused on Internet access offered to customers in which the customers were automatically billed for Internet service without their consent. One of the most surprising aspects of this case involved the altering of electronic evidence by an attorney for Best Buy. The attorney, Timothy Block, admitted to altering documents prior to producing the documents in discovery to benefit Best Buy.

Many electronic files can be quickly validated through hash comparisons. An example seen in Figure 11.4 shows two files with different file names, yet their hash values are identical. If one file is known to be valid, perhaps an original evidence file, any file matching the hash values would also be a valid and unaltered copy of the original file.

Alternatively, Figure 11.5 shows two files with the same file name but having different hash values. If there were a claim that both of these files are the same original files, it would be apparent that one of the files has been modified.

FIGURE 11.4 Two files with different file names, but having the same hash value, indicating the contents of the files are identical.

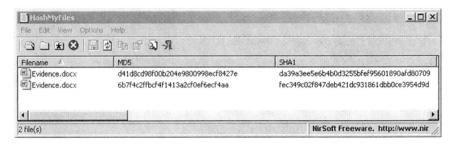

FIGURE 11.5 Two files with the same file names, but having different hash values, indicating the contents are not identical.

Finding the discrepancies or modifications of an electronic file can only be accomplished if there is a comparison to be made with the original file. Using Figure 11.5 as an example, given that the file having the MD5 hash value of d41d8cd98f00b204e9800998ecf8427e is the original, and where the second file is the alleged altered file, a visual inspection of both files should be able to determine the modifications. However, when only file exists, proving the file to be unaltered is more than problematic, it is virtually impossible.

In this situation of having a single file to verify as original and unaltered evidence, an analysis would only be able to show when the file was modified over time, but the actual modifications won't be known. Even if the document has "track changed" enabled, which logs changes to a document, that would only capture changes that were tracked, as there may be more untracked and unknown changes.

As a side note to hash values, in Figure 11.5, the hash values are completely different, even though the only difference between the two sample files is a single period added to the text. Any modification, no matter how minor, results in a drastic different hash value.

The importance in validating files in relation to the identification of a suspect that may have altered a file is that the embedded metadata will be a key point of focus and avenue for case leads. As a file is created, copied, modified, and otherwise touched, the file and system metadata will generally be updated.

Having the dates and times of these updates should give rise to you that the updates occurred on some computer system. This may be on one or more computers even if the file existed on a flash drive. At some point, the flash drive was connected to a computer system, where evidence on a system may show link files to the file. Each of these instances of access to the file is an opportunity to create a list of possible suspects having access to those systems in use at each updated metadata fields.

In the Microsoft Windows operating systems, Volume Shadow Copies may provide an examiner with a string of previous versions of a document, in which the modifications between each version can be determined. Although not every change may have been incrementally saved by the Volume Shadow Service, such as if the file was saved to a flash drive, any previous versions that can be found will allow to find some of the modifications made.

Where a single file will determine the outcome of an investigation or have a dramatic effect on the case, the importance of 'getting it right' cannot be overstated. Such would be the case of a single file, modified by someone in a business office, where many persons had common access to the evidence file before it was known to be evidence. Finding the suspect that altered the evidence file may be simple if you were at the location close to the time of occurrence.

Interviews of the employees would be easier as most would remember their whereabouts in the office within the last few days. Some may be able to tell you exactly where other employees were in the office, even point the suspect out directly.

But what if you are called in a year later? How about 2 or more years later? What would be the odds employees remembering their whereabouts on a Monday in July 2 years earlier? To identify a suspect at this point requires more than a forensic analysis of a computer. It will probably require an investigation into work schedules, lunch schedules, backup tapes, phone call logs, and anything else to place everyone somewhere during the time of the file being altered.

Potentially you may even need to examine the hard drive of a copy machine and maybe place a person at the copy machine based on what was copied at the time the evidence file was being modified. When a company's livelihood is at stake or a person's career is at risk, leave no stone unturned. If you can't place a suspect at the scene, you might be able to place everyone else at a location, and those you can't place, just made your list of possible suspects.

Spoofed call harassment

Scenario: An unidentified suspect continually calls a victim with harassing phone calls. The caller's phone number changes constantly. The phone numbers appear to be fake, or spoofed, numbers. Where do you start?

Investigative Tips: Spoofed calls that are criminal acts, such as conveying threats or harassment, have a devastating effect on the victims. As anonymous as it may feel to the victim, there are actions you can take to help identify the suspect, as long as legal authority exists to demand records.

CASE IN POINT

United States District Court, Western District of Washington at Tacoma v Daniel Christopher Leonard, 2010

A victim was receiving harassing phone calls from a spoofed telephone number. Investigators searched the Internet for spoofing services and discovered the service that was used to spoof these calls. This was based on the victim's phone number existing in the spoofing services logs. A search warrant to the spoofing service provided billing records and call logs related to the victim's phone number. Information provided included the suspect's billing information, date of the account being created, address, and a log of every call made. In this case, there were a total of 1566 calls made.

A spoofed call requires Internet access at some point to at least create an account. This will be important later in the case during a forensic analysis of any seized computer system or smartphone. Although there are free services to spoof phone calls, many of these limit the length of the spoofed call to a few minutes or less, and may only allow one call to be made. Therefore, where there are many spoofed calls being made, the assumption is that an account has been created, a credit used, and at least one legitimate phone number used for the spoofed calls.

As mentioned, at least one legitimate phone number is needed to make a spoofed call. The legitimate phone number, whether it is a landline or cell phone, calls the target and the spoofing service changes the number seen on the target's Caller ID. The evidence trail includes the calling logs maintained by the spoofing service, the credit card information used to purchase the service, the IP addresses recorded to access the spoofing service website, and the call detail records of the suspect's phone used. The call detail records and cell phone itself may provide geolocation records too.

The obstacles placing a suspect with the spoofing phone are only as difficult as the suspect makes it. If the suspect is unaware of the records kept by the spoofing service, and creates an account online using a home computer, their own credit card, and their personal cell phone or landline, the investigation will be fairly quick and easy. The amount of electronic evidence generated across third party providers such as the Internet Service Provider, phone service provider, and credit card service coupled with a forensic examination of the suspect's computer and phone should yield more than enough evidence to close the case with charges. The methods of placing a suspect at specific locations with specific electronic devices fall right in place with this type of electronic communication crime just as it does with an online crime.

However, each step the suspect takes to hide his identity creates extreme difficulty in identifying the suspect. As Internet access is needed to create an account with a spoofing service, public Internet terminals could be used to avoid the suspect disclosing his home or work IP address. Pre-paid credit cards can be used to purchase the spoofing service, thereby avoiding his true name being used. A pre-paid credit cell phone would allow a method where the suspect could dispose of the phone on a regular basis and replace with another. None of these actions require the suspect to use accurate personal information.

But this does not mean the case is impossible. Besides hoping for a break caused by the suspect, the same methods of identifying the physical phone being used and the IP address logged by the spoofing service provider apply. Call detail records of a pre-paid cell phone still yield information with other numbers that may have been called which were not spoofed. Perhaps the suspect called home using his disposable phone, or perhaps the cell tower records give a geo-location that may help identify the suspect.

Once a list of possible suspects is developed, placing the list of suspects at locations as calls have been made will be helpful in reducing the list of suspects. Potentially, the victims in these cases have met the suspect at one or more points in their life, either as friends, acquaintances, or in passing.

Disgruntled employee steals and deletes employer's data

Scenario: An employee, unhappy with his current employer, decides to copy company information consisting of client files and confidential product information onto an external USB hard drive. After he steals the information, he proceeds to delete folders from the company server. A few months after leaving his company, the former employee starts his own business using the stolen information.

Investigative Tips: Intellectual property (IP) theft by employees is a serious threat to any business. The security of information by an organization requires that employees be able to access the information needed to perform their duties, while at the same time, the employer has no option but to trust the information not be stolen. Non-disclosure agreements, employment agreements, and promises do not prevent the theft of IP as it only helps litigate the damage afterwards.

If a suspect has not already been caught with stolen IP, the first course of action is to determine which data has been stolen, when it was stolen, and which persons had access during those times. Many large or high tech companies secure confidential data through a series of safeguards. One safeguard could be allowing the fewest persons necessary to have access to the data. Another safeguard is requiring a series of secure logins to access the data, which every login is recorded with as much detail as possible.

In cases where the company employs a high level of security, identifying those employees with access requires a review of the logs showing access to the files.

CASE IN POINT

United States of America v Biswamohan Pani, 2008

Biswamohan Pani was an employee at Intel. While working for Intel, he gave a resignation notice and while on leave from Intel, obtained a job at AMD, a competing manufacturer of computer chips. Having access to both AMD and Intel at the same time, Pani copied electronic files from Intel to an external hard drive. Pani's intention was to use the stolen files to benefit his new position at AMD.

Files in question that were accessed can be collected in order to create a hash database and listing of the files. This list and database can be compared against any storage media devices of possible suspects for matches of identical or near identical files.

In companies where computer security is not as secure requires more hands on effort. In an office in which an employee can access multiple computer systems and access file servers that do not require individual login credentials requires additional work beyond the examination of the computer systems. The suspect that does not want to use their assigned workstation most likely will use an external hard drive or USB flash drive to copy files using another employee's computer. This could also be in an attempt to frame someone else for IP theft.

Since files can easily be copied onto a flash drive, leaving no visible trace by an average computer user, obtaining a list of all USB device information from suspected computers is paramount to start developing leads.

Collecting information about any attached USB storage devices across a broad spectrum of computers allows you to build a timeline of device travel across the computers. As an example, a suspect using his own flash drive to copy files by connecting the flash drive to a co-workers computer leaves traces of that activity on the co-workers computer. One of the artifact traces is the serial number of the flash drive. It would be expected that the suspect would have connected that same USB device in his own assigned workstation or his personally owned computer before copying the files and certainly after copying the files.

Figure 11.6 shows a collection of information about USB devices obtained from a computer system. If a different computer system showed any of the

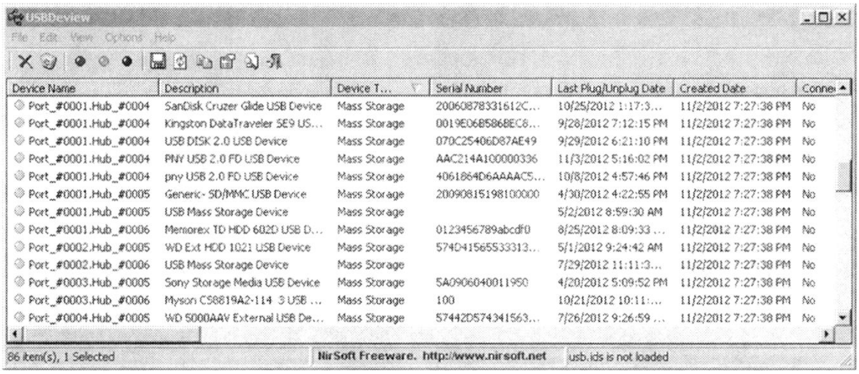

FIGURE 11.6 A list of USB devices collected using USBDeview, http://www.Nirsoft.net.

same devices, then those devices were connected to both systems. As the time stamps of connection are available, an analysis of the files created or accessed after the device being connected can show the files that may have been copied.

Visual depictions of USB activity across systems make an effective impact as to the suspect's physical actions as compared to a spreadsheet of the activity. Figure 11.7 shows a simple diagram of one USB flash drive connected to three computers and the files accessed. In this example, without explaining anything other than showing the movement of the flash drive, an assumption would be that Taylor connected his flash drive to Smith's workstation, copying files. About a half hour later, he then connected the flash drive to his computer and opened several files, probably to make sure the files copied correctly. Finally, later in the evening, he connected the same flash drive to his home computer, copying the files onto it.

This graphic strongly implies Taylor is the suspect and is probably correct. Effectively, Taylor has been placed at three different locations by mere use of his USB flash drive. If Taylor used this same flash drive across many other computers in the company, it would be that much more impactful as a graphic representation of his movements and activity.

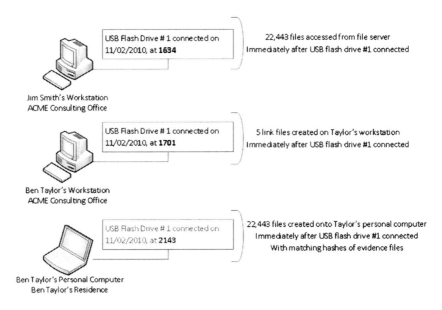

FIGURE 11.7 An easy-to-understand flow of historical USB history, as it was connected to three different computers.

Another method of IP theft includes the suspect emailing copies of files as attachments using web-based email to his own email or to others. Webmail evidence can be recovered from systems, but will not be as complete as having legal access to the webmail account through the provider. IP can also be copied by physically copying pages of paper, where the originals never leave the premises. Most modern copy machines have standard hard drives where images of each copy made are stored.

The forensic analysis of a copy machine hard drive could show IP being copied, such as computer-aided design (CAD) drawings, which may have had no reason to be copied by an employee. If CAD drawings were being copied, it can be suspected that these same drawings could have been stolen, causing an investigation into determining which employee was copying the drawings at that time. The goal then becomes placing the suspect at a copy machine, which could be more difficult than at a computer.

Missing evidence

Scenario: Suspect claims to have provided all electronic storage media, yet according to the forensic examiner, there are missing storage devices. Several devices that have been provided have never been connected to the suspect's computer and devices that have been connected were not produced. What is happening and how do you keep track?

Investigative Tips: At some point of every investigation, you have to get a handle on the evidence, insofar as counting the evidence you have on hand and the evidence that you should have, but either has not been found or produced yet. Beyond the electronic storage devices you have in your possession for examination, there most certainly will be references in your current evidence media that point to other devices relevant to your case.

As the previous case study showed, one computer system had information that many storage devices had been connected to it, any of which may contain

---

CASE IN POINT

Justin Lee Firestone v Hawker Beechcraft International Service Company, 2012

Defendants claimed the Plaintiff copied or removed confidential information from the Defendants' computer system. A forensic examination of the Plaintiff's assigned computer was conducted and between eight and twelve USB devices were discovered to have been connected to the computer. Upon request, the Plaintiff produced USB devices, but not all the devices that were found to have been connected to the computer.

evidence. Your list of evidence should include evidence which you do not have but has been discovered as attached devices, such as USB flash drives. These removable devices connect computers together and connect suspects to computers by sharing connections at different times. One flash drive, possessed by a suspect that has been shown to have been connected to multiple computers, shows a nexus between the suspect and all the systems by way of the flash drive connections. This also helps place a person at a specific location by date and time.

Almost by design, the hard drive you may be examining contains a listing of every device connected to that system. This includes the name, serial number, dates and times of connections, and a plethora of details to help you create a list of evidence items that you do not have. For the most part, this information is found in the Windows registry and in some logs, such as the setupapi.log. Two of the most comprehensive sources of guides for USB forensics come from Colin Cree's Tracking USB Storage Devices, and Rob Lee's Guides to Profiling USB Keys/Thumbdrives (Lee 2009). Both of these resources cover all things "USB" in regard to forensics and the information you can gleam from their artifacts left behind in a computer system.

In reality, the production of every storage device ever connected to a computer system may be impossible. Flash drives, especially the micro size variety, are easily lost or misplaced. Flash drives are sometimes shared among co-workers and they eventually fail and are thrown away. Co-workers sometimes will use another person's computer, plugging in a flash drive during that time to save a file, and the assigned user may never know that a flash drive was just logged in their system's registry. Time and proximity of use should guide common sense as to if an external storage device is relevant, as a flash drive connected only once 4 years prior to an incident may not exist today.

Bomb threats by email

Scenario: An anonymous suspect emails bomb threats to a local high school. The email used is a freely available webmail. A search warrant for IP address information for the email shows origination from another Russia, yet the contents of the email appear to be created by a person local to the area. It appears that an Internet proxy was used to obscure the actual IP address. The odds of tracing the email through anonymous proxy servers are too low to even try. What to do?

Investigative Tips: In cases where there is a threat to public safety, such as a bomb or weapons of mass destruction threat, consider a wiretap on the account, or using CIPAV or similar spyware. Not every threat is credible, but every actual incident that was preceded by a threat, was. Taking chances that a threat may not be credible could end in a preventable tragedy.

FBI "timberlinebombinfo" Investigation (Sanders & Western District of Washington. 2007)

Former Timberline High School student, Josh Glazebrook sent, multiple threats of bombs using email and enticing others to link to the suspect's MySpace page. The IP address was obtained from the emails and comments, with the location being a compromised computer in Italy. The FBI obtained a search warrant to remotely and covertly install a spyware to the MySpace account. The spyware, Computer & Internet Protocol Address Verifier, or CIPAV, to be installed on the account would send the FBI information about the suspect once the suspect logged into the account. This would include the actual IP address of all outbound and inbound communications, MAC address of the network device used, open ports, running programs, last visited URL, and logged in user.

In conjunction with attempts to place tracking code or spyware on the suspect's machine, online searches for any related information may be helpful. For example, given a suspect's user name, a search across the Internet for that user name may result in finding a posting or comment with the same user name. Identifying that person to either rule out the possibility or confirm the possibility of being the suspect is worth the effort. There is always the possibility of the suspect making mistakes. A suspect may use the same account in threats as in an innocent comment on an online forum, but without using a proxy to hide his IP address. That one post with the real IP address could resolve directly to your suspect's physical address.

Another method would be to collect any other Internet users with a connection to your suspect. Forums, social networking sites, and bulletin boards may all provide clues to the suspect's identity through associations with others. Some associations online may be personal contacting the suspect and worth giving a second look.

ID the suspect

Scenario: An unknown suspect is wreaking havoc on network systems with denial of service attacks on several local government agencies. The suspect continually posts his exploits online in various hacker forums. All IP addresses lead to locations all over the world, obviously none being the suspect's actual IP address. How to make it stop?

Investigative Tips: Never underestimate the power of a suspect's mistake and arrogance, but also, keep in mind that you have to find the mistakes to be useful. In this case study, an investigator had to know that metadata might exist in the photo of Ochoa's girlfriend, and then take the effort to

CASE IN POINT

United States of America v Higinio O. Ochoa III, 2012

Higinio Ochoa gained unauthorized access to a police department's entire user database containing usernames, passwords, and personal information of the law enforcement employees in the agency. This information was posted online and resulted in threatening phone calls to several police employees. Ochoa also posted taunting comments on Twitter about the intrusion. On one of the postings, a photo of a female taken from the neck down, in a bikini top with a sign on her skirt reading, "PwNd by w0rmer & CabinCr3w < u BiTch's!," an obvious taunt to investigators. The sign is shown in Figure 11.8.

FIGURE 11.8 The taunting message pinned to skirt of Ochoa's girlfriend, ultimately leading to his capture.

Ochoa may not have realized at the time, but the photo contained embedded metadata that included geolocation information, pointing to an address in Australia. Further investigation found an Internet posting by the user name "w0rmer" on a software programming website. The posting was signed "Higino Ochoa AkA w0rmer." A further search for information on Ochoa led investigators to Ochoa's Facebook page, in which his profile listed Ochoa being in a relationship with Kylie Gardner, who lived in Australia. Other information was developed leading to the identification of Ochoa, but it was the EXIF metadata of Ochoa's girlfriend photo that 'broke the case' by giving investigative leads to Ochoa's identity.

check. Had this not been done, Ochoa may still be hacking into government databases.

Still, these mistakes may not come to light and other investigative means need to be started. Basic Internet searching can result in some useful information. Advanced searching more than likely will yield better information. Using the information at hand, such as a user name, email address, or even a tagline of a suspect could have a hit somewhere on the Internet. An Internet forum, online club, or social networking site could each hold the one key piece of information leading to the identity of the suspect.

If not the suspect, the friends and family of the suspect could lead to the identification. A friend of the suspect could innocently brag about an incident perpetrated by his friend the suspect, in an online forum or social networking site. The identification of a known associate or family member can quickly lead to the suspect through interviews or more detailed online investigation of the friend.

Online extortion

Scenario: Suspect extorts victims by holding gaining control of their computers and encrypts the victim's data offering to decrypt it in exchange for fund wired to an overseas account. The suspect communicates via email and threatens to wipe the data or expose personal information publicly if payment is not made or the victims contact law enforcement. As this is all conducted online, you assume that there can be dozens or hundreds of victims being extorted by one suspect.

Investigative Tips: As mentioned before, consider pen registers on email addresses in hopes of discovering a lead through other email addresses of correspondence. As in many cases, online investigations through social networking sites, forums, and blogs usually will lead to your suspect. Sooner or later, suspects will create a link between that information which is legitimate to that which is their anonymous identity.

CASE IN POINT

United States of America v Luis Mijangos, 2010

Scenario: Luis Mijangos infected computers with a malware that allowed him to gain control of the computers of more than 100 computers, affecting about 230 people including dozens of juveniles. He also installed keylogging software on the victim computers, stealing their credit card numbers and personal information, which he used to make credit card purchases. Mijangos covertly recorded videos of the victims, in compromising and intimate acts. Mijangos demanded the victims to create and send sexually explicit videos to him or he would release the videos he made online.

As investigators were able to obtain his email from the victims, a search warrant of the email address identified the victims of Mijangos through the emails produced. Further investigation led to domain names associated with the email address that was registered in the name of Luis Mijangos. The break in the case was Mijangos apparently not aware his email address was associated with several of his registered domain names that used his real name.

Once a possible suspect is identified, investigative methods to place him behind the keyboard can be put into play, using any of the techniques in this book or with an ingenious method you might create.

Placing suspect at a location

Scenario: An identified suspect in a hacking case denies being at a location determined to be the origin of an intrusion based on an IP address. A forensic examination of the suspect's computer does not turn up any information as being used in the crime. How do you place the suspect at any of the locations used to access the Internet during the crimes without electronic evidence to support this belief?

CASE IN POINT

United States of America v Timothy James McVeigh, 1995

Timothy McVeigh was convicted of bombing the Murrah Federal Building in Oklahoma City, Oklahoma in 1995. The evidence in the case was substantial, with a large focus on the historical locations of McVeigh during the planning and commission of the bombing. Of particular note is that McVeigh was captured on at least one security cameras prior to the bombing. The Ryder rental truck used in the bombing can be seen in the snapshot of security footage in Figure 11.9 as it drove past a hotel. Although McVeigh cannot be seen in the truck, a combination of evidence placing McVeigh at the rental truck company and other locations shows that this security camera caught McVeigh in the truck.

FIGURE 11.9 Security footage of the Ryder rental truck occupied by Timothy McVeigh prior to the bombing of the Murrah Federal Building, http://law2.umkc.edu/faculty/projects/ftrials/mcveightrial.html.

Investigative Tips: Think outside the CPU. Placing your suspect at the scene of a crime and in particular, behind a keyboard, requires thought as to the many ways this can be accomplished outside of a forensic analysis of a computer. If the actual location is known through an IP address where the suspect accessed an Internet connection, it is only expected that you visit the scene to visually inspect the location. Are there security cameras inside the business? Are there security cameras in the parking lot? Does any adjacent business have security cameras? Are there red light cameras? In the businesses, do the employees seem to take notice of their customers? Perhaps they would remember your suspect and be able to pick out his photo from a montage of photos. You will only be able to answer these questions by surveying the location personally.

If the crime scene location does not have security cameras, perhaps the suspect also used an adjacent business for an unrelated purpose, such as a gas station. Any of these businesses may have caught your suspect on video. Also, if the suspect was security conscious, he certainly wouldn't use his credit card at the same coffee shop that he would be committing online crimes. That doesn't mean he wouldn't use his credit card across the street to fill up his car with gas or buy a pack of cigarettes.

Placing the suspect at an Internet café without evidence that he even had a computer with him at the time is not worthless. If he can be placed at the location, with or without a computer, this one fact placed before him could discredit an alibi and lead to an admission of guilt. You just don't know which piece of the puzzle will end up breaking the case wide open, so you try one by one until you find the piece that fits.

Placing the suspect in the office at a specific location

Scenario: An employee is suspected of accessing classified information, copying electronic files, and taking photos of confidential products under development. Unfortunately, he denies all claims of being in the area of the information. Sometimes this is an easy task, other times, a bit more difficult.

Investigative Tips: With many workplaces, there is usually some physical action needed to move about the area. Sometimes a RFID badge is needed to unlock doors or a door must be opened by a Security Officer upon display of identification and signing in. Some workplaces may have security cameras covering all areas while other workplaces may only have a security camera in the employee parking area for safety.

With a small location, an investigation may take only a few minutes to determine if there are any records of employee movement at all, besides perhaps a punch card. Other workplaces may be extensive in geography, open Wi-Fi access, and unrestricted access to all areas. Regardless of the workplace, the best method of determining how an employee moves about is to move about in that area as if you were an employee.

In a case where an alleged cybercrime occurred on a commonly accessed computer workstation, being able to understand who may have access to the workstation based on any recorded activity will help narrow the list of suspects. The recorded activity could be security cameras, entering passcodes to locked doors, or being seen by other employees that remember the suspect being at the computer on a certain date, at a specific time. Computers used in a cybercrime, in which many employees have open access, require determining their whereabouts during the incident. Obviously, this is a lot of effort, but if you want to narrow your list to one possible suspect, it is more than worth the time.

Stolen property

Scenario: A burglary victim finds items for sale on the Internet that appears to be her stolen property. In one of the photos posted in the classified, the floor looks to be the same floor in her home as if the burglar took photos of the property in her home. Easy enough, but let's take it a little further.

Investigative Tips: Just as you shouldn't discount a suspect's mistakes, you should also not underestimate the effort of a victim trying to find their property. In the scenario of a victim finding their property for sale through the Internet, the easiest resolution for law enforcement would be arrange a meeting place with the seller/criminal, and make an arrest upon finding the property was stolen.

Taking this a step further, consider that the items for sale may not be the only stolen items in possession, nor is this one victim the only victim. The goal is to resolve more than one case and give more than one victim closure. The common thread with investigations involving the Internet is obtaining IP addresses and this type of investigation is not different. Online classified advertising websites typically require the user to create an account before posting an advertisement. This process captures the IP address of the user, which may lead directly to the physical residence through search warrants or subpoenas to the classified ad website service and Internet Service Provider.

This newly identified location might contain evidence of many crimes and the recovery of victim property. This location most likely will also contain one or more computer systems used to post the online ads. And don't forget the actual photos used in the ads. If they were taken by a smartphone, you may have a treasure chest of historical geolocation data in a phone that may have traveled with the burglar during commission of his crimes.

With a little elbow grease, you could solve a series of burglaries, recover dozens or hundreds of stolen items, and maybe even identify a conspiracy of burglaries through an analysis of the smartphone call detail records that was used by one burglar to communicate with other burglars.

IP addresses aren't enough

Scenario: You have been given a tip that harassing emails have been originating from several IP addresses. You have the name of the resident living at the addresses and decide to make an arrest based on the content of the emails. So, do you?

CASE IN POINT

United States Court of Appeals for the Ninth Circuit, Todd M. Chism v Washington State; Washington State Patrol, 2011

Investigators for the Washington State Patrol received a tip that child pornography was contained in a website. Warrants were served to obtain any IP addresses used to create and access the website as well as the names used. The results of the search warrants showed the name to be Mr. Nicole Chism. A search warrant on the residence of Todd and Nicole Chism was served where charges were filed. The end result of this investigation concluded that the IP address alone was not enough information for probable cause, particularly when the IP addresses did not resolve to the residence or workplace of either of the Chisms.

Investigative Tips: An IP address is not a person. An IP address alone most likely will not answer all the questions needed for your case. An IP address is a lead or a clue to where you can start. Sometimes it may point directly to a physical location in which the name of the subscriber is listed. But still, the IP address by itself does not mean the subscriber is your suspect.

IP addresses are extremely easy to manipulate through anonymous proxies. Even the use of an open Wi-Fi access point can provide misleading information as to the identity of the suspect. By all means, collect all the IP addresses related to your case, but treat them like the fragile eggshells they are. There are still Internet users that use Wi-Fi in their residences, without security configured. Even those home users that enable Wi-Fi security can still be compromised by a number of means by anyone determined to break their way into the network.

The easiest cases involve the suspect using his own Internet at home, with his real name and personal information. In today's world, it is common knowledge among cybercriminals to avoid using their own Internet service at all costs, and if possible, pin the crime on someone else by using an innocent person's Internet service. Placing a suspect behind the keyboard on IP address alone does not make for a solid case.

Planted evidence

Scenario: An employee at a business is accused of downloading child pornography on his work computer. He has also accused of emailing child pornography to his coworkers. During an interview with the employee, he flatly denies ever

---

CASE IN POINT

United States of America v Barry Vincent Ardolf, 2012

Barry Ardolf was mad at his neighbors, Matt and Bethany Kostolniks, so much so, he exacted an anonymous reign of terror for years on the family. Shortly after moving next to Ardolf, one of the Kostolnikses' very young sons was picked up by Ardolf and Ardolf kissed him on the mouth. The police were called by the Kostolnikes and Ardolf began his campaign of terror.

During the next 5 years Ardolf focused on revenge. He hacked into their wireless network by breaking the encryption password. Ardolf also created email accounts and social networking sites in the name of Matt Kostolnikes without his knowledge or permission.

Ardolf, using the Kostolnikeses' IP address, sent sexually explicit emails to Matt's coworkers. He uploaded child pornography to the MySpace page created with Matt's name. Ardolf also emailed threats to the Vice President of the United States, the Governor of Minnesota, and a US Senator. Ardolf also emailed child pornography using the email account he created with Matt's name.

A forensic examination by the Secret Service, which included examining the Internet traffic on the Kostolnikes' network, showed that their neighbor, Ardolf, was the suspect. A search warrant for Ardolf recovered more than enough information needed to prove.

even seeing child pornography or having anything to do with the allegations. Is there something that sticks out in this case?

Investigative Tips: If something in your investigation doesn't seem right, it probably isn't. In the scenario above, where an employee denies sending emails containing child pornography using his work provided computer, does it make sense? Is this something a person would do, at work, where the network oversees computer activity?

This type of allegation where the acts do not fit the alleged suspect should scream out that something is wrong. As with the Kostolnikes case, the all too obvious criminal contraband posted publicly on the Internet along with emailing contraband to others using a real name doesn't seem plausible. Of course, it can happen, but given the background of the alleged suspect and the audacity of the crimes that are obvious attempts to bring law enforcement attention, what is the motivation? Consider that the planting of electronic evidence is a simple process. A flash drive containing contraband can be connected to a computer perhaps that of a supervisor at a company, and the files copied onto the supervisor's computer by a disgruntled employee. Later, an anonymous 911 call results in the supervisor having his computer seized and his reputation slandered, not to mention having potential criminal charges. Hacking or accessing a home owner's Wi-Fi can lead to the same type of allegations or worse.

When working to place the suspect behind the keyboard, be aware that the suspect you have identified may be an innocent victim, chosen by the actual suspect. Verify. Validate. Corroborate. Double-check. You have nothing to lose by doing a thorough job and a lot to lose if you don't.

THE LIFE AND CASEWORK OF A CYBER INVESTIGATOR

This investigative field is not just digital forensics. This field encompasses all things digital, not just computers, from the flash drive to a global network. Our personal electronic devices become interconnected and our personal devices connect to the devices of others around the world instantly, sharing information. Each person has their own personal virtual network consisting of social networking websites, home networks, work networks, and mobile devices connected wirelessly to their personal networks.

Of course this doesn't help explain to a client or case agent that even if digital forensics on a hard drive may be easy, but proving a particular person was at that keyboard is not. There are many factors to consider beyond the electronic data to build enough circumstantial evidence identifying the suspect.

So from now, take a different look at your suspects. Look at each suspect as having their own personal network of connectivity between devices and people. There are connections to be found. A connection that links your suspect to a crime could be an IP address or a username or a posting on a blog. There certainly will be a connection between the victim and suspect, at least an electronic connection. Just make sure the connections are real and not planted as red herrings to mislead your investigation.

Technical knowledge and skills

The vast amount of technical knowledge needed to place a suspect behind a keyboard makes this task difficult. No longer are cybercrime investigations just the forensic analysis of a computer hard drive. Cybercrimes require the identification of any and all devices connected to the crime which can be any number of devices and many different types of devices. Smartphones, tablets, flash drives, and digital cameras add to the complexity of cyber cases if not just for the sheer number of devices involved but also the technical skills needed for analysis.

Today's cybercrime fighter must have an overall grasp of how any electronic device may be used to facilitate a crime as well as having specific and specialized knowledge to examine these devices. Just as one device may contain evidence that supports allegations, another device may give evidence that is exculpatory to those allegations. Keeping up with technology is challenging when you are constantly trying to keep up with your cases. So what can you do to keep up with your skills?

One of the ways to keep up with your analysis skills is to modify your reading habits. Instead of reading a fictional love story, read a non-fiction book on file systems. Find and evaluate the casework of others, either found online or in your own office. Review cases you have completed in the past and see if there is anything you would do different today. Maybe you have since learned new methods or now use better software that could have resulted in better results. To keep up on your skills means evaluating and improving yourself constantly.

One of the quickest methods of learning about a newly discovered forensic artifact or method is through the sharing of others. Many of us painfully learn from our own mistakes while some of us choose to learn from the mistakes of others. Those that have suffered through a forensic analysis and solved difficult problems usually tried many different methods and tools to overcome obstacles. When these examiners share their efforts of what worked and what didn't, everyone can benefit. Ideally, these successful efforts with sharing will result in further advancements of forensic analysis and sharing with the community.

Not sharing the discovery of a new forensic artifact can be considered selfish, but no one will know about it anyway. The concept of not sharing advanced skills and knowledge with the community at large stymies the development of the digital forensics field as well as not allowing the newly discovered process to be vetted by the community.

In order for common practices and procedures to become accepted, they must be commonly used and practiced by a community of practitioners. Courts generally approve of commonly used practices without little, if any, questioning. Those that have kept the "secret sauce" to themselves run the risk of having to have their efforts and work vetted, and potentially destroyed, in court.

There are many examples of how sharing information among the community results in more effective forensic analysts. One example is that of collecting physical memory. Not so many years ago, physical memory was not considered a primary evidence source, so much so, that computers were forcefully and abruptly shut down by pulling the power cord from the back of computers while they were running. Today, that same action will destroy gigabytes of electronic data. Had not those that researched, tested, and shared their findings about physical memory, we'd still be yanking power cords on every machine we find, including the machines that absolutely need physical memory preserved.

This case is different from that case

Every investigation is unique because people are unique. Forensic artifacts in one case may not be exist in another. Even within the same case, the storage media being analyzed will be different, requiring different skill sets and tools. Motives are different from each other suspect, as is each suspect's technology skill level.

Knowing that every suspect is different from the next, that there are many ways to commit the same crime, and that the technology used is dependent upon the choices of the suspect, take a breath and think before going fishing in an ocean of electronic data. If your job is solely digital forensics, where you have no interaction with victims or suspects, you need to have constant communication with the case agent. The forensic examiner needs to know the objectives and goals of the investigation. Already, analyzing terabytes of data is akin to searching for a needle in a haystack of needles. Being made aware of the case details and needs of the investigator will prevent frustration for everyone involved in the case.

Investigations, whether criminal or civil in nature, where the forensic examiner is purposely not made aware of intimate case details will only result in a massive amount of time spent needlessly hoping to find evidence that miraculously jumps out during an exam. In most cases, knowing the details of an investigation will enable the forensic analyst to target specific data, in specific areas, that may resolve the case or lead to investigative leads that will satisfy case goals. It is up to the forensic examiner to ask just as much as it is the responsibility of the case agent (or client) to inform the forensic examiner of important information.

TESTIFYING TO YOUR WORK

Your work does influence the odds of being deposed, going to trial, or even having to personally present your findings to your internal company in a corporate matter. If you do a comprehensive analysis, detailing your findings succinctly and accurately, where the facts are clearly established, there may be no need to go further in the investigation regarding testimony. The facts may speak loud enough to cause a suspect to plea guilt and your testimony is avoided.

However, I do not believe that doing great work will always mean you never go to trial. Your great work may only reduce the amount of personal testimony you have over a period of time. Some suspects may face such great lengths of incarceration that they have to go to trial as a last ditch hope, no matter how high the evidence is stacked. Others may have nothing to lose and want to go to trial.

So prepare every examination as if you will be testifying to it. A seemingly simple internal corporate matter can quickly be made into a federal criminal case with a single piece of evidence. Companies with government contracts that involve national security are always at risk of any internal investigation becoming a federal investigation. The discovery of child pornography during an employee Internet abuse internal investigation automatically reaches a criminal investigation.

Any forensic examiner risks being called to testify to their work. That includes the interns. That includes the person who may not be a trained forensic examiner that was fishing around a hard drive for evidence. Any person who wishes to touch evidence must also know that touching evidence means risking testifying to everything you saw and did in regard to that evidence. Many organizations, corporate and government alike, take great steps to minimize the number of hands and eyes that interact with evidence. The more eyes and hands involved increases that many more persons risking giving testimony that could negatively affect the case.

Testimony that negatively affects the case doesn't only affect that one case. It can affect every case like it in the future, for everyone. To give testimony which a court accepts as factual means that other cases may use those findings to support future cases, even if the facts weren't accurately stated originally. This means that testimony in other cases, even in a different state, will require arguments between opposing counsels to accept your version of the facts compared to another court's acceptance of different facts in a different case.

The best advice for preparing your testimony is to start before you leave your office to collect the first piece of evidence. Make a plan, be sure everyone involved is using the same plan, and stick to the plan unless an unexpected event comes up during the execution. If you are not the plan maker and have suggestions, give them. Don't let someone else make mistakes because everyone involved will potentially pay for it later.

The best advice for giving testimony is simply following the court's instructions to tell the truth and nothing but the truth. When you don't know an answer, just state you don't know the answer. There is no need to fill in the blanks or guess. Let someone else fill in the blanks to an investigation with facts, not conjecture. And as difficult as it may seem, if you are called on an error you made, admit the error because we all make one sooner or later.

A personal rule I have for evidence is to have a single point of entry for all evidence. You may have as many evidence collectors as necessary, each collector copying files, imaging hard drives, or bagging physical items, but have each collector report to a single evidence handler. One person with the one master list as a sole duty will be one of the best ideas you will ever have in evidence collection as it directly affects testimony regarding evidence admission in your case.

SUMMARY

The point of the above exercises in case studies was to show how different cases have placed the suspect behind the keyboard using a variety of investigative and forensic analysis means. Not one method always worked, was needed, or could be used every time. The software and hardware used did not make the cases, as nothing has been developed yet that automatically finds the evidence for you. These cases used a combination of technical know-how and pure gumshoe detective work to put the cases together.

As a forensic examiner or general investigator that has electronic evidence in a case, your duty and responsibility requires awareness beyond your primary duty. The investigator must be aware of technology and the potential of evidence available through forensic analysis of storage media. The forensic analyst also needs to be aware of the case outside the hard drive. The goal of both jobs is not just to collect mounds of evidence, but it is to place the suspect behind the keyboard, in the name of justice for the victim. Otherwise, all this work is for nothing.

Bibliography

Arredondo M., Federal Bureau of Investigation, Search warrant (2008). Retrieved from US District Court website: <http://www.fbi.gov/about-us/history/famous-cases/anthrax-amerithrax/08-489-m-01.pdf/at_download/file>.

Cree C., Tracking USB devices (2009). Retrieved from <https://encaseondemand.adobeconnect.com/_a799910323/p80426859>.

Justin Lee Firestone v Hawker Beechcraft International Service Company (2012).

Lee R., (2009, September 09). Computer forensic guide to profiling USB device thumbdrives. Retrieved from <http://computer-forensics.sans.org/blog/2009/09/09/computer-forensic-guide-to-profiling-usb-thumbdrives-on-win7-vista-and-xp/>.

Mandylion Research Labs. <http://www.mandylionlabs.com/>.

Odom v. Microsoft and Best Buy (United States Court of Appeals 2006).

Paul D. Ceglia v Mark Elliot Zuckerberg, and Facebook Inc. (US District Court 2012).

Sanders N., US District Court, Western District of Washington (2007). Search warrant. Retrieved from website: <http://politechbot.com/docs/fbi.cipav.sanders.search.warrant.071607.pdf>.

State of Kansas v Dennis Rader (District Court of Kansas 2005).

State of Missouri v Gary D Heggins (Missouri Circuit Court 2012).

State of Wisconsin v Brian Pierick (Waukesha County Circuit Court 2010).

Stexbar. <http://code.google.com/p/stexbar/>.

The People of the State of Illinois v Steven Zirko (Circuit Court of Cook County 2009).

United States Court of Appeals for the Ninth Circuit. Todd M Chism v Washington State; Washington State Patrol (US Court of Appeals 2011).

United States District Court for the Eastern District of Virginia v Robert Philip Hanssen (US District Court 2001).

United States District Court. Western District of Washington at Tacoma v Daniel Christopher Leonard (US District Court 2010).

United States of America v Barry Vincent Ardolf (US District Court 2012).

United States of America v Biswamohan Pani (US District Court 2008).

United States of America v Higinio O. Ochoa III (US District Court 2012).

United States of America v Luis Mijangos (US District Court 2010).

United States of America v Timothy James McVeigh (US District Court 1995).

US District Court v Clifton Dwayane Brooks (US District Court 2012).

US District Court. Eastern District of Wisconsin v Harry J Janikowski (US District Court 2009).

USBDeview. <http://www.nirsoft.net>.

Index

CPSIA information can be obtained
at www.ICGtesting.com
Printed in the USA
FFOW03n2331171014
8169FF